Oracle Database 12c Release 2 In-Memory

Tips and Techniques for Maximum Performance

Joyjeet Banerjee

New York   Chicago   San Francisco
Athens   London   Madrid   Mexico City
Milan   New Delhi   Singapore   Sydney   Toronto

Cataloging-in-Publication Data is on file with the Library of Congress

Oracle Database 12c Release 2 In-Memory: Tips and Techniques for Maximum Performance

1 2 3 4 5 6 7 8 9   LCR   21 20 19 18 17

ISBN   978-1-259-58616-3
MHID   1-259-58616-2

Sponsoring Editor	**Technical Editors**	**Production Supervisor**
Wendy Rinaldi	Deba Chatterjee	Lynn M. Messina
Editorial Supervisor	**Copy Editor**	**Composition**
Jody McKenzie	Lisa Theobald	Cenveo Publisher Services
Project Manager	**Proofreader**	**Illustration**
Anubhav Singh,	Lisa McCoy	Cenveo Publisher Services
Cenveo® Publisher Services	**Indexer**	**Art Director, Cover**
Acquisitions Coordinator	James Minkin	Jeff Weeks
Claire Yee		

*This book is dedicated to my mom; my dad; my sisters,
Joyeeta and Tiya; my brothers-in-law, Sagar and Riju;
my little sweet niece, Saanjh; and my lovely nephew, Manav.*

About the Author

Joyjeet Banerjee works as an enterprise solutions architect with Amazon Web Services, where he crafts highly scalable, flexible, and resilient cloud architectures that address customer business needs. Joyjeet helps organizations understand best practices around advanced cloud-based solutions and how to migrate existing workloads to the cloud. Prior to working with Amazon Web Services, Joyjeet worked as an enterprise architect with Oracle's Engineered Systems team at Oracle headquarters in California. His primary function was to help Oracle Enterprise customers migrate from legacy systems to engineered systems. Before joining the Engineered Systems team, Joyjeet was with Oracle Consulting, where he assisted Oracle Database, RAC, and EBS customers to implement Oracle products. Joyjeet joined Oracle in 2003 as a database administrator in the E-Business Suite development organization, where he specialized in application performance on Oracle Database.

Joyjeet is a regular guest speaker at Oracle Applications Users Group (OAUG) Collaborate and Oracle OpenWorld. He served on the panel of Oracle University that reviewed the course content and set up questions for the OCP for the Oracle Database, RAC, and Oracle Applications track.

Joyjeet earned an MBA in Systems and Operations Management and has recently been honored as an Oracle Innovator (www.oracle.com/us/products/applications/ebusiness/conversations-with-innovators-070240.html).

About the Technical Editor

Deba Chatterjee is the director of products at Robin Systems. Prior to serving in his current role, he was a senior principal product manager at Oracle Corporation and was responsible for the Oracle Multitenant option and Oracle Diagnostics and Tuning packs. Before his work in product management, Deba worked for the performance services team in Oracle Product Development IT, where he was responsible for managing the performance of large data warehouses. He has previously worked at Oracle Consulting; Oracle India; Michelin Tires in Clermont-Ferrand, France; and Tata Consultancy Services. Deba has a Master's degree in Technology Management, a joint program by Penn Engineering and Wharton Business School.

Contents

Acknowledgments

Many people have contributed a lot to the successful completion of this book. I would like to use this opportunity to thank all of you. Without all your help, it would have been difficult for me to finish this book.

I would like to thank Wendy Rinaldi, editorial director at McGraw-Hill Professional, for her enthusiastic support and motivation throughout the book, helping me in all possible ways to make this book a reality; Claire Yee, acquisitions coordinator at McGraw-Hill Professional for managing this project; Anubhav Singh of Cenveo Publisher Services for helping me in all phases of the production of this book; Lisa Theobald for helping me in editing this book; and Lisa McCoy for the proofreading.

I would like to thank Deba Chatterjee, Director of Products at Robin Systems, for technical review of this book and for providing his valuable feedback and advice at every step. I would also like to thank Maria Colgan, Master Product Manager for Oracle Database In-Memory option, for reviewing the core chapters and providing her valuable input.

I would like to thank Andy Mendelsohn of EVP Database Server Technologies for quickly approving this project; Sheila Cepero for following up in getting me all the required approvals very quickly; and Todd Alder, managing counsel, and Mark Schreier from the Oracle legal team for providing all the necessary approvals.

Last, but not the least, I would like to thank all my friends and colleagues who, without fail, motivated and encouraged me to make this happen.

Introduction

There has been a paradigm shift in the way businesses work. Today's businesses want to be empowered with tools that can help them make quick and effective decisions easily. Often, to cope quickly with increases in demand, companies run analytics directly on their operation systems in addition to their data warehouses. This leads to a precarious balancing act between transactional workloads, which are subject to frequent inserts and updates, and reporting style queries that need to scan large amounts of data.

With Oracle Database In-Memory, a single database can now efficiently support mixed workloads, delivering optimal performance for transactions while simultaneously supporting real-time analytics and reporting. Oracle Database In-Memory's unique dual-format architecture makes this possible by maintaining the data in row format for OLTP operations and in the In-Memory columnar format for analytical processing, which is the essence of this book.

The In-Memory option in Oracle Database is compatible with existing applications and leverages all existing Oracle Database functionality. It can be implemented without changes in the application.

With this book, you will learn and perform the following:

- Configure Oracle Database 12c and construct In-Memory–enabled databases.

- Edit and control In-Memory options from the graphical interface.

- Implement In-Memory with Oracle Real Application Clusters.

- Use the In-Memory Advisor to determine what objects to keep in memory.

- Optimize In-Memory queries using groups, expressions, and aggregations.

- Maximize performance using Oracle Exadata Database Machine and the In-Memory option.

- Use Swingbench to create data and simulate real-life system workloads.

This book comprises eight chapters.

Chapter 1: Database Architecture

In this chapter, you will read about the Oracle Database architecture. You will learn the components involved in an Oracle Database. You will learn how the Oracle Database engine works and understand all the background processes. If you are not familiar with Oracle Database, this chapter provides a jumpstart. If you are already familiar with Oracle Database, this chapter will help you to review its features and architecture.

Chapter 2: In-Memory Architecture

This chapter introduces the In-Memory option and its architecture, discusses the advantages of running Database In-Memory, and explains how it works and how the data is stored and processed in memory. You will also learn about all the background processes involved in In-Memory.

Chapter 3: Implementing In-Memory

In this chapter, you will learn how to implement the In-Memory feature in your database. You will allocate the In-Memory area and learn all the initialization parameters related to In-Memory, how to populate data In-Memory, and how to enable In-Memory for various database objects (such as tables, columns, materialized views, and so on).

Chapter 4: How Database In-Memory Works with RAC and Multitenant

In this chapter, you will learn about Oracle Real Application Clusters. You'll learn how a parallel query works, read about the requirements for running

In-Memory on RAC-based systems, learn how the data population happens in RAC, and read about how In-Memory works with the Multitenant option.

Chapter 5: Database In-Memory Advisor

In this chapter, you will learn how to use In-Memory Advisor to determine which objects are best to maintain in memory. You will learn how to install and run the In-Memory Advisor and learn about the various In-Memory Advisor methods. This chapter also offers an example of running the In-Memory Advisor, implementing Advisor recommendations, and comparing results.

Chapter 6: Optimizing Database In-Memory Queries

Here you will learn how to optimize In-Memory queries to gain maximum performance benefits. You will learn how to use join groups, In-Memory expressions, and In-Memory aggregations.

Chapter 7: In-Memory and Engineered Systems

In this chapter you will learn about the Exadata architecture and features, the advantages of Exadata, the benefits of running In-Memory in Exadata, and how to run In-Memory on Exadata.

Chapter 8: In-Memory Lab

In this chapter, you are going to play with the In-Memory features. This chapter consists of examples and scenarios for implementing In-Memory features. You will generate data in your database using the Swingbench tool and will run various queries related to In-Memory against that data set. After you finish this chapter, you will have gained enough exposure to In-Memory to implement it at your workspace.

Appendix: Installing Oracle Database and Enabling In-Memory

This appendix walks through a complete installation of the Oracle Database. It covers using the Oracle software and enabling the In-Memory option.

CHAPTER
1

Database Architecture

Data is the most critical asset for any organization. As companies have continued to expand, their need for information storage and access has expanded exponentially, and there is no end in sight to the need for data storage and retrieval. By now, most organizations have moved from files and folders to the database. The relative ease of use and efficiency of the database accounts for its success in taking on the majority of companies' important data. The database offers a placeholder for storing information, but more importantly, when properly organized, it allows for efficient and meaningful information retrieval.

A *database management system* (DBMS) is the software that controls the storage, organization, and retrieval of data. A *relational database management system* (RDBMS), as defined by Codd's Rules, adapts to the relation model with well-defined object stores or structures. These stores and structures, commonly known as *operator and integrity rules*, are clearly defined actions meant to manipulate and govern operations on the data and structures of the database.

NOTE
According to Edgar F. Codd, a pioneer of the relational model for databases, any DBMS, in order to become an RDMBS, has to follow 12 golden rules, often known as Codd's 12 Rules. If you are interested to know more about Codd's Rules with respect to RDBMS, visit http://dl.acm.org/citation .cfm?id=362685.

Oracle introduced the first commercially available RDBMS database in 1979, with Oracle V2 (Version 2). Oracle Database has evolved far beyond RDBMS through continuous innovation. With every new version, Oracle introduced new features. In 1999, Oracle introduced Oracle8*i* (*i* in *8i* stands for Internet), a database designed for Internet computing that can be deployed in a multitier environment. In 2001, Oracle9*i* introduced a breakthrough in Oracle technology, Oracle Real Application Clusters (RAC). RAC made it possible to access the same database from multiple instances simultaneously, making Oracle Database highly available. In 2003, Oracle10*g* (*g* in 10*g* stands for grid) introduced *grid computing*, which emphasized creating a farm of low-cost commodity servers (grid infrastructure) and running Oracle Database on the same. Oracle11*g* introduced Active Data Guard, which enabled a standby database to be open in read-only mode for reporting purposes.

Oracle Database 12*c* brings the database to a cloud-ready state. Oracle12*c* introduces two new groundbreaking features:

- **Multitenant database architecture**   This enables an Oracle Database to function as a multitenant container database (CDB) that can include a single pluggable database (PDB) or multiple pluggable databases.

- **Database In-Memory**   The focus of this book, Oracle Database In-Memory, transparently accelerates analytic queries by orders of magnitude, enabling real-time business decisions; it also speeds up operational transactions in a mixed workload environment. Embedding the In-Memory capabilities into the existing Oracle Database software ensures that it is fully compatible with all existing features and requires no changes in the application layer.

Before we dive directly into discussing Oracle Database In-Memory, let's first take a look at the architecture of an Oracle database.

Oracle Database and Instance

In simplest terms, a database consists of physical files that store the entire data and instance. An instance includes a set of memory structures and background processes that manage the physical files. The physical files that store data are sometimes also referred to as the database.

Oracle database server = physical files + instance

Or

Oracle database server = database (physical files) + instance

A database can comprise three major structures:

- Storage structure
- Memory structure
- Process structure

The storage structure consists of physical storage (or physical files) and logical storage (the logical distribution of data). Logical storage is in the form of a table, index, tablespace, and so on and helps to manage the physical structure effectively. We will study this in detail in the next section.

Although the storage structure is part of the database, memory structure and process structure are part of the instance as well.

A database can have one or more than one instance. A database with only one instance is called a *single-instance database*. If the database has more than one instance and if all the instances access the same database simultaneously, it is called a *Real Application Cluster (RAC) database*. By default, an RAC database is always *active-active*. If two database instances are configured and only one remains active at any point in time, it is known as *active-passive* configuration. Oracle Database supports both active-active and active-passive configurations. Oracle Database 12c also introduces CDBs and PDBs, which you will learn about in subsequent chapters.

An instance can access only one database at any point in time. Though a database can have multiple instances (RAC), an instance cannot access multiple databases at the same time. Thus, an instance is mapped only to one database at a particular point in time. An instance can be present without the database, and vice versa. Normally, when you create a database using the **create database** command, the instance is there but not the database. Similarly, when you have the backup of a database, you have only the physical files, which constitute the database but not the instance. In order to have a working database, you need both the database and an instance.

Storage Structure of a Database

As discussed, the storage structure of the database consists of the physical and logical storage. Oracle manages physical and logical storage structures separately. Each of these storage structures works independently, so managing one of them does not impact the other. For example, if you rename a table, the database file containing the table is not renamed.

Physical Structure

The *physical structure* of the database comprises the following files:

- Database files
- Control files
- Online redo log files

■   Archived redo log files

■   Parameter file

■   Password file

■   Alert log file, trace files, dumps, and core files

■   Backup files

Database Files

Database files, commonly known as *datafiles*, contain all the data. Every database should have at least one datafile where the data is stored; without the datafile, a database has no meaning. The datafile is a physical file created by Oracle Database. Apart from storing the data, the datafile also contains data structures such as tables, indexes, and materialized views. The data in the datafile is written in a binary format, which cannot be read without the Oracle Database—so, for example, if you open the datafile in vi or some other editor, you won't be able to read it.

For each tablespace, there will be one or more datafile. Thus, if your database has ten tablespaces, it will have at least ten datafiles. A datafile cannot be associated with more than one tablespace.

Normally, datafile names have the extension .dbf (database files). The datafiles can be stored in a storage area network (SAN), network attached storage (NAS), file system, Network File System (NFS), or Oracle Automatic Storage Management (ASM). Oracle recommends using ASM to store the datafiles, since ASM manages the datafiles and requires no manual intervention. ASM also takes care of striping and mirroring the datafiles. Striping provides better performance by spreading data across multiple disks to balance the load. Mirroring protects the data from any failures. In ASM, the Oracle Managed Files (OMF) feature simplifies database creation and names the datafiles, so the DBA does not have to do this manually.

The first block of the datafile stores the *block header*, which contains information about the details of the datafile, the datafile number, whether the datafile is offline or online, how much used space and free space are available in the datafile, and information on datafile checkpoint and recovery.

A temporary file (.tmp) is a type of database file used for temporary operations such as sorting during the execution of queries. The data in these *tempfiles* is stored temporarily and is discarded once the query has completed. The space in tempfiles can be reused for various operations in the database.

Datafiles can be queried from the dictionary view V$DATAFILE, while tempfiles can be queried from the V$TEMPFILE view:

```
SQL> select name from v$datafile ;

NAME
----------------------------------------------------------------
/u01/app/oracle/oradata/orcl/system01.dbf
/u01/app/oracle/oradata/orcl/ts_data.dbf
/u01/app/oracle/oradata/orcl/sysaux01.dbf
/u01/app/oracle/oradata/orcl/undotbs01.dbf
/u01/app/oracle/oradata/orcl/example01.dbf
/u01/app/oracle/oradata/orcl/users01.dbf
/u01/app/oracle/oradata/orcl/ts_data2.dbf
/u01/app/oracle/oradata/orcl/sh1.dbf
/u01/app/oracle/oradata/orcl/enc128_ts0.dbf

9 rows selected
SQL> Select name from v$tempfile;

NAME
--------------------------------------------------------------------
/u01/app/oracle/oradata/orcl/temp01.dbf
```

Control Files

Unlike datafiles, control files do not contain any table, index, or materialized view data; instead, they contain the most critical information about the database. Because control files are of utmost importance, they are mirrored *and* multiplexed. If there is corruption in a control file, Oracle reads from the mirrored copy. The contents of the control files are not stored anywhere else, not even in the datafiles, so it becomes very important to safeguard the control files. The control file contains the following information:

- Database name, date and time when the database was created, and database unique identifier (DBID)

- Details of the datafiles and redo log files, including their size, location, and number of files

- Information about the Recovery Manager (RMAN) backup

- Details about the tablespaces

- Information about redo log files, archived log files, and the log history

- Details about the logging used to recover the database in the event of failure

- Details of checkpoint

- Details of recovery

Whenever there are structural changes in the database, such as adding a datafile or resizing the redo log file, the changes are updated in the control file. A control filename normally has the extension .ctl or .con. The control file location is specified in the **control_files** parameter of the initialization parameter file. Because the control file is always multiplexed, whenever the file is updated, Oracle simultaneously process updates all the copies of the control file, ensuring that all files are in sync. The background process that updates the control file is called a *checkpoint* (CKPT). It is recommended that you create multiple copies of the control file on different disks to override any disk failures.

A control file has multiple sections where the information about the database is stored. Each section includes a set of records about a particular area of the database, such as tracking the records of datafiles and so on. Control files contain the following two types of records:

- **Circular reuse records**   As the name indicates, the records written in this section contain noncritical information, which can be overwritten as required. For example, whenever a new backup is taken using RMAN, the old backup records are overwritten, or when the archived redo log files are old, the information is overwritten.

- **Noncircular reuse records**   These records contain critical information that cannot be overwritten. Most of the information stored here seldom changes—for example, information about the datafiles, tablespaces, redo log files, and so on. In exceptional cases, the records might be reused, such as when a datafile is dropped.

The control file can be queried from the dictionary view V$CONTROLFILE:

```
SQL> select name from v$controlfile ;

NAME
-------------------------------------------------------------------
/u01/app/oracle/oradata/orcl/control01.ctl
/u02/app/oracle/oradata/orcl/control02.ctl
/u03/app/oracle/oradata/orcl/control02.ctl
```

Tip & Technique
The V$CONTROLFILE_RECORD_SECTION view displays information about control file record sections.

Online Redo Log Files

Online redo log files, often known simply as log files, record any change that happens in the database. The main purpose of the redo log files is to protect the database against data loss. Redo log files even capture the undo change information, thereby protecting the undo data as well. Two or more redo log files in a database always capture all the changes.

Redo log files include redo records, or redo entries, which comprise a group of change vectors. Each vector records the change made to a block in a database. In addition to the change vectors, the redo log file contains detailed information about the change, including the timestamp, system change number, transaction ID, committed or uncommitted transaction, operation that made the change, and type of data segment.

The *Log Writer (LGWR)* process writes to the redo log files in a circular fashion. It starts writing the first file, and once it's filled, it starts writing the next, and in a similar fashion it continues to the last one. When the last redo log file is written, the process returns to the first redo log file and starts writing again. This process reuses the existing redo log files, and the contents are overwritten. Of course, before the data is overwritten, the database writer process ensures that the data is written to the datafiles. A filled redo log file is available for reuse after all the changes have been written to the datafiles. If archiving is enabled, a filled redo log file is available for reuse after all the changes have been written to the datafiles and the file has been archived—that is, written to archived log files. We will study the archive log files in the next section.

Whenever a transaction is committed, LGWR assigns a *system change number (SCN)* to identify the committed transaction; the SCN is then written on the datafiles.

Only one redo log is active at a time. The active redo log file where the LGWR is actively writing is the *current* redo log file. The redo log files, which are required for instance recovery, are the *active* redo log files. Redo log files that are not required for instance recovery are *inactive* redo log files.

The redo log files for a particular database instance are the *redo thread*. In a single-instance database, only one redo log thread exists. With a RAC database, a separate redo log thread will exist for each instance; so a four-node RAC database will have four different redo log threads.

As previously discussed, a database should have at least two redo log files so that one file is always available for writing. When the database stops writing to one redo log file and starts writing to the next, the process is called a *log switch*. The log switch normally happens when the current redo log file is full and writing must continue. Apart from this, a log switch can be configured to occur at regular intervals, irrespective of the filled redo log file.

On the occurrence of a log switch, the database assigns a new log sequence number to the redo log file and LGWR begins writing to it. Each redo log file has a unique log sequence number. When a log file is overwritten, a new unique log sequence number is assigned for new writes. When the redo log files are written to the archived redo log files, the same log sequence number is retained in the archived redo log files. The log sequence number is used to recover the database during instance recovery or a crash.

Similar to control files, the redo log files are also multiplexed or mirrored to protect against failures. LGWR writes to all the copies of the redo log files simultaneously, eliminating the possibility of a single point of failure. Mirroring of the log files occurs by creating groups of redo log files; a group of redo log files contains the redo log file and all its mirror copies. Each redo log file that is part of a group is called a *member*. So, for example, if there are two log groups with two members in each group, the total number of log files in the database is four.

Let's look at an example. A database has two log groups, A and B. Each log group has two members—redo log group A has members A1 and A2, and redo log group B has members B1 and B2. When the LGWR writes in log group A, it writes to A1 and A2 concurrently, and whenever there is a log switch, it starts writing to log group B, where it writes to B1 and B2 simultaneously.

Tip & Technique
The members of a log group should be stored on different disks to avoid problems associated with disk failures.

Archived Redo Log Files

Archived redo log files are simply copies of redo log files. Archived log files should not be confused with the mirrored or multiplex copies of the redo log files, which are also called redo log files. The archived log files are written by the Archiver (ARC*n*) process that copies the content of the redo log files to archived log files for archiving the data. Archived log files are created when archiving is enabled and the database runs in *archivelog mode*. When the database runs in *noarchivelog mode*, archiving is disabled and archived redo log files are not created. The log sequence number for the redo log files and the archive log files are the same, since the same data is present in both files.

Archived redo log files provide additional safeguards for data. Though archived redo log files include some overhead in terms of CPU, I/O, and storage, the benefits they provide render the overhead negligible. In case of disk failures, along with the full database backup, redo log files, and archived log files, you should be able to recover all the committed transactions in the database. Enabling the database in archivelog mode also facilitates *online backup*—that is, you can make a backup of the database when it's up and running. Archived redo log files also help to keep the standby database on par with production, since archived redo log files are shipped to the standby database.

As with redo log files and control files, you can have more than one copy of the archived redo log files. The only concern in this case is space management.

Tip & Technique
In a production environment, it makes sense to keep the database in archivelog mode. For a nonproduction environment such as a test environment, patch archiving is not usually needed. Sometimes, however, nonproduction systems such as production support or a user test environment may require that you turn on archiving.

Parameter File

Oracle databases use the *parameter file* to read all the parameters before starting the database. This file contains various parameters related to the functioning of the database. The initialization parameters set the limits for the entire database, users or processes, or a particular database resource. DBAs use this file to control a database, to specify more memory in a database, or to restrict the CPU usage in a database. DBAs can control the maximum number of users, set threshold limits, and enable auditing or tracing using this file.

Hundreds of parameters are available for Oracle databases, which can be divided into two types: basic and optional. Basic parameters are mandatory, without which the database will not start. Optional parameters provide more control over the database, but as the name suggests, they are not mandatory.

Oracle database supports two types of parameter files:

- Initialization parameter file
- Server parameter file

The *initialization parameter file* is a plain-text file containing all the parameters. This file is popularly known as the PFILE or init.ora file. The file contains the names of the parameters and values associated with them. The entries in this file are not case sensitive. The default location of this file is $ORACLE_HOME/dbs. The naming convention used for this file is init<*DB_NAME*>.ora—if your database name is DBIM, for example, the filename would be initDBIM.ora.

The *server parameter file* is the binary version of the initialization parameter file. It is known as SPFILE. This file cannot be edited directly, but you can create a PFILE from SPIFLE, edit it, and convert it to an SPFILE. The SPFILE is also located in the $ORACLE_HOME/dbs directory. The naming convention used for SPFILE is similar to PFILE: spfile<*DB_NAME*>.ora. So if the database name is DBIM, the SPFILE name will be spfileDBIM.ora.

A sample init.ora parameter file is shown next:

```
orcl.__data_transfer_cache_size=0
orcl.__db_cache_size=3238002688
orcl.__java_pool_size=16777216
orcl.__large_pool_size=33554432
orcl.__oracle_base='/u01/app/oracle'#ORACLE_BASE
```

```
orcl.__pga_aggregate_target=1073741824
orcl.__sga_target=3758096384
orcl.__shared_io_pool_size=67108864
orcl.__shared_pool_size=352321536
orcl.__streams_pool_size=33554432
*.audit_file_dest='/u01/app/oracle/admin/orcl/adump'
*.audit_trail='db'
*.compatible='12.1.0.2.0'
*.control_files='/u01/app/oracle/oradata/orcl/control01.ctl',
'/u02/app/oracle/oradata/orcl/control02.ctl',
'/u03/app/oracle/oradata/orcl/control01.ctl'
*.db_block_size=8192
*.db_domain=''
*.db_name='orcl'
*.diagnostic_dest='/u01/app/oracle'
*.dispatchers='(PROTOCOL=TCP) (SERVICE=orclXDB)'
*.inmemory_size=0
*.job_queue_processes=8
*.local_listener='LISTENER_ORCL'
*.memory_max_target=0
*.memory_target=0
*.open_cursors=300
*.pga_aggregate_limit=2147483648
*.pga_aggregate_target=1073741824
*.processes=300
*.remote_login_passwordfile='EXCLUSIVE'
*.resource_manager_plan='DEFAULT_PLAN'
*.sga_max_size=3758096384
*.sga_target=3758096384
*.undo_tablespace='UNDOTBS1'
```

Password File

The *password file* enables users to log in to the database remotely as an administrator. A user can connect as SYS, SYSDBA, SYSOPER, SYSBACKUP, SYSDG, and SYSKM using the password file. The password file is created when the Database Configuration Assistant (DBCA) is run. It can be created or modified at any time using the ORAPWD utility. The location of the password file is $ORACLE_HOME/dbs. The password in the password file is case sensitive.

Tip & Technique
Operating system authentication takes precedence over password file authentication. Password file authentication is used mainly when connecting remotely to the database, whereas operating system authentication is used when logging in directly from the database server.

Alert Log File, Trace Files, and Dump and Core Files

The database *alert log file* keeps a log of all the errors and messages occurring in the database in chronological order. In case of any issues with the database, this is where all the information is written. The DBA can use this tool to analyze any problem occurring in the database. The alert log contains information about start/stop, information about creating or dropping an object, any ORA errors the database is experiencing, and all other database events.

The alert log file is written as both a text file and an XML file. Both files are located in the ADR Home directory. The Automatic Diagnostic Repository is a file system repository for all kind of logs. Each instance has its own ADR directory. Oracle recommends using the XML version of the alert log file for monitoring using either cloud control or the Automatic Diagnostic Repository Command Interpreter (ADCRI) utility, while the text version of the file is kept for backward-compatibility purposes.

The root directory of the ADR, including the ADR Home directory, is ADR base. You can specify the location of the ADR in the initialization parameter file by setting the parameter **DIAGNOSTIC_DEST**. If this parameter is not set in the PFILE/SPFILE, then **DIAGNOSTIC_DEST** is set to the directory designated by **$ORACLE_BASE**. If even **$ORACLE_BASE** is not set, then **DIAGNOSTIC_DEST** is set to **$ORACLE_HOME/log**

Each Oracle Database background process writes information associated with it in its own trace file (.trc). Information related to errors, statuses, warnings, and processes are written in the trace file. The trace file of the database background process is named using the ORACLE_SID and OS process ID. For example, for a database with an ORACLE_SID of DBIM and a process ID of 2239, the Oracle background process trace filename would be dbim_pmon_2239.trc. The server process trace filename includes the ORACLE_SID, the string *ora*, and the process ID. So, for example, for a database with an ORACLE_SID of DBIM and a process ID of 2245, the trace filename would be dbim_ora_2245.trc.

Trace files are sometimes accompanied by additional trace metadata files with .trm extensions; these contain structural information about trace files.

A *dump* is an incident/event–based trace file. It is generally a one-time output of diagnostics data regarding the occurrence of a particular event. The dump is written in the incident directory. Each incident contains an incident number.

Core files are memory dumps. This file is written in binary format. It is mainly used by Oracle Support. The filename contains the string "core" and the operating system process ID.

Tip & Technique
To find the detailed pathname for all the trace, dump, and log directories, run this query:
select * from v$diag_info

Backup Files

Backup files are physical files that are not needed for database function. They are needed in the following cases, however:

- If the database, table, or object needs to be restored

- If you want to restore the database to a particular point in time

- If you want to make a clone of an existing database

- If you want to create a standby database

The backup files can be RMAN backup files that include datafiles, online redo log files, archived redo log files, SPFILEs/PFILEs, and control files. If RMAN is not used, the backup files would include all these files irrespective of the backup methodology. If the backup were taken at the storage level or by using snapshot methodology, the backup files would be the output files using that methodology. The backup files also include a backup of ORACLE_HOME. If the backup is taken using export, the backup files will be the export dump file.

Logical Structure

The *logical structure* of the database enables better control over data in order to process, store, and retrieve it. The four components of the logical structure are blocks, extents, segments, and tablespaces.

Blocks

Data is stored in the Oracle database in units called *data blocks*. Blocks are the smallest unit of data and have a direct relationship with the block size of the operating system (OS)—the size of each block is a multiple of the OS block size. An Oracle block should not be smaller than the operating system block size.

All database data is stored in datafiles, which are made up of OS blocks. An OS block is the minimum unit of data that an OS can read or write; an Oracle block, however, is a logical storage structure. An Oracle database requests data amounts that are multiples of Oracle block size, rather than OS block size. Whenever an Oracle database requests a data block, an OS operation results to translate this request to physical permanent storage—thus separating the physical data block from the logical data block. Hence, the database data can reside on multiple disks, since Oracle knows the address of the logical data blocks.

The block size is specified during database creation; once the database is created, block size cannot be altered. Though some exceptions exist, such as re-creating the database, exporting the whole database, and reimporting it back, these are not easy processes.

Because the data block is the smallest unit of data storage, any query execution Oracle will read is from a minimum of one data block.

Extents

An *extent* is a group of contiguous data blocks obtained in a single allocation. Extents do not have to be contiguous; therefore, an extent can spread across multiple disks. An extent stores a single type of information and is always contained in one datafile.

Segments

A *segment* is a group of extents allocated for a particular object. Segments store physical data; therefore, tables, indexes, partitions, cluster tables, and materialized views all are segments. Objects that do not physically store data are not considered segments, such as sequences, views, synonyms, and procedures. A segment contains data for a logical storage structure within a tablespace. Segments can be divided into three categories:

■ **User segment** Stores data for the user's object, such as the user-created table, index, and so on.

■ **Temporary segment** When sorting a query, Oracle Database often needs a temporary area. Oracle Database creates temporary segments in the temporary tablespaces for that purpose. The tempfiles are mapped with tempfiles. Similarly, for temporary tables and indexes, temporary segments are used.

■ **Undo segment** All the undo data of the database is stored in the undo segments, which are mapped to undo tablespaces.

Tablespaces

Data is stored in the database logically in the form of a *tablespace*. A tablespace is the highest level of unit, as opposed to the smallest unit, in the block. All the datafiles are stored in tablespaces, and a tablespace can contain more than one datafile. A tablespace can be one of two types: permanent or temporary.

Permanent tablespaces store permanent database objects. These permanent objects are always stored in this database. Oracle Database uses two permanent tablespaces for managing the database: SYSTEM and SYSAUX. The *SYSTEM* tablespace is used by the SYS user and includes the data dictionary, tables, views, and other objects containing important information for managing the database. The *SYSAUX* tablespace provides a complement to the SYSTEM tablespace. It reduces the load on the SYSTEM tablespace and is the default tablespace for many of the database features. Neither of these tablespaces can be dropped or renamed; both are mandatory. Oracle recommends that you store user data in its own tablespace and not in SYSTEM or SYSAUX tablespaces.

Undo tablespaces are permanent tablespaces that are used to manage the undo data. Undo tablespaces also contain undo datafiles, just like any other permanent tablespace.

Temporary tablespaces contain temporary data that includes information related to a particular user session. The data in the temporary tablespace is transitory. The datafiles mapped to the temporary tablespaces are *tempfiles*. The temporary tablespace cannot be made permanent.

A tablespace can be in read/write mode or read-only mode. SYSTEM, SYSAUX, and temporary tablespaces are in permanent read/write mode and cannot be changed to read-only mode.

Memory Structure

The *memory structure* resides in the instance of the database. Whenever the instance is started, a portion of the operating system RAM is allocated to the database, and the Oracle database further allocates a memory area. The memory area contains frequently used code, frequently used data, details of the connected sessions, and details of the queries that are being processed by the database. The memory structure of an Oracle database consists of the System Global Area (SGA) and Program Global Area (PGA).

System Global Area (SGA)

Memory in the SGA is allocated whenever the database instance is started and is deallocated when the instance is shut down. The SGA consists of several different types of memory structures. The various components of the SGA store code, data, and important information regarding the current state of the database. Some components of the SGA are mandatory, while others are optional, depending on what database options your system is using. The following are the components of the SGA:

- Database buffer cache
- In-Memory Column Store
- Redo log buffer
- Shared pool
- Large pool
- Java pool
- Streams pool
- Fixed area

Database Buffer Cache

The main purpose of the database buffer cache is to cache the database data blocks into memory. Caching the data in the database buffer cache enables faster execution of SQL queries by eliminating the need to read data from the physical disk. Thus, the database buffer cache provides much faster data access.

Because the database buffer cache is used for storing data, it is the largest area in the SGA. The database buffer cache can cache data from all objects in the database and eventually stores data such as tables, partitions, cluster tables, indexes, and materialized views. Oracle uses a Least Recently Used (LRU) algorithm to manage the data in the database buffer cache.

A buffer (database block) in the database buffer cache can be in one of the following three states:

- **Unused**   The buffer is either unused or has never been used. This data is always available in the database buffer cache for consumption.

- **Clean**   The buffer is ready for reuse. The buffer was used previously, but all the data it contained has been written to disk so there is no harm in overwriting it.

- **Dirty**   The buffer contains data that has not yet been written to disk. The data must be flushed to the disk before this buffer can be reused.

In addition, each buffer has an access mode that specifies whether the data block can be reused or not. If the data buffer has the access mode of "pinned," it has been explicitly kept in the database buffer cache and thus cannot be reused. If the data buffer has the access mode of "free" or "unpinned," it is ready to be reused. An unused buffer state cannot have the access mode of pinned, whereas a clean buffer state can be either pinned or free.

Oracle uses a Least Recently Used (LRU) algorithm to phase out the data from the database buffer cache. A data block that is accessed repeatedly, known as a *hot buffer*, resides in the "hot" end of the LRU; a data block that has not been accessed in a long time is a *cold buffer* and resides in the "cold" end of the LRU. The data from the cold end is phased out first.

When a query reads data from the database buffer cache, depending on the type of SQL statement executed, data in the current mode or consistent mode is retrieved. The database buffer cache contains both committed and uncommitted data. For example, if an uncommitted transaction has updated a row in a block, until the actual commit happens, the data will not be written to the physical disk.

In this case, the data in the database buffer cache and disk are different until the data is written to disk. The database buffer cache has the latest copy of the data, while the datafiles have the read-consistent version of the data. If a SQL query is executed for data modification, data from the database buffer cache will be used—this is called *current mode*. If a SQL query is executed for querying the data, the read-consistent block from the physical disk or datafiles will be retrieved instead of from the buffer cache—this is called *consistent mode*.

On the occurrence of checkpoint, the Database Writer process (DBW*n*) writes the data from the database buffer cache to the physical disk. When the free buffer decreases and drops below a threshold limit, dirty blocks are flushed out to the disk.

To manage the database buffer cache in a better way, the database buffer cache can be divided into one or more *pools*:

- **Default** This is the default database buffer cache. At this location, all the data blocks are cached. This pool will always exist, whether or not you configure other pools. The other two pools are optional and have no impact on the default pool.

- **Keep** This is an optional pool that is created in order to retain the data. If you don't want data to be aged out of the default pool, you can use this space to keep those data blocks always in memory. The keep pool also uses an LRU algorithm.

- **Recycle** This optional pool is used for data blocks that are seldom accessed.

In-Memory Column Store
The In-Memory Column Store is a newly introduced feature in Oracle Database 12*c*. It is the reason why you are reading this book! We will begin covering this topic in detail in Chapter 2.

Redo Log Buffers
The *redo log buffer* is the area in the SGA that stores the redo entries related to changes made in the database. All these captured change records, also called redo entries or change vectors, are written using either Data

Definition Language (DDL) or Data Manipulation Language (DML). These redo entries are helpful if there is a failure in the system; the database uses these redo entries to reconstruct the lost changes.

The redo log buffer is a circular buffer in the SGA. The background process that writes the data from the redo log buffer to the physical disk is the Log Writer (LGWR).

The size of the log buffer can be specified in the initialization parameter file using the parameter **LOG_BUFFER**.

Shared Pool

The *shared pool* is used to store the code, similar to the way a database buffer cache is used to store the data. Any code that is processed by Oracle Database is cached in the shared pool, which contains SQL statements, PLSQL (Procedural Language/Structured Query Language) code, execution plans of SQL statements, data dictionary information, the SQL and PLSQL result cache, and more. The shared pool is further divided into the following components:

- Library cache
- Dictionary cache
- Server result cache
- Reserved pool

Library Cache   The *library cache* is the part of the shared pool that stores the SQL and PLSQL statements. Every time a query executes, the database first checks the library cache to see if the SQL statement exists. If the SQL statement exists in the library cache, the database reuses the same SQL code, or cursor, in a *soft parse*. If the statement does not exist, the database builds a new executable version of the SQL code in a *hard parse*.

The library cache is further subdivided into two areas: a shared SQL area and a private SQL area. The shared SQL area stores the parsed SQL statements, SQL execution plans, and parsed and compiled PL/SQL units. The shared SQL area processes the first occurrence of a SQL statement. All the users in the database share the shared SQL area. When a user or a session issues a SQL statement, it first uses the private SQL area in the PGA. Each user that submits the same statement has a private SQL area that points to the same shared SQL area. Hence, many private SQL areas in separate PGAs can be mapped with the same shared SQL area.

Dictionary Cache   As the name suggests, the *dictionary cache* caches all the dictionary objects of the database. Data dictionary objects contain information about the database and consist of tables and views. During parsing of SQL statements, Oracle uses the data dictionary cache. The data dictionary cache is also known as the row cache because it holds data as rows instead of buffers. Oracle uses the LRU algorithm to maintain the objects in the dictionary cache.

Server Result Cache   The *server result cache* stores the actual result sets of the SQL statements and the PLSQL functions. Thus, it has two parts: one for the SQL and the other for the PLSQL. The server result cache bypasses the execution of the SQL statements, because it enables a user session to directly pick up the end result from here. By using the server result cache, the Oracle database avoids rereading the data and recalculating the results. This provides a system performance boost. For PLSQL blocks, the function result sets are stored here. So for any PLSQL function invocation, if the result exists in the server result cache, the PLSQL statement is not executed again.

Reserved Pool   The *reserved pool* is used to allocate large contiguous chunks of memory. It allows objects (Java, SQL cursor, or PLSQL) larger than 5KB to be loaded directly in memory, without having the need for a single contiguous area. As a result, it reduces memory fragmentation and increases performance.

Large Pool
The *large pool* is an optional area in the SGA. It is used mainly for operations that need large memory allocation. Since the memory required by operations are very large, they cannot be stored in the shared pool. This area is mainly used for RMAN backup and restore, for parallel execution of statements, and for Oracle shared server. The large pool does not use the LRU algorithm. Once the session using the large pool releases the memory, other sessions can then reuse it.

Java Pool

The *Java pool* is another optional area in the SGA. As the name suggests, it is used to store all the Java-related objects. It stores all the Java-related code and data in the Java Virtual Machine (JVM).

Streams Pool

The *Streams pool* is also an optional area in the SGA. It is used to store the buffered queue messages for the Oracle Streams capture and apply process. Because Oracle Streams has been deprecated, Oracle recommends using Oracle GoldenGate to replace all replication features of Oracle Streams.

> **NOTE**
> *Oracle Streams has been deprecated in Oracle Database 12c and may be desupported and unavailable in a later Oracle Database release.*

Fixed Area

The *fixed area* in the SGA is a place for internal housekeeping. It contains the information about the state of the database and the instance, which background process the Oracle database needs to access, or the communication across various processes in the database. Fixed area size is set by the database automatically and cannot be set or altered manually.

Program Global Area (PGA)

The PGA is an area in memory that is outside the SGA. It contains information and data for one process or thread, including session-dependent variables required by dedicated or shared server processes. The dedicated or shared server process allocates memory structure, which is needed in the PGA. The PGA is divided into two main areas: the private SQL area and the SQL work area.

Private SQL Area

The *private SQL area* contains information about parsed SQL statements and other session-specific information for processing. Whenever a server process executes SQL or PLSQL code, the process uses the private SQL area to store the bind variable values, query execution state information, and query execution work areas. The private SQL area contains a *run-time area* that stores the state of the query execution and a *persistent area* that stores the values of bind variables.

SQL Work Area

The *SQL work area* is a private allocation of PGA memory that is used for memory-intensive operations, such as sorting operations, bitmap operations, and hash joins.

Process Structure

An instance of an Oracle database consists of several background processes that are started when the instance is started. An Oracle database uses these background processes to complete several tasks, and each background process has a unique task. Some background processes are dependent on database features. For example, if you are running a RAC database, you will find several RAC-related background processes that are not running in a single-instance database.

   Some of the background processes are mandatory and required for any database configuration. The most important mandatory processes are discussed in the following sections.

Process Monitor (PMON)

The Process Monitor monitors all other background processes running in the database. If a process terminates abruptly or crashes, PMON performs the recovery of the process. PMON also takes care of cleaning the database buffer cache and freeing up resources.

System Monitor (SMON)

The System Monitor monitors the overall system and performs recovery in case of instance failure during startup of an instance. SMON uses the redo log file to perform the instance recovery. If there are multiple RAC nodes and one of the instances fails, SMON can take care of recovering the failed instance. SMON also recovers any skipped transactions, which may have been skipped due to an object being offline, as soon as the object is back online. For example, if a tablespace was offline and recovering terminated transactions were skipped during instance recovery, SMON will recover the transactions when the tablespace is brought back online. In addition, SMON clears the unused temporary segments and takes care of coalescing contiguous free space in the tablespaces.

Database Writer (DBW*n*)

The Database Writer process actually writes to the datafiles. It writes all the dirty buffer contents from the database buffer cache to the datafiles. There can be multiple DBW*n* processes running in the database to parallelize the writes. The first 36 DBW*n* processes are named DBW0–DBW9 and DBWa–DBWz. The names of the 37th through 100th DBW*n* processes are BW36–BW99. The Database Writer (DBW*n*) writes the dirty buffers to the database files on the occurrence of either of these events:

- When a server process cannot find a clean or free buffer after scanning the minimum threshold number
- On the occurrence of a checkpoint

Log Writer (LGWR)

The Log Writer process writes the contents of the log buffer inside the SGA to the online redo log files. Then the log buffer is available for reuse. The LGWR starts writing the log buffer out to the redo logs in the following events:

- Whenever there is a commit
- On occurrence of log switch
- Three seconds after the last write by LGWR
- When the redo log buffer is a third full or contains 1MB of buffered data
- When the DBW*n* writes dirty blocks to the datafiles

As discussed previously, the log files are always mirrored/multiplexed, so the LGWR always writes to multiple copies of the log files simultaneously.

Checkpoint (CKPT)

A checkpoint event triggers a write of data from the database buffer cache to datafiles. When the checkpoint occurs, it updates the control file and datafile headers with the checkpoint information, which includes SCN, location in online redo log file, and other information.

Recoverer (RECO)

The Recoverer process is responsible for resolving failures in distributed transactions. The RECO process of a node automatically connects to other databases involved in an in-doubt distributed transaction. As soon as RECO makes a connection, it automatically resolves all the failed/in-doubt transactions.

Other Processes

Oracle databases run several other processes. Discussing each process in detail is beyond the scope of this book, but several processes and brief descriptions are compiled in Table 1-1. The processes related to the In-Memory Column Store are covered in Chapter 2.

Acronym	Process Name	Description	Required for Basic DB Operation?	Started by Default?
ABMR	Automatic Block Media Recovery background process	Coordinates execution of tasks such as filtering duplicate block media recovery requests and performing flood control.	No	No
AP*nn*	Logical standby/ Streams apply process coordinator process	Obtains transactions from the reader server and passes them to apply servers.	No	No

TABLE 1-1.   *Oracle Background Processes (continued)*

Acronym	Process Name	Description	Required for Basic DB Operation?	Started by Default?
ARCn	Archiver process (30 possible)	Copies the redo log files to archival storage when they are full or an online redo log switch occurs.	No	No
BMRn	Automatic Block Media Recovery Slave Pool process	Fetches blocks from a real-time readable standby database.	No	No
BWnn	Database Writer process (20 possible)	Writes modified blocks from the database buffer cache to the data files. The 37th–100th Database Writer processes are named BW36–BW99. (See the section "Database Writer [DBWn]" and the table entry for DBWn for more information.)	Yes	Yes
CJQ0	Job Queue Coordinator process	Spawns Job Queue slave processes (Jnnn) to execute jobs in the queue.	No	Yes
CKPT	Checkpoint process	Signals DBWn at checkpoints and updates all the datafiles and control files of the database to indicate the most recent checkpoint.	Yes	Yes
CPnn	Database Capture process	Captures database changes from the redo log by using the infrastructure of LogMiner.	No	No
CSnn	I/O calibration process	Issues I/Os to storage as part of storage calibration. There is one slave process per CPU on each node of the database.	Yes	Yes
CXnn	Streams Propagation sender process	Sends LCRs to a propagation receiver.	No	No
CTWR	Change Tracking Writer process	Tracks changed data blocks as part of the RMAN block change tracking feature.	No	No

TABLE 1-1. *Oracle Background Processes (continued)*

Acronym	Process Name	Description	Required for Basic DB Operation?	Started by Default?
DBRM	Database RMAN process	Sets resource plans and performs other RMAN tasks.	No	Yes
DBW*n*	Database Writer process	Writes modified blocks from the database buffer cache to the data files. There can be 1–100 DBW*n* processes. The first 36 DBW*n* processes are named DBW0–DBW9 and DBWa–DBWz. The 37th–100th DBW*n* processes are named BW36–BW99.	Yes	Yes
DIA0	Diagnostic process 0 (although 10 possible, 0 is currently used)	Responsible for hang detection and deadlock resolution. Triggers DIAG to perform diagnostic tasks.	Yes	Yes
DIAG	Diagnostic Capture process	Performs diagnostic dumps and executes global oradebug commands.	Yes	Yes
DM*nn*	Data Pump Master process	Coordinates the Data Pump job tasks performed by Data Pump worker processes and handles client interactions.	No	No
D*nnn*	Dispatcher process	In a shared server configuration, dispatchers place connection requests in a connection request queue.	No	Yes
DW*nn*	Data Pump Worker process	Performs Data Pump tasks as assigned by the Data Pump Master process.	No	No
EMNC	Event Monitor (EMON) Coordinator process	Coordinates the event management and notification activity in the database, including Streams event notifications, Continuous Query Notifications, and Fast Application Notifications. Spawns EMON slave processes.	No	No

TABLE 1-1. *Oracle Background Processes (continued)*

Acronym	Process Name	Description	Required for Basic DB Operation?	Started by Default?
E*nnn*	EMON Slave process	Performs database event management and notifications.	No	No
FBDA	Flashback Data Archiver process	Archives historical rows for tracked tables into Flashback Data Archives and manages archive space, organization, and retention.	No	No
FMON	File Mapping Monitor process	Spawns FMPUTL, an external non-Oracle Database process that communicates with the mapping libraries provided by storage vendors. Responsible for managing the mapping information.	No	No
GEN0	General task execution process	Performs required tasks, including SQL and DML.	Yes	Yes
I*nnn*	Disk and Tape I/O Slave process	Serves as an I/O slave process spawned on behalf of DBWR, LGWR, or an RMAN backup session.	No	No
IMCO	In-Memory Coordinator process	Instigates trickle repopulation for any In-Memory Compression Unit (IMCU).	No	No
J*nnn*	Job Queue Slave processes	Processes jobs in the queue; spawned by CJQ0.	No	Yes
LG*n*	Log Writer Slave process	On multiprocessor systems, LGWR creates slave processes to improve the performance of writing to the redo log. LGWR slaves are not used when there is a SYNC standby destination.	No	No
LGWR	Log Writer process	Writes the log buffer out to the redo logs.	Yes	Yes
L*nnn*	Pooled Server process	Handles client requests in Database Resident Connection Pooling (DRCP).	No	No

TABLE 1-1. *Oracle Background Processes (continued)*

Acronym	Process Name	Description	Required for Basic DB Operation?	Started by Default?
LREG	Listener Registration process	Notifies the listeners about instances, services, handlers, and endpoints.	Yes	Yes
MMAN	Memory Manager process	Serves as the SGA Memory Broker and coordinates the sizing of the memory components.	No	Yes
MMNL	Manageability Monitor Lite process	Performs frequent and lightweight manageability-related tasks such as session history capture and metrics computation.	No	Yes
MMON	Manageability Monitor process	Collects statistics for the Automatic Workload Repository (AWR).	No	Yes
Mnnn	MMON Slave process	Performs manageability tasks on behalf of MMON.	No	No
MSnn	LogMiner Worker process	Reads redo log files and translates and assembles into transactions.	No	No
Nnnn	Connection Broker process	Monitors idle connections and hands off active connections in database resident connection pooling.	No	No
OFSD	Oracle File Server background process	Listens for new file system requests, both management (such as mount, unmount, and export) and I/O requests, and executes them using Oracle threads.	Yes	Yes
PMON	Process Monitor	Recovers failed process resources. If shared server architecture is used, PMON monitors and restarts any failed dispatcher or server processes.	Yes	Yes

TABLE 1-1.   *Oracle Background Processes (continued)*

Acronym	Process Name	Description	Required for Basic DB Operation?	Started by Default?
Pnnn	Parallel Query Slave process	Started and stopped as needed to participate in parallel query operations.	No	No
PRnn	Parallel Recovery process	Performs tasks assigned by the coordinator process performing parallel recovery	No	No
PSP0	Process Spawner process	Starts and stops Oracle processes. Reduces workload of ASM Rebalance Master Process (RBAL) by starting/stopping ASM rebalance slaves.	No	Yes
RCBG	Result Cache Background process	Supports SQL query and PL/SQL function result caches.	No	No
RECO	Recoverer Process	Resolves failures involving distributed transactions.	No	Yes
RM	Real Application Testing (RAT) Masking Slave process	Used with data masking and RAT.	No	Yes
RPnn	Capture Processing Worker process	Processes a set of workload capture files.	No	No
RPOP	Instant Recovery Repopulation daemon	Re-creates and/or repopulates data files from snapshot files and backup files. It works with the instant recovery feature to ensure immediate data file access. The local instance has immediate access to the remote snapshot file's data, while repopulation of the recovered primary data files happens concurrently. Any changes in the data are managed between the instance's DBW processes and RPOP to ensure the latest copy of the data is returned to the user.	No	No

TABLE 1-1. *Oracle Background Processes (continued)*

Acronym	Process Name	Description	Required for Basic DB Operation?	Started by Default?
RVWR	Recovery Writer process	Writes flashback data to flashback database logs in the flash recovery area.	No	No
SA*nn*	SGA Allocator process	A small fraction of SGA is allocated during instance startup. The SA*nn* process allocates the rest of SGA in small chunks. The process exits upon completion of SGA allocation.	No	Yes
SMCO	Space Management Coordinator process	Coordinates the execution of various space management–related tasks, such as proactive space allocation and space reclamation.	No	Yes
SMON	System Monitor process	Performs critical tasks, such as instance recovery and dead transaction recovery, and maintenance tasks, such as temporary space reclamation, data dictionary cleanup, and undo tablespace management.	Yes	Yes
S*nnn*	Shared Server process	In a shared server configuration, shared servers check a connection request queue (populated by dispatchers) and service the connection requests.	No	Yes
VKRM	Virtual Scheduler for RMAN process	Centralized scheduler for RMAN activity.	No	Yes
VKTM	Virtual Keeper of Time process	Responsible for providing a wall-clock time (updated every second) and reference-time counter (updated every 20 ms and available only when running at elevated priority).	Yes	Yes
W*nnn*	Space Management slave process	Slave processes spawned by SMCO to execute space management tasks.	No	Yes

TABLE 1-1.   *Oracle Background Processes*

Summary

In this chapter, you have learned that a database consists of physical files that store the entire data set and an instance. An instance has a set of memory structures and background processes that are used to manage the physical files. Thus, Oracle Database server = physical files + instance.

A database can have one single instance or more than one instance. If the database has only one instance, it is called a single-instance database; if it has more than one instance, it is called a Real Application Cluster (RAC) database.

A database can be divided into three major structures: storage, memory, and processes. The storage structure can again be divided into physical and logical storage. *Physical* storage refers to the physical files, and *logical* storage refers to the logical distribution of data in the form of tables, indexes, tablespaces, and so on.

The physical structure of the database comprises database files, control files, online redo log files, archived redo log files, parameter file, password file, alert log file, trace files, dumps and core files, and backup files.

The logical structure of the database enables better control over data processing, storage, and retrieval. There are four components of the logical structure of the database: block, extent, segment and tablespace.

The memory structure resides in the instance of the database. The memory area contains frequently used code, frequently used data, details of the connected sessions, and details of the queries that are being processed by the database. The memory structure of Oracle Database consists of SGA and PGA. SGA is made up of the database buffer cache, In-Memory Column Store, redo log buffer, shared pool, large pool, Java pool, Streams pool, and fixed area.

The instance of an Oracle database consists of several background processes, which are started when the instance is started. Oracle Database uses these background processes to complete several tasks, and each background process has a unique task. The most important mandatory processes are Process Monitor (PMON), System Monitor (SMON), Database Writer (DBRW), Log Writer (LGWR), Checkpoint (CKPT), and Recoverer (RECO) processes.

CHAPTER
2

In-Memory Architecture

Back in 2005, the average Oracle database was several terabytes in size; at that time, managing a database of just a few terabytes proved to be an arduous task for the database administrator (DBA). This is already an archaic thought, however, because databases these days are measured in petabytes; managing a database of that size is no longer a big deal for the DBA. Technological advancements have enabled the database to perform more functions than ever before. What was fastest yesterday is not even in the race today. Even the definition of *fast* has completely changed!

Businesses must quickly learn and implement new features to keep pace with competition. As service-level agreements (SLAs) have become more and more stringent, the amount of work performed by today's database has increased manifold. A SQL query could once run on small-scale data since the overall size of the database was small, but the substantial increase in the size of the data set now limits that SQL query's effectiveness.

And it's not just existing data sets that must be considered. Businesses continue adding new functionality, locations, and geographies, and these increase the load on the database. As the database size grows, more and more data needs to be processed. Yet businesses cannot afford delays in getting a report or changes in turnaround time—instead, they expect more and more out of the database technology.

Many of today's new technologies are disruptive in nature, requiring a change in either IT or business processes or a change in application code. Implementing these changes comes with a lot of risk. What if businesses were able to manage the transformation without changing any business process, application code, or IT processes? The result would be unprecedented opportunities for growth without the risk and negative impacts. The need for "speed-of-light" processing power brought about Oracle Database In-Memory. Database In-Memory enables you to put the identified set of data or the working set of data into the system memory. So when any query is executed on that data set, the data is fetched straight from the Dynamic Random Access Memory (DRAM) instead of the hard drive, resulting in very fast turnaround time. If the data is accessed straight from the memory, the network layer is completely bypassed, resulting in very low latency and thus providing instantaneous results.

Advantages of Running Database In-Memory

The Database In-Memory option offers several advantages:

- **Reduces total cost of ownership (TCO) and addresses need for increased speed** The main reason why organizations are considering the Database In-Memory option is speed—or, at least, the benefits obtained from speed. With In-Memory, a business can change a few small business processes because the application runs faster; this was not possible previously. Consider a demand forecasting example: A coffee shop at one location sells out all the contents of its bakery by the afternoon. In another coffee shop run by the same company, however, all the baked goods are still available in the evening. This type of issue occurs because the coffee company is not able to run store-level demand forecasting. Using Database In-Memory, however, the company can directly connect to a store and perform the correct demand forecasting to ensure that the appropriate amount of product is available to meet the demand. Similarly, when we visit a store of a company that manufactures electronic tablets, phones, and watches and the product we want is sold out, the sales representative often cannot tell us when the new supplies are due to arrive. This is because they cannot run demand forecasting at the store level. For both the examples if you want to process the massive data without implementing Database In-Memory option, you have to spend at least two to three more times more in hardware. Thus this option reduces TCO.

- **Processes massive amounts of data in real time** The In-Memory database takes advantage of in-memory processing in order to process data in real time, which empowers the business to deliver information at unprecedented speeds. The real-time responsiveness enabled by Oracle Database In-Memory can deliver insights at the moment important decisions need to be made.

- **Expands server memory to 64TB** RAM has become cheap, and some of the biggest servers have up to 64TB of memory, which provides huge headroom to process lots of data in memory.

(continued)

- **Requires no change in application code**   Running Oracle Database In-Memory does not require any changes in the application code, which provides the biggest bang for the buck. In-Memory works transparently with existing applications, business intelligence, and reporting tools. It is compatible with all Oracle and independent software vendor (ISV) tools and applications in addition to custom-written applications.

- **It's easy to deploy**   Implementing Oracle Database In-Memory is an easy and straightforward process. There is no need to migrate any data for implementation. The database stores the data in row format, which is automatically converted into columnar format when populating In-Memory Column Store.

- **Offers improved data persistence**   Oracle Database In-Memory supports data persistence in the memory, and Oracle's engineered system takes care of the data in case of memory failure.

- **Supports In-Memory compression**   Oracle Database In-Memory supports in-memory compression, so more data can be processed with the In-Memory option.

- **Requires no database modifications**   Oracle Database In-Memory can be implemented without modifying the physical structure of the database; there is no need to migrate the database or reorganize the tables.

- **Requires no additional hardware purchases**   The existing servers on which the Oracle Database runs today can be leveraged to implement the In-Memory Option. If the memory of the existing server is inadequate, additional memory can be added to the existing server to allow for more tables and table partitions in memory. Of course, customers can always buy new hardware with massive memory capability, but this is not mandatory.

- **Offers compatibility with other Oracle Database features**   The In-Memory option is compatible with all other features of the Oracle Database, such as Oracle Real Application Clusters (RAC),

Oracle Multitenant, Advanced Compression partitioning, and Active Data Guard. Running the In-Memory option has no impact on these features, and the features work exactly the same way with and without the In-Memory option.

- **Supports Online Transaction Processing (OLTP) and analytics**   Oracle Database In-Memory's unique dual format enables transparent scale-up and scale-out for analytics and OLTP workloads running together.

- **Supports high availability (HA)**   The In-Memory Column Store supports HA. All the database HA features are supported. With RAC, each RAC node has its own In-Memory Column Store; with Oracle Exadata Database Machine, the Column Store is duplicated across Exadata compute nodes.

Row vs. Column Processing

Before we discuss the In-Memory architecture, you need to understand how objects are stored in a table inside the database. Oracle uses rows and columns to store data inside the table. As you are probably aware, every new transaction is stored in a new row in an Oracle database, that row is divided into multiple columns, and each column stores a different attribute about the transaction. We can say that Oracle Database traditionally stores the data in a row format. Storing the data in a row format is optimized for Online Transaction Processing (OLTP) workloads, and it is even optimized for inserts and updates.

OLTP operations tend to access only a few rows, but they normally touch all the columns. For example, when you run a query to select the list of inventory on a particular date (July 4, 2015) for a particular object (say, a chair) for a particular attribute (say, the color red) from the inventory table, the query will provide the details of all red chairs in stock on July 4, 2015. If there were 100 red chairs in stock, the query would fetch the details for all 100 objects. In this case, the query is going to fetch 100 rows, one for each chair, and the columns inside each row will provide more detailed information about each chair. A row format allows quick access to all of the columns in a record, because all the data for a given record is kept together in memory and on

FIGURE 2-1. *Accessing row data*

storage. Since all data for a row is kept together, whenever a query is run, a contiguous row is accessed, resulting in faster data access. Row access is depicted in Figure 2-1.

With analytical workloads, storing the data in row format is not optimal, since an analytical workload mostly scans all the data sets on fewer columns. Say, for example, that you want to run a report on sales numbers; you will be querying only a few columns from the sales table. A column format is ideal for analytics because it allows for faster data retrieval when only a few columns are selected—this is because all the data for a column is kept together in memory and a single memory access will load many column values. Storing data in columnar format provides faster filtering and aggregation, making it the ideal and most efficient format for analytics. For inserts, updates, and delete operations, a column format is not so efficient at processing row-wise Data Manipulation Language (DML). To insert or delete a single record in a column format, all of the columnar structures in the table must be changed. The columnar format is depicted in Figure 2-2.

FIGURE 2-2. *Accessing columnar data*

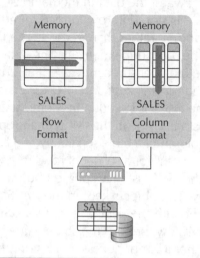

FIGURE 2-3. *Accessing data with In-Memory's dual format*

Thus it can be seen that OLTP benefits the best from the row format, whereas analytics benefits the most from a column format. Choosing one format over the other involves a tradeoff of either suboptimal OLTP or suboptimal analytics.

The Database In-Memory option solves that problem, however, bringing the best of both worlds. With In-Memory, data is stored in a dual format (row and columnar format), benefitting both analytics and OLTP. Figure 2-3 depicts the dual format.

Database In-Memory Architecture

In the last chapter, we studied the various components of the System Global Area (SGA). As you will recall, one component of the SGA was the In-Memory Column Store (IMCS), which we will discuss in detail now.

The In-Memory Area is an optional component in the SGA, which is dedicated for Database In-Memory. The In-Memory Area contains the IMCS, which stores tables, table partitions, and/or materialized views in DRAM in a columnar format for Database In-Memory processing. Once the IMCS is implemented, its size can be increased dynamically without restarting the database. The In-Memory Area is dynamic, which means you can modify the size even if the database is open.

As you are probably aware, the data in the database buffer cache (also a component of the SGA) is stored in row format. In the IMCS, the data is populated in columnar format rather than in rows. The IMCS does not replace the database buffer cache, but supplements it. The database buffer cache stores the data using the LRU (least recently used) algorithm, in which the MRU (most recently used) data is kept and LRU data is phased out.

Data populated in the IMCS is stored in In-Memory Compression Units (IMCUs). An IMCU is a storage unit in the IMCS that is optimized for fast scans. The IMCS stores each column in a table separately and compresses it. Each IMCU contains all the columns for a subset of rows in a specific table segment.

The data stored in the IMCS is never phased out. It is not a cache, but a static pool of memory. The objects kept in the IMCS are always kept transactionally consistent with the database buffer cache, which means a query directed to the IMCS will return the same value if it is directed to the database buffer cache. It is not necessary to store the data populated in the IMCS in the database buffer cache. Thus, the IMCS provides an additional transaction-consistent copy of the table that is independent of the disk format. Again, data is always stored in the storage, so there are no synchronization issues. Storing the data in columnar format makes it highly optimized for rapid scans. Storing data using Oracle's IMCS technology is a pure in-memory format. The in-memory columnar format is not persisted on storage and never causes extra writes to disk. The data is also not logged.

The In-Memory Area can be specified by initialization parameter **INMEMORY_SIZE**. By default, the IMCS is disabled, and the size of the In-Memory Area is 0. The In-Memory Area can be queried from views V$SGA and V$INMEMORY_AREA.

In the following query, the In-Memory Area is allocated to the SGA, which is depicted in boldface:

```
SELECT * FROM V$SGA;

NAME                      VALUE
------------------  ---------
Fixed Size                 5837574
Variable Size      990421802
Database Buffers        83340222431
Redo Buffers       27848521
In-Memory Area          21474836480
```

By combining the database buffer cache and the IMCS, an Oracle database stores data in both row and columnar format, providing the best of both worlds.

The IMCS is not a replacement for the database buffer cache, however, since the data is stored in different formats in each of these memory structures. If you are planning to enable the IMCS, you should increase the size of the SGA to account for this. If you do not want to increase the total size of the SGA, the database buffer cache size is going to take a hit. Figure 2-4 shows the correlation of SGA_TARGET and INMEMORY_SIZE.

Here's an example to illustrate this. Say that today your SGA size is 100GB—that is, the **SGA_TARGET** parameter is set to 100GB. If you want to dedicate 30GB for the In-Memory Area without impacting the database buffer cache, you need to increase the **SGA_TARGET** by an additional 30GB, making it 130GB. If you keep the **SGA_TARGET** as 100GB, even after implementing the In-Memory Area, then only 70GB is available for the database buffer cache and shared pool. This memory area is not affected or controlled by Automatic Memory Management, which means the database does not decrease the size allocated to the In-Memory Area when the shared pool or database buffer cache needs more memory—and vice versa. The only way to increase or decrease the size allocated to the In-Memory Area is by changing the initialization parameter associated with it.

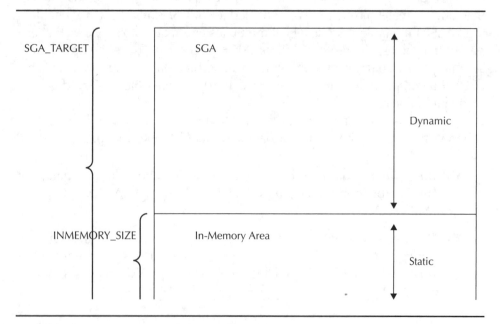

FIGURE 2-4. *Correlation of SGA_TARGET and INMEMORY_SIZE*

Depending on how many objects you want to keep in the IMCS, you need to size it accordingly. You can always start with a very small size and gradually expand it, depending on your needs. The larger the size of the IMCS, the larger the number of objects you can place there.

NOTE
The IMCS is available only with Oracle Database 12.1.0.2 and later versions. The IMCS is included with the Oracle Database In-Memory Option.

The IMCS can be enabled at the following levels:

- Column (virtual or nonvirtual)
- Table
- Materialized view
- Partition of a table or materialized view
- Tablespace

If you enable the IMCS for a table or materialized view, all the columns of that table or materialized view are enabled for IMCS. Similarly, if you enable the IMCS at the tablespace level, all the tables and materialized views that are part of that tablespace are enabled for IMCS. You always have the option of selecting a few columns of a particular table to be a part of the IMCS, which gives you complete flexibility to decide when and what objects should be loaded in the IMCS.

The database internally divides the In-Memory Area into two different subpools for keeping the columnar data and metadata information:

- **The columnar data pool**   This subpool stores the columnar data. This can be identified from the V$INMEMORY_AREA view as the 1MB POOL row.

- **The metadata pool**   This subpool contains metadata for the objects stored in the IMCS. It does not store actual data—just the metadata. This can be identified from the V$INMEMORY_AREA view as the 64KB POOL row.

The subpool sizes cannot be manually modified, since they are managed automatically by Oracle Database. Oracle allocates most of the size for the columnar data pool in order to store more data.

The following query shows the distribution of 1MB pool and 64KB pool:

```
SQL> SELECT POOL, TRUNC(ALLOC_BYTES/(1024*1024*1024),2) "ALLOC_GB",
TRUNC(USED_BYTES/(1024*1024*1024),2) "USED_GB",POPULATE_STATUS
FROM V$INMEMORY_AREA;

POOL        ALLOC_GB USED_GB POPULATE_STATUS
--------- ---------- ---------- ----------------
1MB POOL    15.98      0       DONE
64KB POOL    3.96      0       DONE
```

In the previous example, where we ran the query (**SELECT * FROM V$SGA;**), the In-Memory Area was 20GB. If you add both the pool sizes (15.98 + 3.96), this becomes 19.94GB, not 20GB. This is because the database uses a very small percentage of memory allocated to the In-Memory Area for internal management structures.

The columnar pool stores the In-Memory Compression Units and In-Memory Expression Units, whereas the metadata pool stores the Snapshot Metadata Units (SMUs), which we are going to study in next section.

In-Memory Storage Units

The In-Memory Area can be subdivided into storage units that consist of the following:

- In-Memory Compression Units (IMCUs)

- Snapshot Metadata Units (SMUs)

- In-Memory Expression Units (IMEUs)

Figure 2-5 shows the relationship among the three components.

In-Memory Compression Unit (IMCU)

The IMCU is a compressed storage unit that contains the actual data for columns kept in the memory. Any column of an object can be kept in the database memory by specifying the **INMEMORY** clause. We will explore this in more detail in Chapter 3.

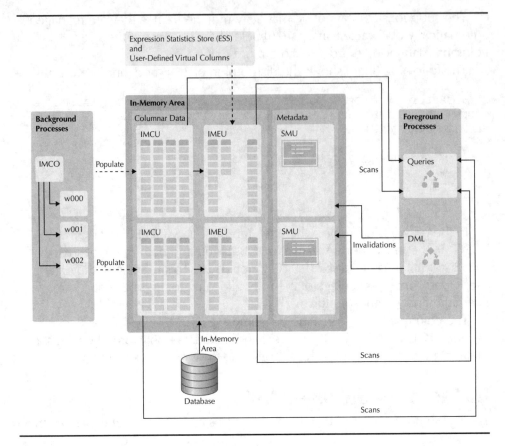

FIGURE 2-5. *Components of in-memory storage units*

An IMCU is a read-only storage unit that is optimized for faster scans. The IMCS stores each column of the object (such as table, partition, materialized view) separately and compresses it. The IMCS consists of multiple IMCUs.

Each IMCU contains a subset of database blocks or rows for a specific object. Each IMCU also contains all columns for a subset of rows (also called granule units) in a specific table segment. There is only one object per IMCU. IMCU also contains null column values.

A one-to-many mapping exists between the IMCU and a set of database blocks. If the rows are stored in *x* number of blocks on disk, then there might be multiple IMCUs to distribute the data of *x* blocks. For example, IMCU1 may store the first 30 database blocks, IMCU2 may store the next 30 database blocks, IMCU3 may store the next 30 database blocks, and so on. It is not necessary that all the IMCUs be the same size. IMCUs can vary in size depending on the data types stored and the compression ratio achieved in the IMCS.

In-Memory Columnar Compression The In-Memory Columnar Compression provides the ability to compress data in the range of 2x to 20x, depending on the data types and the distribution of the data. As a result, the amount of data that can be fit into In-Memory is significant, since we are compressing it as we populate it. In-Memory Columnar Compression is a special query processing algorithm that allows queries to execute directly against the compressed data. The compression format used by IMCS is optimized for access speed rather than storage reduction. In-Memory Columnar Compression in the IMCS is very similar to the Hybrid Columnar Compression (HCC) used in Oracle's popular Exadata Database machines. While HCC is optimized for disk storage, In-Memory Columnar Compression in the IMCS is optimized for memory.

A column compression unit (CU) is the contiguous storage for a single column in an IMCU. A CU is the smallest unit of storage. Each IMCU can have one or more CUs.

A CU includes a body and a header. The body stores all the column values for the range of rows included in the IMCU. The CU always stores the values in the order of rowid. Storing data in this fashion is very helpful, since the database can quickly retrieve the data for a given query by tying the rows back together. The header contains the metadata information about the data stored in the CUs—for example, the header may contain the minimum or maximum value information. As shown in Figure 2-6, the CU header contains a minimum value of California (1) and a maximum value of Texas (2).

A CU may also contain a local dictionary that is used to store the distinct value of data in *dictionary code*. For example, in the State column of the sales

	CU
California	1
Texas	2
Washington	3
California	1
California	1
Texas	2

FIGURE 2-6. *Column CU header*

table, if there are multiple occurrences of a few states, the data might be stored in a local dictionary. Suppose, for example, three states are included: California, Texas, and Washington. The value of California is allocated as 1 in the local dictionary, the value of Texas is allocated as 2, and the value of Washington is allocated as 3. In a CU, whenever there is an occurrence of these states, the corresponding value of 1, 2, or 3 will be stored. This is depicted in Figure 2-6.

The **MEMCOMPRESS** subclause of the **INMEMORY** clause specifies different compression options for each table, partition, or column. To disable the compression, you can use the subclause **NOMEMCOMPRESS**. The six levels of in-memory compression are shown in Table 2-1.

Unless explicitly stated, the default compression algorithm used by IMCS is QUERY LOW. The compression technique used can vary across columns or partitions within a single table. For example, some columns in a table can be optimized for scan speed, and others for space saving.

Compression Level	Purpose/Usage
MEMCOMPRESS FOR DML	Optimizes DML performance by applying minimal compression.
MEMCOMPRESS FOR QUERY LOW	(Default) Provides the fastest read times, because the database does not need to decompress the data. It applies common compression techniques such as dictionary encoding, run-length encoding, and bit packing.
MEMCOMPRESS FOR QUERY HIGH	Optimizes compression for performance and space saving.
MEMCOMPRESS FOR CAPACITY LOW	Optimizes compression for both performance and space saving, but is better for space saving. It applies a proprietary compression technique called OZIP that offers fast compression tuned specifically for Oracle Database. This option can affect performance because Oracle Database must decompress each entry before applying query predicates.
MEMCOMPRESS FOR CAPACITY HIGH	Optimizes compression for space saving. It applies a heavyweight space-saving algorithm with a larger penalty for decompression. This option can affect performance, because Oracle Database must decompress each entry before applying query predicates.
NO MEMCOMPRESS	Data is populated without any compression.

TABLE 2-1. *In-Memory Compression Levels*

During table creation, you can add the columns you want directly to memory. You can also specify the compression algorithm at this time. As shown in the following code example, we have enabled **INMEMORY** across the table, except for the column sku. We have enabled **MEMCOMPRESS FOR QUERY** at the table level, whereas for the column quantity, we have enabled **MEMCOMPRESS FOR CAPACITY HIGH**.

```
CREATE TABLE inventory
( item VARCHAR2( 25),
quantity NUMBER,
location VARCHAR2( 10),
sku CLOB
)
INMEMORY  MEMCOMPRESS FOR QUERY
NO INMEMORY(sku)
INMEMORY MEMCOMPRESS FOR CAPCITY HIGH(quantity);
```

You can use the Oracle Compression Advisor to estimate the compression ratio achieved using the **MEMCOMPRESS** clause. You can run the procedure **DBMS_COMPRESSION.GET_COMPRESSION_RATIO** on a table to analyze the results. The **GET_COMPRESSION_RATIO** is discussed next.

GET_COMPRESSION_RATIO Procedure

This procedure analyzes the compression ratio of a table and provides information about the compressibility of a table. The user can provide various parameters to selectively analyze different compression types.

Syntax

The syntax for **GET_COMPRESSION_RATIO** for an object (table or index) is provided next. The default object is table.

```
DBMS_COMPRESSION.GET_COMPRESSION_RATIO (
    scratchtbsname      IN      VARCHAR2,
    ownname             IN      VARCHAR2,
    objname             IN      VARCHAR2,
```

```
        subobjname              IN      VARCHAR2,
        comptype                IN      NUMBER,
        blkcnt_cmp              OUT     PLS_INTEGER,
        blkcnt_uncmp            OUT     PLS_INTEGER,
        row_cmp                 OUT     PLS_INTEGER,
        row_uncmp               OUT     PLS_INTEGER,
        cmp_ratio               OUT     NUMBER,
        comptype_str            OUT     VARCHAR2,
        subset_numrows          IN      NUMBER   DEFAULT COMP_RATIO_MINROWS,
        objtype                 IN      PLS_INTEGER DEFAULT OBJTYPE_TABLE);
```

The syntax for **GET_COMPRESSION_RATIO** for LOBs is provided next:

```
DBMS_COMPRESSION.GET_COMPRESSION_RATIO (
        scratchtbsname          IN      VARCHAR2,
        tabowner                IN      VARCHAR2,
        tabname                 IN      VARCHAR2,
        lobname                 IN      VARCHAR2,
        partname                IN      VARCHAR2,
        comptype                IN      NUMBER,
        blkcnt_cmp              OUT     PLS_INTEGER,
        blkcnt_uncmp            OUT     PLS_INTEGER,
        lobcnt                  OUT     PLS_INTEGER,
        cmp_ratio               OUT     NUMBER,
        comptype_str            OUT     VARCHAR2,
        subset_numrows          IN      number DEFAULT COMP_RATIO_LOB_MAXROWS);
```

In the syntax for **GET_COMPRESSION_RATIO** for all indexes on a table, the compression ratios are returned as a collection:

```
DBMS_COMPRESSION.GET_COMPRESSION_RATIO (
        scratchtbsname          IN      VARCHAR2,
        ownname                 IN      VARCHAR2,
        tabname                 IN      VARCHAR2,
        comptype                IN      NUMBER,
        index_cr                OUT     compRecList,
        comptype_str            OUT     VARCHAR2,
        subset_numrows          IN      NUMBER DEFAULT COMP_RATIO_INDEX_MINROWS);
```

Following are the parameters for the **GET_COMPRESSION_RATIO** procedure:

Parameter	Description
scratchtbsname	Temporary scratch tablespace that can be used for analysis
ownname/tabowner	Schema of the table to analyze
tabname	Name of the table to analyze
objname	Name of the object
subobjname	Name of the partition or subpartition of the object
comptype	Compression types for which analysis should be performed
blkcnt_cmp	Number of blocks used by compressed sample of the table
blkcnt_uncmp	Number of blocks used by uncompressed sample of the table
row_cmp	Number of rows in a block in compressed sample of the table
row_uncmp	Number of rows in a block in uncompressed sample of the table
cmp_ratio	Compression ratio, **blkcnt_uncmp** divided by **blkcnt_cmp**
comptype_str	String describing the compression type
subset_numrows	Number of rows sampled to estimate compression ratio
objtype	Type of the object; should be a constant to indicate object types defined in this package
lobname	Name of the LOB column
partname	In case of partitioned tables, the related partition name
lobcnt	Number of LOBs actually sampled to estimate compression ratio
index_cr	List of indexes and their estimated compression ratios

In-Memory Storage Index (IMSI) For every column in the IMCS, the database automatically creates and manages an In-Memory Storage Index (IMSI). The IMSI is created by the IMCU header for its CUs. An IMSI stores the minimum and maximum values for each IMCU. IMSIs allow data pruning to occur based on the filter predicates supplied in a SQL statement. Whenever a query specifies a where clause, the IMSI is referenced and checked to determine if the data queried for is in the range of minimum and maximum values of the IMCU. If the column value is outside the minimum and maximum range, the scan of that IMCU is avoided.

Let's look at an example. Suppose the sales table has millions of orders with unique order numbers. Now let's assume an IMCU stores 10,000 orders. IMCU 1 will store order numbers from 1 to 10,000, IMCU 2 will store order numbers 10,001 to 20,000, IMCU 3 will store order numbers 30,001 to 40,000, and so on. The IMSI will have the corresponding entries of the minimum and maximum values of the IMCU—that is, IMCU 1 has a minimum value of 1 and maximum value of 10,000, IMCU 2 has a minimum value of 10,001 and a maximum value of 20,000, and so on. Now if you run a query looking for the order number 251,098, the database optimizer will check the IMSI and will find that IMCU 25 has the minimum value of 250,001 and maximum value of 260,000. Thus, it will eliminate the scan of all other IMCUs and just fetch the data directly from IMCU 25.

Snapshot Metadata Units (SMUs)

Snapshot Metadata Units (SMUs) contain the metadata and transaction information for an IMCU. For each IMCU in the IMCS, a transactional journal is created and always maintained. The transactional journal associated with the IMCU takes care of keeping the data transactionally consistent with the row format. Let's see how the IMCU and SMUs actually work.

Suppose that a table exists both in the database buffer cache and IMCS. If a DML updates a row in the database buffer cache in the traditional way (just as it would be without Database In-Memory enabled), then the change must be reflected in the IMCS. The buffer cache and the IMCS are kept transactionally consistent via the In-Memory Transaction Manager. All logging is done on the base table, just as it was before; there is no logging needed for IMCS.

Similarly, when a DML statement changes a row in an object that is populated to the IMCS, the corresponding entries for that row are marked stale in the IMCU by recording the rowid for the row in the In-Memory transaction journal.

NOTE
In the context of Database In-Memory, population is the automatic transformation of row-based data on disk into columnar data in the IMCS.

Any transaction executing against this object in the IMCS that started before the DML occurred needs to see the original version of the entries. Read consistency in the IMCS is managed via system change numbers (SCNs), just as it is without Database In-Memory enabled. The original entries in the IMCU are not immediately replaced in order to provide read consistency and maintain data compression. When a query with a newer SCN is executed against the object, it will read all of the entries for the columns in the IMCU except the stale entries. The stale entries will be retrieved from the base table (buffer cache) via the rowids in the transaction journal.

If there are more stale entries in the IMCU, scans become slow. When the stale entries reach a certain threshold, Oracle Database automatically repopulates an IMCU. The repopulation is an online operation that is taken care of by background processes. The process of repopulation of data is directly proportional to the amount of stale data. The overhead for repopulation and keeping the IMCS transactionally active depends on a number of factors, including the compression level, rate of change, types of operations being performed, and location of the changed rows or those IMCUs that are accessed frequently. Tables with higher compression levels will incur more overhead than tables with lower compression levels. Changed rows that are co-located in the same block will incur less overhead than changed rows that are spread randomly across a table.

In-Memory Expression Units (IMEUs)

An *expression* is a combination of one or more values, operators, and SQL functions that evaluates to a value. When the In-Memory expression optimization is enabled, the database automatically calculates and caches results of frequently evaluated expressions. By default, this optimization is disabled.

The In-Memory expression is useful when querying a large data set, including extensive computation expressions. It provides immense performance benefits. If the IMCS does not populate the expression results, then the database must compute them for every row returned by the query, which is very resource intensive. In-Memory expression takes advantage of vector processing and IMCU pruning.

While In-Memory expression can be compared with materialized views, In-Memory expression has advantages over MVs:

- An MV must have all columns listed in the query, or the query must join the view and the base tables. In contrast, any query containing an In-Memory expression can benefit.

- In-Memory expressions are created automatically, whereas MVs need to be created manually.

- The database uses an LRU algorithm to keep only frequently used In-Memory expressions in memory.

The database computes and populates the result of an In-Memory expression in a container called an In-Memory Expression Unit (IMEU). Each IMEU maps to one In-Memory Compression Unit (IMCU). The IMEU contains expression results that correspond to the data contained in its associated IMCU.

The database treats materialized expressions just like other columns in the IMCU.

The database dedicates a small percentage of the IM column store for IMEUs. Depending on the access pattern, the database may or may not choose to populate the same IMEUs for every IMCU in an object.

The database automatically loads IM expressions into the IMEUs using background processes. The database calculates the values for the IM expressions during the initial load. If the source data changes, the database automatically changes the derived data in the IM expression.

The statistics about expressions are stored in the Expression Statistics Store (ESS), which is maintained by the database optimizer. The ESS resides in the SGA and is independent of the IMCS. Apart from residing in SGA, the ESS is also persisted in the disk. The optimizer extensively uses the ESS to evaluate whether an expression is a candidate for IM expressions.

The ESS maintains statistics about an expression in terms of number of times executed, cost of evaluation, and time when evaluated. Every time an expression is evaluated, the optimizer allocates a score in terms of cost, cardinality, and number of times evaluated. The higher the score, the more the chances of evaluating that expression as an IM expression.

SIMD Vector Processing

Another advantage of the In-Memory columnar representation is the ability to perform vector processing using very fast single instruction, multiple data (SIMD) values processing. The SIMD process is similar to array processing. It was originally designed for accelerating computer-generated animation and high-performance scientific computing. In our previous example, to count the number of chairs, we simply need to count the column chair and the number of its occurrences. SIMD allows up to 16 values to be checked in one CPU cycle, resulting in faster scan and filter operations. It is capable of scanning billions of rows per second per CPU core, providing exceptional speed. For example, imagine that an application issues a query to find the total stock in the inventory table using the tag 888, and the inventory table resides in the IMCS. The query begins by scanning only the inventory.tag column, as shown in Figure 2-7.

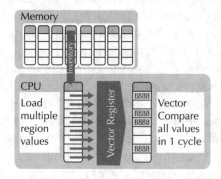

FIGURE 2-7. *SIMD processing a query*

The CPU evaluates the data as follows:

1. It loads the first eight values (the number varies depending on data type and compression mode) from the tag column into the SIMD register and then compares them with the value 888 in a single instruction.

2. It discards the entries that are not a match and keeps entries that do match.

3. It loads another eight values into the SIMD register and continues in this way until it has evaluated all the entries.

Data Load in In-Memory Column Store

The IMCS is populated (loaded in memory) by background processes, so the database is fully active and accessible while this occurs. In data warehouse environments, the data is often populated via bulk load. A bulk load operation is always conducted as a direct path load in which the input data is parsed and converted to an Oracle data type for each input field; then a column array structure is built for the data. These column array structures are used to format Oracle data blocks and build index keys. The data blocks are written directly to the database, and the direct path load bypasses the SQL processing engine and database buffer cache.

Since the data does not go through the database buffer cache, the operation cannot be committed until all data has been loaded. If anything goes wrong in the data load process, the entire operation needs to be restarted, because nothing is saved until the operation completes. A direct path load inserts data into database blocks that are created above the segment high water mark (the maximum number of database blocks used so far by an object or segment). Once the direct path load is committed, the high water mark is moved to encompass the newly created blocks into the segment, and the blocks will be made visible to other SQL operations on the same table. Until this point, the IMCS is not aware that the data change occurred.

Once the data is committed, the IMCS instantly realizes that the data is not populated in the IMCS. The size of the missing data will be visible in the BYTES_NOT_POPULATED column of the v$IM_SEGMENTS view. Depending on the **PRIORITY** specified, the data will be automatically added to the IMCS, or the background worker processes will be triggered to begin populating the missing data, assuming there is free space in the IMCS.

NOTE
*You will learn about specifying **PRIORITY** and populating data in the IMCS in detail in Chapter 3.*

Oracle always recommends partitioning all the larger tables or fact tables in the data warehouse. Partitioning helps to load data quickly, with minimal impact on users, via the **EXCHANGE PARTITION** command. This command allows the data in a nonpartitioned table to be swapped into a particular partition in a partitioned table. It does not physically move data, but rather updates the data dictionary to exchange a pointer from the partition to the table, and vice versa. Because there is no physical movement of data, a redo is not generated and performance is not compromised.

In this scenario, the IMCS is not aware of a partition exchange load until the operation has been completed. At that point, the data in the temporary table is part of the partitioned table. If the temporary table had the **INMEMORY** attribute set and all of its data has been populated into the IMCS, nothing else will happen. The data that was in the temporary table will simply be accessed via the IMCS along with the rest of the data in the partitioned table the next time it is scanned. If the temporary table did not have the **INMEMORY** attribute set, then all subsequent accesses to the data in the newly exchanged partition will occur via the buffer cache.

Two background processes are responsible for data population and managing the IMCS:

- In-Memory Coordinator (IMCO) process
- Space Management Slave process (W*nnn*)

The IMCO is mainly responsible for populating the data into the IMCS. It converts the row data into columnar format, compressing it at the same time. It gets invoked automatically and starts populating objects into memory when the objects have any priority other than **NONE**. IMCO uses the W*nnn* process to populate the objects that have a priority of **NONE**.

In addition to the standard repopulation algorithm, another algorithm attempts to clean all stale entries. The IMCO background process may also instigate "trickle repopulation" for any IMCUs in the IMCS that have some stale entries but do not currently meet the staleness threshold. Trickle repopulation is a constant background activity. By default, the IMCO wakes up every two minutes and checks whether any trickle repopulation task needs to be completed. When the IMCO wakes up, it also checks to see if there are any IMCUs with stale entries in the IMCS. The moment it finds stale entries, it triggers the slave processes to repopulate them.

The W*nnn* process gets into action whenever it is called by the IMCO. As discussed previously, this process is responsible for populating objects with priority **NONE**. When it populates the data, the W*nnn* process also creates IMCUs, SMUs, and IMEUs. While creating the IMEUs, it also identifies and creates virtual columns for data population. The W*nnn* process also associates the IMEUs with their corresponding IMCUs.

IM FastStart

In-Memory FastStart enables the database to open faster by sorting columnar data on disk. Whenever you restart the database, or if the database gets restarted due to any reason, the data in the IMCS needs to be repopulated. If you have a large amount of data, the repopulation operation can take a lot of CPU cycles and can result in poor performance. When IM FastStart is enabled, the database saves the columnar data into disk at regular intervals so that database population is faster in the event of database restart. The area where the columnar data is saved into the disk is called the FastStart area. Now, whenever the database is restarted or the database reads the columnar data from the FastStart area, it populates it into the IM column store, ensuring that all transactional consistencies are maintained. When the data is populated from the FastStart area to IMCS, the data population is governed by priority settings. You will learn about priority in Chapter 3. The FastStart area is used only for storing and managing the INMEMORY objects and nothing else.

The FastStart area is actually a tablespace that is dedicated for IM FastStart operations. There is only one tablespace created for the FastStart area per database. If you are using the multitenant option, then one tablespace is permitted for each PDB or non-CDB.

Once the FastStart area is enabled, while populating the data or repopulation after FastStart area is enabled, the database creates the FastStart area. This is how the database manages the FastStart area:

- When the data population or repopulation occurs, the database writes columnar data to the FastStart area. The Space Management Worker Processes (*Wnnn*) write IMCUs to the SecureFiles LOB named SYSDBinstance_name_LOBSEG$. The database writes FastStart metadata to the SYSAUX tablespace.

- If the attribute of the object is changed to NOINMEMORY, the database automatically removes the corresponding IMCUs from the FastStart area.

- If the FastStart area runs out of space, the database uses an internal algorithm to drop the oldest segments and continues writing to the FastStart area. For some reason if there is no space available, the database stops writing in the FastStart area.

- If you define an ADO policy on a segment, the database manages the segment in the FastStart area based on the rule in the policy. For example, if ADO specifies that an object changes its attribute to NO INMEMORY based on a policy, the IM column store removes its data from the FastStart area.

In-Memory with Automatic Data Optimization (ADO)

Heat Map is a feature in Oracle Database 12c that automatically tracks table/partition usage information at the row and segment levels. Data modification times are tracked at the row level and aggregated to the block level; modification times, full table scan times, and index lookup times are tracked at the segment level. Heat Map gives you a detailed view of how your data is being accessed and how access patterns are changing over time. Programmatic access to Heat Map data is available through a set of PL/SQL table functions, as well as through data dictionary views. For example, to obtain the read and write time for In-Memory objects, query the ALL_HEAT_MAP_SEGMENT view. When an IM column store is enabled, Heat Map tracks access patterns for columnar data.

Automatic Data Optimization (ADO) allows you to create policies for data compression and data movement, and to implement storage and compression tiering. Oracle Database periodically evaluates ADO policies and uses the information collected by Heat Map to determine when to move and/or compress data. All ADO operations are executed automatically and in the background, without user intervention. ADO policies can be specified at the segment or row level for tables and/or partitions. Policies will be evaluated and executed automatically in the background during the maintenance window. ADO uses the Job Scheduler to perform population. The job scheduler calls the In-Memory Coordinator (IMCO) process behind the scenes, which performs the actual data population.

In the 12.2 database release, ADO has been extended to encompass the IM column store. You can create ADO policies to set INMEMORY attributes on objects in the IM column store. ADO manages the content of the IM column store by executing user-defined policies to move tables or partitions in and out of the IM column store and adjusting the compression level of objects within the IM column store from a lower compression level to a higher compression level. For example, a policy can evict the customers table from the IM column store after 30 days of no access.

In-Memory ADO features require the initialization parameter settings HEAT_MAP=ON and a nonzero setting for INMEMORY_SIZE.

Three new policies have been added that enable managing objects in the IM column store, as shown in Table 2-2.

Restrictions and Usage

Almost all the objects in the database can be populated to the IMCS, yet there are some restrictions. The following object types cannot be populated in the IMCS:

■ Index-organized tables (IOTs)

■ Cluster tables

■ Objects owned by the SYS user and stored in the SYSTEM or SYSAUX tablespace

In addition to these objects, the following data types are not supported in IMCS:

■ LONGs

■ Out-of-line large objects (LOBs)

If you have a table or an object with these data types, all other columns with data types other than these will be eligible for the IMCS population. Note that any object smaller than 64KB will not be populated into the IMCS,

Policy Name	Description
SET INMEMORY	Enables the INMEMORY attribute on a specified segment
MODIFY INMEMORY	Changes the compression level of an object from a lower level of compression to a higher level
NO INMEMORY	Removes, or evicts, an object from the IM column store

TABLE 2-2. *Policies for Managing Objects in IMCS*

because the memory inside the IMCS is allocated in 1MB chunks. Any size smaller than this will waste a lot of space inside the IMCS.

The IMCS is hardware independent and is available on all hardware platforms and in the following common scenarios:

- Performing fast full scans of large tables

- Evaluating predicate filters that use operators such as =, <, >, and IN

- Querying a subset of columns in a table (such as selecting 5 of 100 columns)

- Accelerating joins by converting predicates on small dimension tables into filters on a large fact table

- Improving analytic query performance by caching the results of virtual columns and other frequently evaluated expressions

The analytics workload benefits the most from IMCS. Let's look at an example to see how the benefits are obtained from an IMCS. Suppose we have a table inventory, shown in Table 2-3, with four rows and six columns.

The inventory data is stored in row format, where each row contains detailed information about a particular type of inventory. Now if this table has

Name	ProductID	Color	Location	Quantity	Cost
Table	2245	Black	DEN	56	120
Chair	2284	Blue	PHX	12	45
Table	13323	Brown	DEN	198	240
Sofa	1214	Green	SFO	212	450

TABLE 2-3. *Inventory Table Example*

to be stored in the IMCS, we need to rotate it by 90 degrees and then reverse it, as shown in the following illustration:

Name	ProductID	Color	Location	Quantity	Cost
Table	2245	Black	DEN	56	120
Chair	2284	Blue	PHX	12	45
Table	13323	Brown	DEN	198	240
Sofa	1214	Green	SFO	212	450

Name	ProductID	Color	Location	Quantity	Cost
Table	2245	Black	DEN	56	120
Chair	2284	Blue	PHX	12	45
Table	13323	Brown	DEN	198	240
Sofa	1214	Green	SFO	212	450

This is how the table looks when the data is stored in the columnar format, in which the current rows used to be columns. Now let's take a closer look at the table in row format. The first row contained Table,2245,Black,Den,56,120; the second row contained Chair,2284,Blue,PHX,12,45. If we write the rows and the corresponding data, it would appear like so:

1:Table,2245,Black,DEN,56,120-2:Chair,2284,Blue,PHX,12,45-
3:Table,13323,Brown,DEN,198,240-4:Sofa,1214,Green,SFO,212,450

To represent this in columnar format, the structure will change to this:

Table:**1**,Chair:**2**,Table:**3**,Sofa:**4**;2245:**1**,2284:**2**,13323:**3**,1214:**4**,Black:**1**, Blue:**2**,Brown:**3**,Green:**4**;56:**1**,12:**2**,198:**3**,212:**4**;120:**1**,45:**2**,240:**3**,450:**4**

If you observe carefully, you'll see that the first part of the table structure (which is underlined) is the first column, and the first value is associated with the first rowid, then the second value with the second rowid, and so on.

Now look carefully at the first part of the table structure: Table:**1**,Chair:**2**, Table:**3**,Sofa:**4**. The second value of the Name column is "Table"; thus, you can compress the data, keeping only one entry for Table: Table,**1**:**3**,Chair:**3**, Sofa:**4**.

Summary

In this chapter, you have learned the advantages of Database In-Memory, which include reduced total cost of ownership, the ability to process massive amounts of data in real time, no requirement to change application code, improved data persistence, and support for Online Transaction Processing (OLTP) and analytics.

Oracle uses rows and columns to store data inside a table. Oracle Database traditionally stores the data in a row format. Storing the data in a row format is optimized for OLTP workloads as well as for inserts and updates. In the case of analytical workloads, storing the data in row format is not a good idea, since an analytical workload mostly scans all the data sets on a few columns. A column format is ideal for analytics: it allows for faster data retrieval when only a few columns are selected, because all the data for a column is kept together in-memory and a single memory access will load many column values. OLTP benefits the best from the row format, whereas analytics benefits the most from a column format. Choosing one format over the other has a trade-off of either suboptimal OLTP or suboptimal analytics. The Database In-Memory option solves that problem by storing the data in dual format (rows and columns) in the database.

The IMCS is an optional component in the SGA, and is dedicated for the Database In-Memory. The IMCS stores copies of the table and table partitions in memory (DRAM) for the Database In-Memory processing. The IMCS can be enabled at the following levels:

■ Column

■ Table

■ Materialized view

■ Partition of a table or materialized view

■ Tablespace

The IMCS consists of In-Memory Compression Units (IMCUs), In-Memory Expression Units (IMEUs), and Snapshot Metadata Units (SMUs).

In-Memory Columnar Compression provides the ability to compress data in the range of 2x to 20x, depending on the data types and the distribution of the data. As a result, the amount of data that can be fit into In-Memory is significant. Five types of compression are available: MEMCOMPRESS FOR DML, MEMCOMPRESS FOR QUERY LOW, MEMCOMPRESS FOR QUERY HIGH, MEMCOMPRESS FOR CAPACITY LOW, and MEMCOMPRESS FOR CAPACITY HIGH. The default compression algorithm used by IMCS is QUERY LOW.

An In-Memory Storage Index (IMSI) stores the minimum and maximum values for each IMCU. IMSIs allow data pruning to occur based on the filter predicates supplied in a SQL statement. IMSIs are created and managed by the database automatically.

In-Memory also has the ability to perform vector processing using very fast SIMD processing. SIMD allows checking up to 16 values in one CPU cycle, resulting in faster OLTP workloads. It is capable of scanning billions of rows per second per CPU core, providing exceptional speed.

The IMCS enable queries to scan only the required column, thereby eliminating unnecessary columns and increasing efficiency. The IMCS also helps in joining and combining data, providing the ability to join and aggregate, as well as scan, data.

The IMCS is populated (loaded in memory) by two background processes: the In-Memory Coordinator process (IMCO) and the Space Management Slave process (W*nnn*).

The database is fully active and accessible while this occurs. In data warehouse environments, the data is often loaded via bulk load. You have also studied the benefit of In-Memory FastStart and how creating the FastStart area helps to improve the performance of the database after restart.

CHAPTER
3

Implementing In-Memory

In Chapter 2 you learned about the architecture and various components of Database In-Memory. This chapter will take a deeper dive into those features and how to implement them. Because the In-Memory Column Store (IMCS) is embedded in Oracle Database, it is fully compatible with all existing features and requires absolutely no changes in the application layer. Any application that runs against the Oracle Database will transparently benefit from the IMCS.

Allocating the In-Memory Area

To use the In-Memory option, your first step—after you obtain the license, of course—is to allocate space for the In-Memory. The In-Memory Area is an optional area in the System Global Area (SGA) where you define how much space you want to allocate to the In-Memory option.

The area you allocate for In-Memory depends on several factors:

- **The amount of physical RAM on your server**   Because the In-Memory Area resides in the machine's physical RAM, it cannot exceed the size of the RAM. You also need to consider the size of the SGA/SGAs, because SGA also resides in RAM, along with memory used by Program Global Area (PGA) and operating system overhead. To determine the maximum size you can allocate for the In-Memory option, use this formula:

    Total RAM – (size of SGA/SGAs + RAM usage of PGA/PGAs + operating system overhead + any other program/tool that uses RAM)

NOTE
SGAs and PGAs comes into picture when you have more than one database running in the server.

Suppose, for example, that your server has 512GB of RAM and you are running three databases. The first database has 100GB of SGA allocated, the second database has 55GB of SGA allocated, and the third database has 10GB of SGA allocated. You have seen the PGA is using about 12GB of RAM in the first database, 8GB of RAM in the second, and 1GB of RAM in third database. You also have some Java programs running on the server, which use about 16GB of RAM, and the operating system uses around 20GB. In this case, to determine the amount of memory in the system that can be used for the In-Memory option, you'd use this formula:

$$512 - \{(100 + 55 + 10) + (12 + 8 + 1) + 16 + 20\} = 290GB$$

So you have around 290GB of memory available to allocate for In-Memory Area. If you want to use the In-Memory option for all three of the databases running on the server, you would divide the 290GB across three databases. Your next question would be, How will I divide this 290GB across the three databases? The answer depends on the size of data set.

- **Data set**   The data set is another factor that governs how big the In-Memory footprint would be. The bigger the data set you want to put in memory, the more In-Memory Area you need. Since there is always a hard limit on the amount of physical memory available in the system, you need to plan well in advance if you are going to need more memory, and you may want to influence the purchase decision to obtain hardware with more memory.

- **Compression**   Compression greatly helps in reducing the memory footprint, since it means that more objects can be stored in the memory. Your choice of compression algorithm depends on which offers the greatest reduction in memory size or the best query performance.

Because the In-Memory option is an optional component, by default this option is not enabled when Oracle Database is installed. Check the Appendix for database installation steps. You need to enable it manually. Once In-Memory is enabled, the SGA shows an In-Memory Area.

Let's query a freshly installed database to see if the In-Memory option is included:

```
SQL> show sga ;

Total System Global Area 9663676416 bytes
Fixed Size                  4592552 bytes
Variable Size            1543507032 bytes
Database Buffers         8086618112 bytes
Redo Buffers               28958720 bytes
SQL>
```

We can see that in our newly installed database, the SGA does not include an entry for In-Memory. Let's check the In-Memory Area to see if the system has allocated some area by default:

```
SQL> select * from v$inmemory_area;
```

```
POOL          ALLOC_BYTES USED_BYTES POPULATE_STATUS          CON_ID
------------- ----------- ---------- ------------------------ ------
1MB POOL          0            0 OUT OF MEMORY                 1
64KB POOL         0            0 OUT OF MEMORY                 1
1MB POOL          0            0 OUT OF MEMORY                 2
64KB POOL         0            0 OUT OF MEMORY                 2
1MB POOL          0            0 OUT OF MEMORY                 3
64KB POOL         0            0 OUT OF MEMORY                 3

6 rows selected.
```

We can see that no space has been allocated for the In-Memory option in the In-Memory Area. We'll need to set up the In-Memory Area explicitly after installing Oracle Database. We can enable In-Memory by running the following query. (In this example, we are allocating 100MB for the In-Memory Area. You would need to change this number to the size you want to allocate.)

```
SQL> ALTER SYSTEM SET INMEMORY_SIZE = 100M SCOPE=SPFILE;

System altered.
```

Next, restart the database to initialize the IMCS if you are running an Oracle Database version earlier than 12c R2. With Oracle Database 12c R2, you can set this parameter dynamically, which means that you can set the parameter without restarting the database. To increase the size of the In-Memory Area dynamically, run the following command. Note that you can increase the size dynamically only if the new size is greater than 128MB.

```
SQL> ALTER SYSTEM SET INMEMORY_SIZE = 300M;

System altered.
```

As soon as you change the size of the In-Memory Area, the change is immediately reflected in the v$view:

```
SQL> select * from v$inmemory_area;

POOL      ALLOC_BYTES USED_BYTES POPULATE_STATUS              CON_ID
------    ----------- ---------- ---------------------------- ----------
1MB POOL   229638144           0 DONE                              1
64KB POOL   66519040           0 DONE                              1
1MB POOL   229638144           0 DONE                              2
64KB POOL   66519040           0 DONE                              2
1MB POOL   229638144           0 DONE                              3
64KB POOL   66519040           0 DONE                              3

6 rows selected.
```

If you want to disable the In-Memory option, you can simply set the value of the parameter **INMEMORY_SIZE** as 0, which is also the default value.

Since the IMCS is part of the SGA, you also need to ensure that the **SGA_TARGET** parameter is set large enough to accommodate the new IMCS and all the other existing components (buffer cache, shared pool, large pool, and so on).

Initialization Parameters for In-Memory

When the Oracle Database starts, it reads the initialization parameter file for all the parameters related to the Oracle instance. Thus, all the parameters related to In-Memory are also read from this file. Let's examine these parameters in detail since you are going to use them for anything related to In-Memory. Each parameter and its description are provided.

INMEMORY_SIZE This parameter specifies the size of the IMCS. The default value for this parameter is 0, which means IMCS is disabled. The value for this parameter can be set from 0 to the amount of memory left in the SGA after other allocations. The minimum value for the parameter is 100MB, which also means that the minimum size for the IMCS should be 100MB. The database must be restarted after setting this parameter for the first time to enable the IMCS. This parameter is dynamic, which means subsequent changes in size do not require database bounce. Note that all subsequent change increments should be more than 128MB. Whenever you change the parameter size, the change is reflected immediately in the V$INMEMORY_AREA.

For Real Application Clusters (RAC) implementations, it is recommended that you specify the same value for all the RAC nodes. If you're using Oracle Multitenant, this parameter can also be set per pluggable database (PDB) to limit the maximum size of the IMCS for that PDB. Note that the sum of the PDB values does not have to equal the container database (CDB) value, and the sum of the PDB values may even be greater than the CDB value. Unless this parameter is specifically set on a PDB, each PDB inherits the CDB value, which means they can use all of the available IMCS. This parameter can be modified by running the **ALTER SYSTEM** command:

```
SQL> ALTER SYSTEM SET INMEMORY_SIZE = 300M;
```

INMEMORY_FORCE   This parameter enables tables and materialized views, which are specified with **INMEMORY**, to be populated in the IMCS automatically. The default value is **DEFAULT**. When this value is in effect, the IMCS is populated only with tables and materialized views specified as **INMEMORY**. This parameter can also have the value of **OFF**. When the value is specified as **OFF**, no tables or materialized views are populated in memory, despite configuring the IMCS. In case of Oracle RAC, all the nodes should have same value. This parameter can be modified by running the **ALTER SYSTEM** command:

```
SQL> ALTER SYSTEM SET INMEMORY_FORCE = OFF;
```

INMEMORY_CLAUSE_DEFAULT   Using this parameter, you can specify a default IMCS for new tables and materialized views. When this parameter is set, any newly created table or materialized view specified as **INMEMORY** will inherit unspecified attributes from the parameter. If this parameter is unset or set to an empty string (value), only tables and materialized views explicitly specified as **INMEMORY** will be populated into the IMCS. The default value of this parameter is an empty string, and it has same effect as setting it to **NO INMEMORY**.

This parameter can have the following values:

```
INMEMORY_CLAUSE_DEFAULT = '[INMEMORY] [NO INMEMORY] [other-clauses]'.
```

The other clauses and the subclauses within it can have the following values:

- **other-clauses** `[compression-clause] [priority-clause] [rac-clause]`

- **compression-clause** `NO MEMCOMPRESS | MEMCOMPRESS FOR { DML | QUERY [ LOW | HIGH ] | CAPACITY [LOW | HIGH] } *`

- **priority-clause** `PRIORITY { LOW | MEDIUM | HIGH | CRITICAL | NONE }*`

- **rac-clause** `[distribute-clause] [duplicate-clause] *`

- **distribute-clause** `DISTRIBUTE [ AUTO | BY ROWID RANGE | BY PARTITION | BY SUBPARTITION ] *`

- **duplicate-clause** `NO DUPLICATE | DUPLICATE [ ALL ] *`

The syntaxes and the descriptions for the **INMEMORY_CLAUSE_DEFAULT** parameter are shown in Table 3-1.

Syntax	Description
INMEMORY	Specifies that all newly created tables and materialized views populate the IMCS unless they are specified as **NO INMEMORY** in the SQL **CREATE TABLE** or **CREATE MATERIALIZED VIEW** statement.
NO INMEMORY	Specifies that only tables and materialized views explicitly specified as **INMEMORY** in the SQL **CREATE TABLE** or **CREATE MATERIALIZED VIEW** statement populate the IMCS.

TABLE 3-1. *Syntaxes and the Descriptions for the **INMEMORY_CLAUSE_ DEFAULT** Parameter (continued)*

Syntax	Description
compression-clause	Specifies that In-Memory compression should be used for the instance. Use the **MEMCOMPRESS FOR** values to specify the In-Memory compression level.
NO MEMCOMPRESS	When specified, no In-Memory compression is done in the IMCS.
MEMCOMPRESS FOR	Used to indicate the In-Memory compression level for the IMCS.
DML	When specified, the IMCS is optimized for DML operations, and some lightweight In-Memory compression may be done.
QUERY	When specified, the In-Memory compression level is for high performance. If **QUERY** is specified without **LOW** or **HIGH**, it defaults to **QUERY LOW**.
QUERY LOW	When specified, the In-Memory compression level provides the highest performance.
QUERY HIGH	When specified, the In-Memory compression level provides a balance between compression and performance, weighted toward performance.
CAPACITY	When specified without **LOW** or **HIGH**, it defaults to **CAPACITY LOW**.
CAPACITY LOW	When specified, the In-Memory compression level is a balance between compression and performance, weighted toward capacity.
CAPACITY HIGH	When specified, the In-Memory compression level is for highest capacity.
priority-clause	Specifies the priority to use when populating tables in the IMCS. Use the **PRIORITY** values to specify the priority. By default, the population of a table in the IMCS can be delayed until the database determines it is useful. On database instance startup, tables are populated in priority order.

TABLE 3-1. *Syntaxes and the Descriptions for the **INMEMORY_CLAUSE_ DEFAULT** Parameter (continued)*

Syntax	Description
PRIORITY NONE	When specified, the population of a table in the IMCS can be delayed until the database determines it is useful. This is the default value when no priority is specified.
PRIORITY LOW	When specified for a table or tables, the population of those tables in the IMCS is done before tables that have no priority specified.
PRIORITY MEDIUM	When specified for a table or tables, the population of those tables in the IMCS is done before tables that have no priority or **PRIORITY LOW** specified.
PRIORITY HIGH	When specified for a table or tables, the population of those tables in the IMCS is done before tables that have no priority, **PRIORITY LOW**, or **PRIORITY MEDIUM** specified.
PRIORITY CRITICAL	When specified for a table or tables, the population of those tables in the IMCS is done before tables that have no priority, **PRIORITY LOW, PRIORITY MEDIUM**, or **PRIORITY HIGH** specified.
rac-clause	Specifies how tables in the IMCS will be managed among Oracle RAC instances. Use the distribute-clause and duplicate-clause to specify how tables in the IMCS will be managed in Oracle RAC instances. For a non-Oracle RAC database, these settings have no effect, because the whole table or partition has to be on the single instance.
distribute-clause	Specifies how a table is distributed among Oracle RAC instances.

TABLE 3-1. *Syntaxes and the Descriptions for the **INMEMORY_CLAUSE_ DEFAULT** Parameter (continued)*

Syntax	Description
DISTRIBUTE AUTO	Specifies that the database will automatically decide how to distribute tables in the IMCS across the Oracle RAC instances based on the type of partitioning and the value of the duplicate-clause. **DISTRIBUTE AUTO** is the default, and it is also used when **DISTRIBUTE** is specified by itself.
DISTRIBUTE BY ROWID RANGE	Specifies that the tables in the IMCS will be distributed by rowid range to different Oracle RAC instances.
DISTRIBUTE BY PARTITION	Specifies that partitions in the IMCS will be distributed to different Oracle RAC instances.
DISTRIBUTE BY SUBPARTITION	Specifies that subpartitions in the IMCS will be distributed to different Oracle RAC instances.
duplicate-clause	Specifies how many copies of each In-Memory Compression Unit (IMCU) of the tables in the IMCS will be spread across all the Oracle RAC instances. Note that the duplicate-clause is applicable only if you are using Oracle RAC on an engineered system. Otherwise, the duplicate-clause is ignored and there is only one copy of each IMCU in memory.
NO DUPLICATE	Data is not duplicated across Oracle RAC instances. This is the default.
DUPLICATE	Data is duplicated on another Oracle RAC instance, resulting in data existing on two Oracle RAC instances.
DUPLICATE ALL	Data is duplicated across all Oracle RAC instances. If you specify **DUPLICATE ALL**, the database uses the **DISTRIBUTE AUTO** setting, regardless of whether or how you specify the distribute-clause.

TABLE 3-1. *Syntaxes and the Descriptions for the **INMEMORY_CLAUSE_ DEFAULT** Parameter*

The following statement causes new tables and materialized views to populate the IMCS with a low capacity compression level. Note that tables that are specified as **NO INMEMORY** will not be populated by this statement.

```
SQL> alter system set INMEMORY_CLAUSE_DEFAULT='INMEMORY MEMCOMPRESS

FOR CAPACITY LOW' scope=spfile;
```

INMEMORY_QUERY   This parameter is used for enabling or disabling the Database In-Memory queries at the system or session level. This parameter is very useful when you see how a query will run with and without using the IMCS. This parameter can be used for testing workloads before implementing IMCS.

When the **INMEMORY_SIZE** parameter is specified, this parameter enables In-Memory queries for the entire database by default. The default value of this parameter is **ENABLE**; set the value to **DISABLE** if you do not want to use this parameter.

Since this parameter can be set at both the database system level and session level, you can run the **ALTER SESSION** and **ALTER SYSTEM** clauses:

```
SQL> ALTER SESSION set INMEMORY_QUERY = { ENABLE| DISABLE } ;
SQL> ALTER SYSTEM set INMEMORY_QUERY = { ENABLE| DISABLE } ;
```

If you are using an RAC database, make sure all the instances use the same value. This parameter is modifiable at the PDB level.

INMEMORY_MAX_POPULATE_SERVERS   This parameter specifies the maximum number of background populated servers (processes) to use for IMCS population. The parameter makes sure that processing for In-Memory does not take all the CPU cycles. The parameter depends on the number of cores in the system. You can allocate a certain percentage of the cores for In-Memory processing.

Make sure that you size this parameter appropriately. Oversizing the parameter will impact other activities of the database, while undersizing will impact the In-Memory background processing.

The population is taken care of by a new set of background processes, **ora_w001_orcl**.

This parameter is used only when the parameter **INMEMORY_SIZE** is also set to a positive value.

The default value of this parameter is half the effective CPU thread count (**CPU_COUNT**), or the **PGA_AGGREGATE_TARGET** value divided by 512M, whichever is less. If you want to disable population tasks on the system from executing, set this parameter to 0. With RAC databases, all the instances should use the same value. This parameter is not modifiable in a PDB.

```
SQL> Alter system set INMEMORY_MAX_POPULATE_SERVERS='10';
```

INMEMORY_TRICKLE_REPOPULATE_SERVERS_PERCENT   This parameter limits the maximum number of background populated servers used for IMCS repopulation, since trickle repopulation is designed to use only a small percentage of the populated servers. The value for this parameter is a percentage of the value of the parameter **INMEMORY_MAX_POPULATE_ SERVERS**.

The default value for this parameter is 1, and the value can be set up to 50. Any value more than 50 is not allowed so that half of the populated servers are available for repopulating.

With RAC databases, the value for this parameter should be the same across all the RAC instances, and this parameter is not modifiable in a PDB.

```
SQL> ALTER SYSTEM set INMEMORY_TRICKLE_REPOPULATE_SERVERS_PERCENT ='25';
```

INMEMORY_EXPRESSIONS_CAPTURE   In-Memory expressions improve the performance of queries that are compute intensive and that access large data sets. This parameter controls the detection of frequently used In-Memory expressions. The parameter has two possible values: **ENABLE** and **DISABLE**. When enabled, Oracle Database automatically detects and captures IM expressions. When disabled, the automatic capture of IM expressions is stopped. By default, this parameter is disabled. With RAC databases, this parameter should be the same across all the instances. This parameter is modifiable at the PDB level and can be changed using the **alter system** command.

```
SQL> Alter system set INMEMORY_EXPRESSIONS_CAPTURE = 'ENABLE';
```

INMEMORY_EXPRESSIONS_USAGE   This parameter controls the use of In-Memory expressions—that is, which IM expressions are populated into the IMCS and which are available for queries. This parameter can have one of four values:

- **STATIC_ONLY**   Tables containing certain data types such as Oracle numbers or JSON (JavaScript Object Notation) will have these columns populated in the IMCS using a more efficient representation. Setting this value increases the In-Memory footprint for some tables.

- **DYNAMIC_ONLY**   Frequently used expressions detected within the capture window will be automatically created and populated into the IMCS. Setting this value also increases the In-Memory footprint for some tables.

- **ENABLE**   Both static and dynamic IM expressions will be populated into the IMCS and will be used by queries. This is the default value.

- **DISABLE**   IM expressions will not be populated into the IMCS.

This parameter can be changed using the **alter system** command. With RAC databases, all instances should have the same value. This parameter is modifiable at the PDB level.

```
SQL> Alter system set INMEMORY_EXPRESSIONS_USAGE='STATIC_ONLY';
```

INMEMORY_VIRTUAL_COLUMNS   This parameter controls which user-defined virtual columns are stored as In-Memory virtual columns. IM virtual columns eliminate the repeated calculations, thereby improving query performance. Using techniques such as single instruction, multiple data (SIMD), the database can scan and filter IM virtual columns. This parameter can have one of three values:

- **ENABLE**   For any table or partition that has been enabled for In-Memory, all virtual columns will be stored at the default table or partition memcompress parameter value unless they have been altered to have a different memcompress parameter value other than a base table or partition or they have been explicitly excluded by using **NO INMEMORY**.

■ **MANUAL**   This is the default value for the parameter. For any table or partition that has been enabled for In-Memory storage, virtual columns will not be stored in memory unless they have been marked with a different memcompress parameter value than the base table or partition or they have been explicitly marked for In-Memory, in which case they will be stored in memory at the table or partition memcompress parameter value.

■ **DISABLE**   In this case, no virtual columns will ever be stored in memory for all tables or partitions that have been enabled for In-Memory storage.

This parameter can be changed using the **alter system** command. In case of RAC, all instances should have the same value. This parameter is modifiable at the PDB level.

```
SQL> alter system set INMEMORY_VIRTUAL_COLUMNS = 'ENABLE';
```

OPTIMIZER_INMEMORY_AWARE   This parameter enables or disables all of the optimizer cost model enhancements for In-Memory. The default value for this parameter is true, and the accepted values are true and false. If this parameter is set to false, it causes the optimizer to ignore the In-Memory property of tables during the optimization of SQL statements. This parameter can be modified at session as well as system levels. With Oracle RAC databases, the same value should be used by all the instances, and this parameter is modifiable at the PDB level.

```
SQL> Alter system set OPTIMIZER_INMEMORY_AWARE='false';
```

You can query all the In-Memory–related parameters by running this query:

```
SQL> show parameter inmemory;

NAME                                    TYPE        VALUE
--------------------------------------- ----------- -------
inmemory_clause_default                 string
inmemory_expressions_capture            string      DISABLE
inmemory_expressions_usage              string
```

```
inmemory_force                                   string      DEFAULT
inmemory_max_populate_servers                    integer     0
inmemory_query                                   string      ENABLE
inmemory_size                                    big integer 0
inmemory_trickle_repopulate_servers_percent      integer     1
optimizer_inmemory_aware                         boolean     TRUE
```

Populating Data in the IMCS

As discussed previously, data population is the process of reading the data from the row format and converting it into the columnar format and storing them at the IMCS. When the IMCS is enabled, the object's data (for which IMCS is enabled) is populated in two ways:

- Oracle Database controls when the data is populated in IMCS.

- You can set up priority for populating the data in IMCS.

By using the **INMEMORY PRIORITY** subclause included in Oracle SQL, you can set the priority of the database population at a more granular level. Unless explicitly stated, Oracle Database takes control when the data is going to be populated in IMCS. The database analyzes all the workload before populating the data for a particular object before another.

There are two kinds of data population:

- **Initial populate**   The initial creation of the IMCS.

- **Repopulate**   Re-creation of the IMCS after it has been modified. It can be either threshold based (after exceeding the threshold of changes to IMCU) or trickle-driven from constant background activity. Any modification to an IMCU causes a background process to act on it. Since IMCUs are read-only structures, when the data in the row changes, Oracle Database does not populate the data immediately. Instead, it records all the changes in a transactional journal and then creates a new IMCU as part of the repopulation of data.

There are five levels of priority for populating data in IMCS:

■ **PRIORITY NONE** When **PRIORITY** is set to **NONE**, Oracle Database controls when the database object's data is populated in the IMCS. This happens *on demand*—that is, whenever there is a scan of the database objects, Oracle Database triggers the population of the object into the IMCS. If the object is not scanned, is never accessed, or is accessed through an index scan or a fetch using the rowid, the population never happens. **NONE** is the default level when **PRIORITY** is not included in the **INMEMORY** clause. If **PRIORITY** is set to a value other than **NONE**, Oracle Database uses the queue of priority (**LOW, MEDIUM, HIGH, CRITICAL**) to populate the data. In this scenario, there is no need to access the data in order to populate it. Oracle Database starts populating the data automatically according to the priority level and as long as the IMCS has sufficient space.

■ **PRIORITY LOW** The database object's data is populated in the IMCS before database objects with the priority level of **NONE**. The database object's data is populated in the IMCS after database objects with the priority levels **MEDIUM, HIGH**, and **CRITICAL**.

■ **PRIORITY MEDIUM** The database object's data is populated in the IMCS before database objects with the priority level of **NONE** or **LOW**. The database object's data is populated in the IMCS after database objects with priority levels **HIGH** and **CRITICAL**.

■ **PRIORITY HIGH** The database object's data is populated in the IMCS before database objects with the priority level of **NONE, LOW**, or **MEDIUM**. The database object's data is populated in the IMCS after database objects with the priority level of **CRITICAL**.

■ **PRIORITY CRITICAL** The database object's data is populated in the IMCS before database objects with the priority level of **NONE, LOW, MEDIUM**, or **HIGH**.

Data population is a constant process that happens in the background. During this process, the data is not only converted from the row format to the column format, but it is also compressed simultaneously. You can specify the number of background processes by using the initialization parameter **IN_MEMORY_MAX_POPULATE_SERVERS**, which we have already studied in the "Initialization Parameters for In-Memory" section of this chapter. The number of workers is directly proportional to the speed of data population—that is, the greater the number of workers, the faster the data population will be.

The data for the objects with the priority **CRITICAL** are populated first, followed by **HIGH**, then **MEDIUM**, and then **LOW**. If the size of IMCS becomes full while data is being populated, the data population is suspended until space becomes available.

NOTE
The priority-level settings must apply to an entire table or to a table partition. Specifying different IMCS priority levels for different subsets of columns in a table is not allowed.

Enabling the IMCS at the Database Level

The IMCS must be enabled at the database level before you can start enabling IMCS for tables, tablespaces, or materialized views. Following are the steps for enabling the IMCS:

To start, the Oracle Database should be compatible with version 12.1.0:

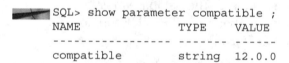

```
SQL> show parameter compatible ;
NAME                  TYPE    VALUE
----------------      ------- ------
compatible            string  12.0.0
```

If the database is compatible with a version earlier than 12.1.0, follow these steps to change the parameter:

If you are using a server parameter file…

1. Perform a full database backup before changing the **COMPATIBLE** initialization parameter. Raising the **COMPATIBLE** initialization parameter might cause your database to become incompatible with earlier releases of Oracle Database, and having a backup ensures that you can return to the earlier release if necessary.

2. Run the following command:

```
SQL> ALTER SYSTEM SET COMPATIBLE = '12.1.0' SCOPE=SPFILE;
```

3. Restart the instance.

If you are using an initialization parameter file...

1. Shut down the instance using the command

```
SQL> Shutdown immediate
```

2. Edit the initialization parameter file to set or change the value of the **COMPATIBLE** initialization parameter:

```
COMPATIBLE = 12.1.0
```

3. Start the instance using the **startup** command:

```
SQL> Startup
```

Here are the steps for enabling the IMCS:

1. Set the **INMEMORY_SIZE** initialization parameter to the size you want to allocate for In-Memory operations. This parameter must be greater than 0.

```
SQL> ALTER SYSTEM SET INMEMORY_SIZE = '500M' SCOPE=SPFILE;
```

If you are using the initialization parameter file, add the value for **INMEMORY_SIZE** and restart the database. The database must be restarted irrespective of the server parameter file (SPFILE) or init.ora file in order to initialize the IMCS in SGA.

2. Verify the amount of memory currently allocated to IMCS by running the following query:

```
SQL> show parameter INMEMORY_SIZE
```

Enabling/Disabling IMCS for Tables

The IMCS must be enabled at the database level before it can be implemented at the table level. The IMCS for a table can be enabled either during creation of the table or after the table has been created. The IMCS can be enabled by including an **INMEMORY** clause in the **CREATE TABLE** or **ALTER TABLE** syntax.

It can be disabled easily by adding a **NO INMEMORY** clause in the **CREATE TABLE** or **ALTER TABLE** syntax.

```
SQL>  CREATE TABLE <TABLE_NAME> ( <column_defination,

2nd_column_defination.....) INMEMORY ;

SQL>  CREATE TABLE DBIM_FIRST_TABLE ( in_memcolumn VARCHAR2(20)) INMEMORY ;
```

The table DBIM_FIRST_TABLE is created with the **INMEMORY** option enabled. When a table is created using the default **INMEMORY** clause, **MEMCOMPRESS FOR QUERY** and **PRIORITY NONE** are used. (Refer to Table 3-1 for details.)

A table can also be enabled for IMCS after it has been created by running the following commands:

```
SQL> ALTER TABLE <TABLE_NAME> INMEMORY;

SQL> ALTER TABLE DBIM_SECOND_TABLE INMEMORY;
```

Since we have not explicitly added any **PRIORITY** or **MEMCOMPRESS** in the syntax, the table has taken the default value. We can change the default value at any time by using the **ALTER TABLE** syntax.

To change the **PRIORITY** from default (**NONE**) to **HIGH**,

```
SQL> ALTER TABLE DBIM_SECOND_TABLE INMEMORY PRIORITY HIGH;
```

Similarly, to change the **MEMCOMPRESS** to **CAPACITY HIGH**,

```
SQL> ALTER TABLE DBIM_SECOND_TABLE INMEMORY MEMCOMPRESS FOR CAPACITY HIGH;
```

Here's how to change **MEMCOMPRESS** to **CAPACITY HIGH** and **PRIORITY** to **HIGH** at the same time:

```
SQL> ALTER TABLE DBIM_SECOND_TABLE INMEMORY MEMCOMPRESS

FOR CAPACITY HIGH PRIORITY HIGH;
```

In a table, only a few selected columns can also be enabled for IMCS. Similarly, different columns can have different compression methods for the columns enabled for the IMCS:

```
ALTER TABLE DBIM_SECOND_TABLE
INMEMORY MEMCOMPRESS FOR QUERY
( product_category, product_name, category_id, supplier_id)
```

```
INMEMORY MEMCOMPRESS FOR CAPACITY HIGH
(product_details, warranty_status, list_price)
   NO INMEMORY (inventory, sku);
```

In this example, the columns product_category, product_name, category_id, and supplier_id use **MEMCOMPRESS FOR QUERY**; columns product_details, warranty_status, and list_price use **MEMCOMPRESS FOR CAPACITY HIGH**; and the IMCS has been disabled for the columns inventory and sku.

NOTE
The V$IM_COLUMN_LEVEL view can be used to determine the selective column compression levels that are defined for a database object.

To disable a table for IMCS, use the **NO INMEMORY** clause:

```
SQL> ALTER TABLE <TABLE_NAME> NO INMEMORY;

SQL> ALTER TABLE DBIM_FIRST_TABLE NO INMEMORY;
```

If a table is partitioned, In-Memory can be implemented at the partition level as well. Not all partitions need to have the **INMEMORY** attribute. Partitions can have different compression levels, which allows for easy information lifecycle management (ILM) strategies, as data can be added or removed from memory by partition. Let's take an example to see how we can implement the same for ILM.

In the following example, you can see that different partitions of a table can have different compression levels:

```
CREATE TABLE SALES
PARTITION BY RANGE
   (PARTITION p1 ......
    NO INMEMORY
    PARTITION p2 ......
    INMEMORY MEMCOMPRESS FOR DML,
    PARTITION p3 ......
    INMEMORY MEMCOMPRESS FOR QUERY,
    :
    PARTITION p10 ......
    INMEMORY MEMCOMPRESS FOR CAPACITY
   );
```

Enabling/Disabling IMCS for a Virtual Column

A virtual column is just like any other column of a regular table, except a virtual column is derived by evaluating an expression. You can enable or disable the IMCS for a virtual column in the same way you would for a regular column—with one extra step: the virtual column needs to be enabled. Here are the steps:

1. Enable the IMCS at the database level.

2. Enable the table that contains the virtual columns for IMCS.

3. Set the init.ora parameter for **IN_MEMORY_VIRTUAL_COLUMNS** either to **ENABLE** or **MANUAL**.

NOTE
*If you are running Oracle Database 12.2, you can also specify the **INMEMORY** clause at the column level on an object that is not yet specified as **INMEMORY**. In the release 12.1, a column level **INMEMORY** clause was valid only when the underlying table or partition had an **INMEMORY** clause.*

Enabling/Disabling IMCS for a Tablespace

A tablespace can be enabled for IMCS during its creation by adding the **INMEMORY** clause along with the **CREATE TABLESPACE** statement. Similarly, a tablespace can be altered after its creation to include the **INMEMORY** clause with an **ALTER TABLESPACE** statement to enable IMCS.

```
SQL> CREATE TABLESPACE IM_TS DATAFILE '+DATADG' SIZE 500M

  ONLINE   DEFAULT INMEMORY;
```

You can also use the **ALTER TABLESPACE** statement to change the **MEMCOMPRESS** and **PRIORITY** after the tablespace has been created:

```
SQL> ALTER TABLESPACE IM_TS DEFAULT INMEMORY  MEMCOMPRESS

FOR CAPACITY LOW     PRIORITY HIGH;
```

When you enable the IMCS at a tablespace level, objects in that tablespace (tables and materialized views) are enabled for IMCS by default. Also by default, all the tables, materialized views, and tablespaces will have the same **INMEMORY** clause that has been specified in the **CREATE TABLESPACE** statement or the **ALTER TABLESPACE** statement.

If you create a table or materialized view with an In-Memory setting that is different from the tablespace-level setting, the settings for individual database objects override the settings for the tablespace. For example, if the tablespace is set to **PRIORITY LOW** for populating data in memory but a table in the tablespace is set to **PRIORITY HIGH**, then the table uses **PRIORITY HIGH**.

The IMCS in a tablespace can be disabled by including a **NO INMEMORY** clause in a **CREATE TABLESPACE** or **ALTER TABLESPACE** statement:

```
SQL> ALTER TABLESPACE IM_TS NO INMEMORY;
```

Enabling/Disabling IMCS for a Materialized View

A materialized view can be enabled for an IMCS by including an **INMEMORY** clause in the **CREATE MATERIALIZED VIEW** or by altering the materialized view later by issuing an **ALTER MATERIALIZED VIEW** statement:

```
SQL> CREATE MATERIALIZED VIEW DBIM_FIRST_MV INMEMORY
   AS SELECT * FROM DMIM_FIRST;
```

The materialized view can be changed to a different **MEMCOMPRESS** or **PRIORITY** setting later on using the **ALTER MATERIALIZED VIEW** command:

```
SQL> ALTER MATERIALIZED VIEW DBIM_FIRST_MV INMEMORY PRIORITY LOW;
```

You can disable a materialized view for the IMCS by including a **NO INMEMORY** clause in a **CREATE MATERIALIZED VIEW** or an **ALTER MATERIALIZED VIEW** statement:

```
SQL> ALTER MATERIALIZED VIEW DBIM_FIRST_MV NO INMEMORY;
```

Enabling IM FastStart

In order to implement FastStart, the following steps need to be done:

1. Create a tablespace for the FastStart area.

   ```
   SQL> CREATE TABLESPACE FASTSTART DATAFILE '+DATADG' SIZE 1G
   AUTOEXTEND ON ;
   ```

2. When you create the tablespace, make sure you have enough size in the tablespace to hold all the data. Oracle recommends that you create the FastStart tablespace with twice the size of the INMEMORY_AREA setting.

3. Run the DBMS_INMEMORY_ADMIN.FASTSTART_ENABLE procedure as shown here.

   ```
   SQL> EXEC DBMS_INMEMORY_ADMIN.FASTSTART_ENABLE('FASTSTART');
   ```

Enabling ADO and In-Memory

In order to implement ADO along with In-Memory option, you must set the initialization parameters related to ADO and In-Memory. Table 3-2 shows the related parameters.

You also need to know important views that contain information about ADO and IMCS. They are given in Table 3-3.

In order to enable ADO, you must set the following init.ora parameters, as discussed previously:

- Set the INMEMORY_SIZE initialization parameter to a nonzero value and restart the database.

- Set the value of HEAT_MAP initialization parameter to ON.

- The COMPATIBLE initialization parameter must be set to 12.2.0 or higher.

Initialization Parameter	Description
COMPATIBLE	Specifies the release with which the database must maintain compatibility. For ADO to manage the IM column store, set this parameter to 12.2.0 or higher.
HEAT_MAP	Enables both the Heat Map and ADO features. For ADO to manage the IM column store, set this parameter to ON.
INMEMORY_SIZE	Enables the IM column store. This parameter must be set to a nonzero value.

TABLE 3-2. *Initialization Parameters Related to ADO and In-Memory*

View	Description
DBA_HEAT_MAP_SEG_HISTOGRAM	Displays segment access information for all segments visible to the user.
DBA_HEAT_MAP_SEGMENT	Displays the latest segment access time for all segments visible to the user.
DBA_HEATMAP_TOP_OBJECTS	Displays heat map information for the top 10,000 objects by default.
DBA_HEATMAP_TOP_TABLESPACES	Displays heat map information for the top 10,000 tablespaces.
DBA_ILMDATAMOVEMENTPOLICIES	Displays information specific to data movement–related attributes of an ADO policy in a database. The action_type column describes policies related to the IM column store. Possible values are COMPRESSION, STORAGE, EVICT, and ANNOTATE.
V$HEAT_MAP_SEGMENT	Displays real-time segment access information.

TABLE 3-3. *Views for ADO and IMCS*

To create an ADO policy, do the following:

1. Log in as a sysdba or a user with proper privileges.

2. Use an ALTER TABLE statement with the ILM ADD POLICY ... INMEMORY clause.

You can create various ADO policies depending on your requirement. Policies to set, modify, or remove the INMEMORY clause for objects are based on Heat Map statistics.

To create an ADO IM column store policy, specify the ILM ADD POLICY clause in an ALTER TABLE statement, followed by one of the following subclauses:

- SET INMEMORY ... SEGMENT

  This option is useful when you want to mark segments with the INMEMORY attribute only when DML activity subsides or when a certain time has elapsed. For example, if we want to specify a policy on a customer's table to enable the INMEMORY attribute after 10 days it was created, the SQL command would be

  ```
  SQL> ALTER TABLE CUSTOMERS ILM ADD POLICY SET INMEMORY AFTER
  10 DAYS OF CREATION;
  ```

- MODIFY INMEMORY ... MEMCOMPRESS ... SEGMENT

  Storing data uncompressed or at the MEMCOMPRESS FOR DML level is appropriate when it is frequently modified. The alternative compression levels are more suited for queries. If the activity on a segment transitions from mostly writes to mostly reads, then you can use the MODIFY clause to apply a different compression method. For example, here we are changing the CUSTOMER table to increase the compression level to QUERY HIGH seven days after it stops getting modified.

  ```
  SQL> ALTER TABLE CUSTOMER ILM ADD POLICY MODIFY INMEMORY
  MEMCOMPRESS FOR QUERY HIGH AFTER 7 DAYS OF NO MODIFICATION;
  ```

- NO INMEMORY ... SEGMENT

  This option is useful when access to a segment decreases and you don't want to keep it in memory anymore.

Let's look at a policy that will evict the CUSTOMERS table from the IM column store after it has not been accessed for 60 days:

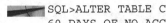

```
SQL>ALTER TABLE CUSTOMERS ILM ADD POLICY NO INMEMORY SEGMENT AFTER
60 DAYS OF NO ACCESS;
```

IMCS and Data Pump

You can import database objects that are enabled for the IMCS using the **TRANSFORM=INMEMORY:y** option of the **impdp** command. With this option, Data Pump keeps the IMCS clause for all objects that have one. When the **TRANSFORM=INMEMORY:n** option is specified, Data Pump drops the IMCS clause from all objects that have one.

You can also use the **TRANSFORM=INMEMORY_CLAUSE:string** option to override the IMCS clause for a database object in the dump file during import. For example, you can use this option to change the IMCS compression for a database object being imported.

Objects that Cannot Be Populated in IMCS

Almost all objects in the database are eligible to be populated into the IMCS, but there are a small number of exceptions. The following database objects cannot be populated in the IMCS:

- Any object owned by the SYS user and stored in the SYSTEM or SYSAUX tablespace
- Index-organized tables (IOTs)
- Clustered tables

The following data types are also not supported in the IMCS:

- LONGs (depreciated beginning in Oracle Database 8i)
- Out-of-line large objects (LOBs)

Note all of the other columns in an object with these data types are eligible to be populated into the IMCS. Any query that accesses only the column residing in the IMCS will benefit from accessing the table data via the IMCS.

In-Memory Views

There are various views related to In-Memory. Some of these views fall under the category of DBA views, and some of them fall under V$ views. All these views are given in the following table.

Initialization Parameter	Description
DBA_EXPRESSION_STATISTICS	Provides expression usage tracking statistics for all the tables in the database.
DBA_FEATURE_USAGE_STATISTICS	Displays information about database feature usage statistics. When the IMCS is accessed, the NAME column shows "In-Memory Column Store."
DBA_HEAT_MAP_SEGMENT	Displays the latest segment access time for all segments. The timestamps in the view are coarse with a granularity of a day reflecting the flush times of the heat map.
DBA_ILMDATAMOVEMENTPOLICIES	Contains information specific to data movement–related attributes of an Automatic Data Optimization policy in a database.
DBA_IM_EXPRESSIONS	Describes the IM expressions that have the column prefix SYS_IME that also have the **INMEMORY** attribute.
DBA_JOINGROUPS	Describes join groups in the database. A join group is a user-created object that lists two columns that can be meaningfully joined.

Initialization Parameter	Description
DBA_TABLES	Indicates which tables have the **INMEMORY** attribute set (the **INMEMORY** column is **ENABLED**) or not set (**DISABLED**).
V$HEAT_MAP_SEGMENT	Displays real-time segment access information.
V$IM_COLUMN_LEVEL	Presents the selective column compression levels that are defined using the **INMEMORY** clause of the **CREATE TABLE** statement. SYS_IME hidden virtual columns are not shown in this view.
V$IM_IMECOL_CU	Provides details about the expressions or virtual columns that are populated in the IMCS in the form of In-Memory expressions.
V$IM_SEGMENTS	Presents information about all In-Memory segments in the database. Only segments that have an In-Memory representation are displayed. If a segment is marked for the IMCS but is not populated, the view does not contain a corresponding row for this segment.
V$INMEMORY_AREA	Displays information about the space allocation inside the In-Memory Area.
V$SGA	Displays the size of the In-Memory Area.

Summary

In this chapter you have learned how to implement the In-Memory option. The In-Memory Area is an optional area in the System Global Area (SGA) where you define how much space you want to allocate to the In-Memory option.

To determine the maximum size you can allocate for the In-Memory option, use this formula:

Total RAM – (size of SGA/SGAs + RAM usage of PGA/PGAs + operating system overhead + any other program/tool that uses RAM)

You can enable the In-Memory by specifying the size of In-Memory area and restarting the database. You can simply set the value of the parameter **INMEMORY_SIZE** to the desired value to set the In-Memory area. For example

ALTER SYSTEM SET INMEMORY_SIZE = 100M SCOPE=SPFILE;

sets the In-Memory area to 100M.

If you want to disable the In-Memory option, you can simply set the value of the parameter **INMEMORY_SIZE** to 0, which is also the default value.

Data population is the process of reading the data from the row format and converting it into the columnar format and storing it at the IMCS. When the IMCS is enabled, the object's data (for which IMCS is enabled) is populated in two ways:

- Oracle Database controls when the data is populated in IMCS.

- You can set up the priority for populating the data in IMCS.

The following database objects cannot be populated in the IMCS:

- Any object owned by the SYS user and stored in the SYSTEM or SYSAUX tablespace

- Index-organized tables (IOTs)

- Clustered tables

- LONGs (depreciated beginning in Oracle Database 8*i*)

- Out-of-line large objects (LOBs)

CHAPTER
4

How Database
In-Memory Works with
RAC and Multitenant

S o far, we have studied the Database In-Memory architecture and how it works in context with a single-instance database. In real life, you will often see lots of database implementations with Real Application Clusters (RAC). Because a database is critical for many applications, most customers prefer to implement a high-availability solution along with their database implementation. Therefore, you will often find Database In-Memory being implemented as a part of RAC, or you will be required to implement Database In-Memory in a RAC system.

The Oracle Multitenant option was introduced in Oracle Database 12*c*. It delivers a unique architecture that allows a multitenant container database (CDB) to hold many pluggable databases (PDBs).

In this chapter, you are going to learn how Database In-Memory works with RAC and the Multitenant option.

RAC Basics

In a single-instance database, the database instance and Oracle software both run on a single server. With Oracle RAC, the database software and the Oracle instance (which includes the background processes and memory structure) run on more than one server that are connected to shared storage, which provides high availability to Oracle Database. If one database instance goes down, there is no impact to the users, since other nodes run additional database instances.

Let's quickly cover some basic concepts of RAC to get you started.

RAC Architecture and Concepts

Oracle RAC allows multiple instances of a database to run across multiple clustered servers. The database files are stored in a file system that is shared across all the nodes of the cluster.

Figure 4-1 shows the RAC architecture. Because the instance runs across multiple servers, if one server goes down, the workload will failover to a different node without impacting the application. RAC ensures that the business can run 24/7.

Following are some of the advantages of RAC:

■ *RAC provides a highly available solution to the business.* RAC ensures continuity in business by providing redundancy. For example, in the event of unplanned downtime, such as a server going down due to

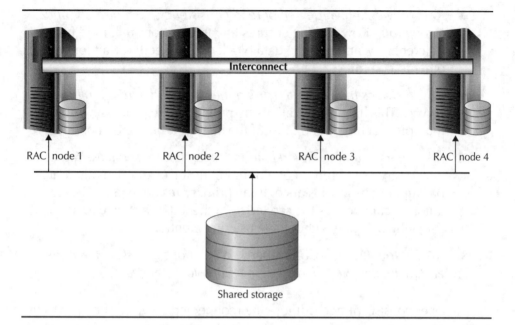

FIGURE 4-1. *RAC architecture*

some hardware failure, the application can still access the database on surviving instances.

■ *RAC provides horizontal scalability to the database.* The biggest disadvantage of vertical scaling is that only a certain number of CPUs can be added before the system hits the maximum limit. With horizontal scaling, more nodes can be added/decreased depending on the application workload. Customers can run up to 64 nodes of RAC clustered together. Adding more nodes can occur online without any downtime.

■ *RAC allows online patching, a better availability solution for planned downtime.* It helps in OS patching as well as database patching, patch set updates (PSU), and critical patch updates (CPU).

■ *RAC provides transparency.* To implement RAC, no code changes in the application are needed. From an application perspective, RAC environments are functionally equivalent to single-instance Oracle Database configurations.

■ *RAC provide a high degree of read consistency, concurrency, and throughput.* Row locking ensures that transactions that modify different rows in the same data block do not need to wait for each other to commit.

■ *RAC provides the ability to spread the workload across multiple servers.* This helps applications by providing the processing power of multiple machines, and most of the tasks can be done in parallel.

■ *RAC offers automated workload management for services.* You can assign services to run on one or more instances or on an alternate, backup, or failover instance. If the primary instance fails, Oracle automatically moves the service from the failed instance to a surviving instance without any user intervention.

■ *RAC automatically load balances connections across all the nodes and maintains the balance across multiple instances.*

A cluster consists of two or more interconnected servers. The important feature of clustering is that to an application, it appears as a single server. Thus, RAC helps to manage multiple servers and database instances as a single group—although there are multiple instances, all are running the same database. Each instance has its own memory structure and background process.

The servers are clustered together using clusterware software, such as Oracle Clusterware or a third-party software certified to run with Oracle RAC. The RAC software manages data access so that changes are coordinated between the instances, and each instance sees a consistent image of the database. RAC synchronizes the data stored in the buffer cache of each instance using the Cache Fusion technology. Cache Fusion uses interconnect to transfer the data residing in the buffer cache from one instance to another when requested. Cache Fusion take cares of coordination of the data blocks across multiple nodes of the RAC and acts as though the data resided in a single buffer cache. Figure 4-2 shows how RAC Cache Fusion works.

The interconnect has a very important role in Oracle RAC. It is the dedicated private connection across the RAC nodes through which all the internode communication happens. The interconnect is always redundant within an RAC cluster.

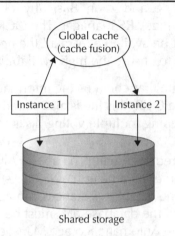

FIGURE 4-2. *RAC Cache Fusion*

Tip & Technique
*If you are interested in knowing how much data
is flowing through the interconnect, you can find
this out from the Automatic Workload Repository
(AWR) reports.*

Oracle recommends running Oracle Clusterware with RAC. It provides all of the features you need to manage the cluster database—for example, node membership, group services, global resource management, and high availability functions. Oracle Clusterware is designed to be tightly integrated with Oracle RAC and thus manages all the resources in the cluster. The services that Oracle Clusterware manages are called Cluster Ready Services (CRS) resources. A CRS resource can be a database, a listener, an instance, a virtual IP (VIP) address, or an application process.

Oracle Clusterware has two major components:

- **Oracle Cluster Registry (OCR)**   Maintains the cluster configuration information and stores all the detail information about all the databases within the cluster. It contains information such as which database joins the cluster, which database leaves the cluster, which database instance runs on which node, what services are running in a particular node, and so on. Basically it has information about all the processes that CRS manages. The OCR must reside in shared storage and must be available from all the nodes in the cluster. The OCR is mirrored to ensure the high availability of this file.

■ **Voting disk**   A file that contains the information about the node membership. Like OCR, this file is also stored on a shared disk. Oracle recommends keeping multiple voting disks for high availability.

Oracle RAC is a "shared everything" database. All the database files, log files, control files, and server parameter files (SPFILEs) need to be kept on a shared disk so that all the database instances can access these files. The storage used for storing all the database files must be cluster-aware. Oracle recommends using Oracle Automatic Storage Management (ASM) as a volume manager for running RAC databases. ASM provides lots of benefits. It is based on the SAME (Stripe and Mirror Everything) methodology, so it takes care of striping and mirroring the data. It provides a choice of two-way and three-way mirroring of data. It also does automatic rebalancing of data when the hard drive fails. ASM also protects from block corruption: when a read operation identifies a corrupt block on a disk, ASM automatically copies the block from the mirrored copy to a different portion of the disk.

RAC vs. Single-Instance

Let's take a deeper look at how RAC is different from single-instance. In a single-instance database, whenever a resource such as a row in a table needs to be updated, locking coordinates the access. The process that updates the row locks it, and therefore it prevents two processes from changing the same row at the same time. With RAC, apart from locking, it is very important to communicate across the different nodes for internode synchronization, since that is the only way to maintain data consistency. Internode synchronization makes sure that each instance sees the updated version of the block in the buffer cache.

RAC uses the Global Resource Directory (GRD) to log all the information about how resources are being used within the database clusters. Two processes, the Global Cache Service (GCS) and Global Enqueue Service (GES), manage all the information in the GRD.

Each instance keeps a part of the GRD in the System Global Area (SGA). The GCS and GES processes use one instance to manage all the information about a particular resource, which is known as the *master instance*. Any update to that particular resource is coordinated via the master instance, and each instance knows which instance is master for which resource.

Here's an example to help clarify how this works. For this example, there are three instances of the database.

1. From the application, the first instance gets a request to update the data block.

2. The first instance sends a write request to the GCS.

3. GCS finds that the master for that particular data block is the second instance, so it forwards the request to the second instance.

4. The second instance receives the request and forwards the request to the instance that is holding the current version of the data block.

5. The instance with the current version of the data block ships the same to the first instance via interconnect.

6. After receiving the database block, the first instance updates the data block.

7. The first instance updates the GCS that has written the data block.

8. The GCS notifies the other instances that the data block has been updated and orders those instances to discard the data block if they were holding any past images of it.

When an instance within an RAC cluster dies, the GRD portion needs to be redistributed across the remaining nodes. In addition, if you add a new node to the cluster, GRD needs to be redistributed. For redistribution, Oracle RAC does object remastering, or dynamic remastering, and assigns new master nodes for the resource. During this process, GCS, which is tightly integrated with the buffer cache, enables the database to migrate resources in the GRD automatically. While doing the remastering, instead of remastering all the resources across all the nodes, RAC remasters only a minimal number of resources during a redistribution. As a result, there is a minimal performance impact in the system.

RAC Background Processes

A lot of processes work in the background for Cache Fusion. It is important that you know about them:

- **Atomic Controlfile to Memory Service (ACMS)**   In an Oracle RAC environment, the ACMS per-instance process is an agent that contributes to ensuring a distributed SGA memory update is either globally committed on success or globally aborted if a failure occurs.

- **Global Transaction Process (GTX0-j)**   The GTX0-j process provides transparent support for XA global transactions in an Oracle RAC environment. The database auto-tunes the number of these processes based on the workload of XA global transactions.

- **Global Enqueue Service Monitor (LMON)**   The LMON process monitors global enqueues and resources across the cluster and performs global enqueue recovery operations.

- **Global Enqueue Service Daemon (LMD)**   The LMD process manages incoming remote resource requests within each instance.

- **Global Cache Service Process (LMS)**   The LMS process maintains records of the data file statuses and each cached block by recording information in a GRD. The LMS process also controls the flow of messages to remote instances and manages global data block access and transmits block images between the buffer caches of different instances. This processing is part of the Cache Fusion feature.

- **Instance Enqueue Process (LCK0)**   The LCK0 process manages non–Cache Fusion resource requests such as library and row cache requests.

- **Oracle RAC Management Processes (RMSn)**   The RMSn processes perform manageability tasks for Oracle RAC. Tasks accomplished by an RMSn process include creation of resources related to Oracle RAC when new instances are added to the clusters.

- **Remote Slave Monitor (RSMN)**   RSMN manages background slave process creation and communication on remote instances. These background slave processes perform tasks on behalf of a coordinating process running in another instance.

Tip & Technique
You can run `ps -ef | grep <owner of oracle software>` *to check all of the processes related to RAC and the database.*

Parallel Execution with RAC

The real advantage of RAC is the ability to run a parallel query across multiple nodes. The in-memory database (IMDB) running on RAC also leverages this feature extensively, so it is important that you understand these concepts.

RAC provides both intra-node and inter-node parallelism. The optimizer decides if a query will be executed in parallel during the parsing phase. If it decides to run the query in parallel, the user session takes the role of coordinator. If, for example, a query needs ten query processes to complete the work, the parallel execution coordinator, which runs on the instance the client connects to, first finds out how many parallel servers are required to complete the task. Then it checks the local node to determine how many parallel execution servers are idle on the local node. If it finds all ten execution servers are idle on the local node, the query is processed by using only the local resource. But if all ten local parallel execution servers are not available locally—say only four are available—the four servers are started locally and six parallel execution servers are started in other nodes. The parallel execution servers perform each operation in parallel wherever possible. When the parallel servers finish their task, the query coordinator performs any pending tasks. In this fashion, both inter- and intra-node parallelism are used to speed up operation.

When a parallel query is executed, the query executor examines the execution plan of the SQL statement and determines the way in which each operation within the SQL statement can be distributed across the parallel execution server. Consider the following query:

```
EXPLAIN PLAN FOR
SELECT /*+ PARALLEL(4) */ inventory.product_name, inventory.brand
  MAX(QUANTITY_SOLD), AVG(QUANTITY_SOLD)
FROM sales, inventory
WHERE sales.product_id=inventory.product_id
GROUP BY inventory.product_name, inventory.brand;

Explained.
```

Figure 4-3 shows a data flow diagram for joining the table in the code example. As the figure shows, the optimizer chooses two parallel servers—one for scanning the INVENTORY table and a second one for scanning the SALES table. As you can see from the explain plan given next, we have given a parallel hint of four; therefore, each parallel server (let's call them PS1 and PS2) has four execution processes.

The operation that produces output independently is known as the *producer operator,* whereas the operation that needs the output of other operations is known as the *consumer operator.* An Oracle server always creates parallel execution sets for both producer and consumer operators in order to run a query in parallel. The execution set for the producer operator directly connects with the execution set of the consumer operator and is directly in proportion to the degree of parallelism. The greater the degree of parallelism, the greater the number of connections. The communication channel requires memory, which is allocated from a shared pool. Each channel needs up to four memory buffers, which facilitates asynchronous communication among the parallel execution servers. In case of single-instance, the communication channel is created by passing the buffers back and forth in shared pool memory. With RAC, the messages are sent using

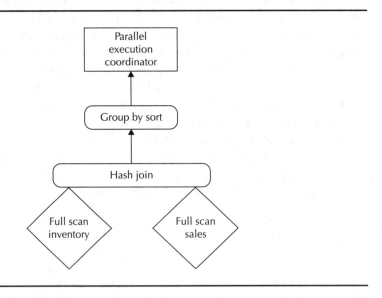

FIGURE 4-3. *Data flow for joining the table*

interconnect, and then they go back and forth in the shared pool memory across the RAC instances. Figure 4-4 shows how the message buffers pass across parallel execution servers across instances. (In the figure, DOP stands for degree of parallelism, which you will read about next.)

NOTE
The parallel server execution is totally dependent on memory; therefore, it is important to size the shared pool accordingly. If the shared pool is inappropriately sized, the parallel server fails to start.

The producer operator server retrieves rows from tables, and the consumer operator server performs operations such as joins and sorts, and any Data Manipulation Language (DML) or Data Definition Language (DDL) operations on these rows. As shown in Figure 4-3, the GROUP BY SORT operation is the consumer of the HASH JOIN operation, because GROUP BY SORT requires the HASH JOIN output.

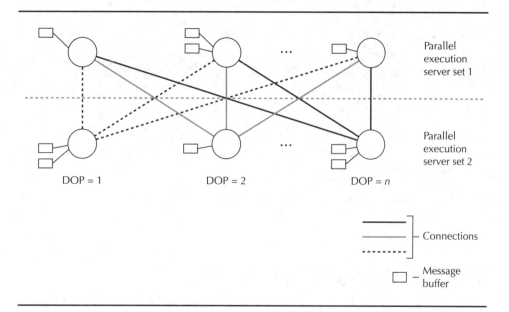

FIGURE 4-4.   *Parallel execution*

The set PS1 (first parallel execution server) first scans the INVENTORY table and sends rows to PS2 (second parallel execution server), which builds a hash table on the rows. In this case, PS1 is the producer and PS2 is the consumer, and they work concurrently: one in scanning INVENTORY in parallel, while the other is consuming rows and building the hash table to enable the hash join in parallel. This is an example of inter-operation parallelism.

Once PS1 has scanned the INVENTORY table, it scans the SALES table in parallel. Then it sends its rows to servers in PS2, which then finishes the hash-join in parallel. After PS1 has scanned the SALES table in parallel and sent the rows to PS2, it switches to performing the GROUP BY operation in parallel. This shows how two server sets run concurrently to achieve inter-operation parallelism across various operators in the query tree.

Following is the explain plan of the SQL query:

```
PLAN_TABLE_OUTPUT
--------------------------------------------------------------------------------
-------
Plan hash value: 4060011603
--------------------------------------------------------------------------------
| Id  | Operation                  | Name      | Rows | Bytes | TQ    |IN-OUT| PQ Distrib |
--------------------------------------------------------------------------------
|   0 | SELECT STATEMENT           |           |  925 | 25900 |       |      |            |
|   1 |  PX COORDINATOR            |           |      |       |       |      |            |
|   2 |   PX SEND QC (RANDOM)      | :TQ10003  |  925 | 25900 | Q1,03 | P->S | QC (RAND)  |
|   3 |    HASH GROUP BY           |           |  925 | 25900 | Q1,03 | PCWP |            |
|   4 |     PX RECEIVE             |           |  925 | 25900 | Q1,03 | PCWP |            |
|   5 |      PX SEND HASH          | :TQ10002  |  925 | 25900 | Q1,02 | P->P | HASH       |
|*  6 |       HASH JOIN BUFFERED   |           |  925 | 25900 | Q1,02 | PCWP |            |
|   7 |        PX RECEIVE          |           |  630 | 12600 | Q1,02 | PCWP |            |
|   8 |         PX SEND HASH       | :TQ10000  |  630 | 12600 | Q1,00 | P->P | HASH       |
|   9 |          PX BLOCK ITERATOR |           |  630 | 12600 | Q1,00 | PCWC |            |
|  10 |           TABLE ACCESS FULL| INVENTORY |  630 | 12600 | Q1,00 | PCWP |            |
|  11 |        PX RECEIVE          |           |  960 |  7680 | Q1,02 | PCWP |            |
|  12 |         PX SEND HASH       | :TQ10001  |  960 |  7680 | Q1,01 | P->P | HASH       |
|  13 |          PX BLOCK ITERATOR |           |  960 |  7680 | Q1,01 | PCWC |            |
|  14 |           TABLE ACCESS FULL| SALES     |  960 |  7680 | Q1,01 | PCWP |            |
--------------------------------------------------------------------------------
----

Predicate Information (identified by operation id):
---------------------------------------------------

   6 - access("SALES"."PRODUCT_ID"="INVENTORY"."PRODUCT_ID")


inventory , item
```

Degree of Parallelism (DOP)

For executing any query in parallel, the *degree of parallelism (DOP)* plays a very crucial role. DOP defines how many parallel processes/slaves will be used while running a query. When a parallel query runs, the query coordinator breaks the query into various parts and executes each part in parallel with parallel slaves. The query coordinator gets the output from each parallel slave and produces the final output. With this process, the overall query processing timing greatly improves compared to running it single-threaded.

If you set the DOP to a very high value, system resources will be overallocated, resulting in poor performance. Setting the value too low will also cause performance degradation. Therefore, it is important that you set the optimal value for the DOP to obtain good performance. If you are new to the world of parallel processing, it may be tricky to determine the optimal value, since one size does not fit all. The more familiar you get with the data pattern, how the data is being queried, data usage, and so on, the better you will understand how to determine DOP in parallel processing.

The DOP can be set automatically, or you can specify it manually. Several initialization parameters control the DOP settings. You can specify the DOP at the table or index level by running the following command:

```
SQL > alter table <table_name> parallel <number> ;
```

or

```
SQL > alter index <index_name> parallel <number> ;
```

So, for example, if you want to specify a DOP of 5 for your INVENTORY table and a DOP of 10 for your SALES table, you would run the following:

```
SQL > alter table inventory parallel 5;
SQL > alter table sales parallel 10;
```

Any query that accesses the INVENTORY table will use a DOP of 5 for processing the query, whereas any query that accesses the SALES table will use a DOP of 10. Now, there may be a situation in which a query accesses both tables (SALES and INVENTORY). When a query accesses multiple tables and each table has a different value of DOP, Oracle uses the maximum value. Thus, in this case, the query would be processed with a DOP of 10.

If you don't specify a DOP manually, the default setting is used for the object when a query accesses it. Oracle uses the following formula to calculate the default DOP:

- For a single instance: DOP = PARALLEL_THREADS_PER_CPU × CPU_COUNT

- For RAC configurations: DOP = PARALLEL_THREADS_PER_CPU × CPU_COUNT × NUMBER_OF_INSTANCE

Therefore, for a three-node RAC cluster, where each has six CPU cores (two threads per processor), the default DOP would be $3 \times 6 \times 2 = 36$.

The initialization parameter **PARALLEL_DEGREE_POLICY** governs whether any query would be run in parallel or serial. This parameter can have three values: **MANUAL**, **AUTO**, and **LIMITED**. The default setting for this parameter is **MANUAL**. To use parallelism, you must change the value to **AUTO**.

- **MANUAL** Disables automatic degree of parallelism, statement queuing, and in-memory parallel execution.

- **LIMITED** Enables automatic degree of parallelism for some statements but statement queuing and in-memory parallel execution are disabled.

- **AUTO** Enables automatic degree of parallelism, statement queuing, and in-memory parallel execution.

When **PARALLEL_DEGREE_POLICY** is set to **AUTO**, the database decides whether a query should be executed in parallel or not, and if in parallel, then what DOP it should use. If the resources are available, the query is executed immediately; if the resources are not available immediately, the queries are queued in the system and executed when resources are available in the system. You can set the PARALLEL_DEGREE_POLICY to AUTO by running the following command:

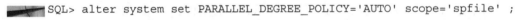

```
SQL> alter system set PARALLEL_DEGREE_POLICY='AUTO' scope='spfile' ;
```

Tip & Technique
*Automatic degree of parallelism is applied only to those statements that access tables or indexes decorated explicitly with the **DEFAULT** degree of parallelism using the **PARALLEL** clause. Statements that do not access any tables or indexes decorated with the **DEFAULT** degree of parallelism will retain the **MANUAL** behavior.*

Next comes the concept of *statement queuing*. Not all queries are queued in the system. Figure 4-5 shows the overall flow.

The parameter **PARALLEL_MIN_TIME_THRESHOLD** determines whether a statement should be executed in parallel or in serial. If the execution time is less than the threshold, the statement is run serially. The default value of the parameter **PARALLEL_MIN_TIME_THRESHOLD** is 10 seconds. Only when the estimated execution time is greater than **PARALLEL_MIN_TIME_ THRESHOLD** will a statement become eligible for automatic DOP.

From the execution plan, the optimizer looks at the cost of the scan operations (full table scan, index scan, and so on) and then determines the DOP for a statement. Most of the time, the DOP is proportional to the resource required. The optimizer, however, limits the actual DOP at times to make sure the resources do not choke the system. The optimizer uses the value of the parameter **PARALLEL_DEGREE_LIMIT** to set the limit of the DOP. The default value for this parameter is PARALLEL_THREADS_PER_CPU × CPU_COUNT × NUMBER_OF_INSTANCE, as you saw previously. The value of **PARALLEL_DEGREE_LIMIT** can be increased or decreased manually to fine-tune the DOP settings.

Thus, the two main parameters that control the DOP are **PARALLEL_ DEGREE_POLICY** and **PARALLEL_MIN_TIME_THRESHOLD**. The DOP

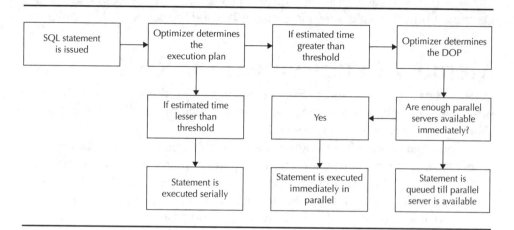

FIGURE 4-5. *Flow of statement queueing*

can also be set at the session level by issuing the **ALTER SESSION** command, as shown next:

```
ALTER SESSION SET parallel_degree_policy = limited;
ALTER TABLE inventory parallel (degree default);
```

For a particular statement, you can manually enable or disable force parallelism by providing a **PARALLEL** or **NO_PARALLEL** hint in the statement. Note that the **NO_PARALLEL** hint overrides a **PARALLEL** parameter in the DDL that created or altered the table.

```
SELECT /*+parallel */ * FROM inventory  WHERE product_name like '%s';
SELECT /*+parallel(10) */ * FROM inventory  WHERE product_name like '%s';
SELECT /*+no_parallel */ * FROM inventory  WHERE product_name like '%s';
```

Whenever you are using auto-DOP, it is always recommended that you use it in conjunction with Oracle Database Resource Manager. Using Resource Manager, you can create various resource plans and enforce a cap on the DOP depending on the workload. Using Resource Manager, you can make better use of DOP, can use the resources available in the system more appropriately, and can protect statements from downgrading to serial through queuing. You can make sure that one statement does not use all the system resources, you can prioritize an important job with more DOP, and so on. (The Resource Manager can be created using Enterprise Manager or from the command line. Discussing how to create a resource plan is beyond the scope of this book.)

Memory Requirement for RAC

In RAC, data blocks may be cached across instances; therefore, you must provision for additional memory. RAC-specific memory is allocated in the shared pool when the SGA is created.

If you are migrating from single-instance to RAC, assuming the same workload, you need to provision about 10 percent more memory for the buffer cache and 15 percent more for the shared pool to run RAC. These are general guidelines provided by Oracle and are good starting points. Again, each workload is different, so you may have to increase or decrease the number accordingly. You can monitor the exact RAC memory usage of the shared pool by running the following query:

```
select * from v$sgastat where name like 'g_s% or name like 'KCL' ;
```

Alternatively, you can query the V$RESOURCE_LIMIT view of each instance and check the current and maximum utilization for the GCS and the GES.

```
Select resource_name,
       current_utilization, max_utilization
from v$resource_limit
where resource_name like 'g_s' or name like KCL' ;
```

NOTE
In RAC, for each v$ view, there is a corresponding gv$ view (global v$ view). The v$ view provides information about the instance from which the query is run, whereas the gv$ view provides information from all the RAC nodes. The gv$ view has an additional column, called inst_id, which displays the instance.

RAC and DBIM

Once you have sized the memory requirements for RAC, the next step is to add the memory for the Database In-Memory option. The size you specify for the parameter **INMEMORY_SIZE** should be equal across all the RAC nodes (although you can use different values, it is not recommended). You also need to set up other initialization parameters related to RAC and implement the RAC-specific instructions for running DBIM on RAC, as discussed in Chapter 3.

Because there are multiple instances in RAC and each instance has its own SGA, each instance will also have its own In-Memory Column Store (IMCS). So, for example, if you have a three-node RAC cluster, you will have three separate IMCSs, each residing in its own instance. Since each node has its own IMCS, it is possible that completely different sets of data are populated on different nodes. When an object is populated in the IMCS, it will be spread equally among all the different IMCSs across multiple nodes. When a query runs, it fetches data residing in all the different IMCSs. The in-memory column units are never shipped across the RAC instances; therefore, parallelism plays a crucial role. Parallelism must be used when fetching objects residing in memory across multiple RAC nodes. When an object (data populated) resides in a particular RAC node, it is called *data affinity*. Suppose, for example, that you run a query and the data resides in the second and third nodes of a three-node cluster. The query must search the IMCU of the second and third instances to fetch the data. In order to complete the process, it must use parallelism.

Oracle recommends that you set the **PARALLEL_DEGREE_POLICY** parameter to **AUTO** for RAC with In-Memory to ensure optimal performance. When the In-Memory option is used, the value for the parameter **PARALLEL_ MIN_TIME_THRESHOLD** is automatically set.

Auto-DOP must be used to guarantee parallelism. When you set auto-DOP, at least one parallel server process is started per instance. The parallel query coordinator is aware of where IMCUs are located, so when the object is affinitized to a specific RAC instance, DOP guarantees that the object will be picked from the IMCU. Suppose that you don't specify the auto-DOP—in this case, though, the parallel query coordinator is aware of the home location of IMCU—the query coordinator still will not be able to make use of IMCU and therefore there is no guarantee that the data will be read from IMCU.

IMCS Data Population in RAC

When the data is populated in RAC, by default, it is populated across all the RAC nodes. The parameter that controls how the data is distributed is the **DISTRIBUTE** subclause. Here's an example:

```
SQL> alter table inventory inmemory distribute by partition;
```

By default, the **DISTRIBUTE** subclause is set to **AUTO**, which means Oracle will find the best way to distribute the data (object) across the multiple IMCSs in RAC nodes. Needless to say, if the data is very small and does not span more than one IMCU, it won't be spread across multiple RAC nodes. When the **DISTRIBUTE** subclause is set to **AUTO**, Oracle distributes the data in three ways:

- By rowid range
- By partition
- By subpartition

If you want to manually distribute the data instead of using **AUTO**, you can do this in four ways:

- **Distribute by rowid range**   When you choose this option, IMCUs are distributed across the range of a rowid in a RAC cluster. For example, in a three node RAC, say you have rowids from 1 to 1000 and you divide the range like so: 1–251, 251–501, 501–751, and 751–1000. When you distribute the rowid range, the range 1–251 goes to the first RAC node, 251–501 goes to the second RAC node, 501–751 goes to the third RAC node, and 751–1000 goes to the first RAC node. When this option is chosen, the IMCUs are distributed by uniform hash on the first rowid, which ensures uniform distribution across all the instances. You should choose this option when a table is not partitioned or if you have a partition table with skewed access across partitions.

- **Distribution by partition**   This parameter specifies that partitions in IMCS will be distributed across different RAC nodes. For example, say you have four partitions in a big table: P1, P2, P3, and P4. When distributed by partition, P1 goes to the first RAC node, P2 goes to the second RAC node, P3 goes to the third RAC node, and P4 goes to the first RAC node. This type of distribution is recommended for hash partitions and other partition types where data is uniformly accessed. Distribution by partition also allows in-memory partition-wise joins.

- **Distribution by subpartition**   This parameter specifies that subpartitions in IMCS will be distributed across different RAC nodes. This type of distribution is recommended for subhash partitions and other subpartition types where data is uniformly accessed. Distribution by subpartition also allows in-memory partition-wise joins. The only difference between this and distribution by partition is distribution by partition takes care of the full partition, whereas distribution by subpartition takes care of a subset of a partition.

- **Distribution for service**   This parameter distributes the objects in IMCS across various RAC nodes using a service. Before we explain this option, let's learn more about the distribution of data using a service.

IMCS Data and Services

Services can be used in conjunction with IMCS to achieve node affinity for particular object types. They can be used to control node access and to control IMCS population. You may be required to do this in several situations. For example, suppose your application needs all GL (general ledger) data to have affinity to a particular RAC node and all your supply chain planning (SCP) data to go to another RAC node. In this situation, you are forced to keep all the GL data in RAC node 1 and SCP data in RAC node 2. The way to achieve this would be to create services and run the services on corresponding RAC nodes. For example, you can create a service for GL and another for SCP like so:

```
srvctl add service -db imdbrac -service GL -preferred exa10db01
srvctl add service -db imdbrac -service SCP -preferred exa10db02
srvctl start service -db imdbrac -service "GL.SCP"
srvctl status service -db imdbrac
Service GL is running on instance(s) exa10db01
Service SCP is running on instance(s) exa10db02

GL =
  (DESCRIPTION=
    (ADDRESS=(PROTOCOL=TCP)(HOST=exa10db01.us.oracle.com)(PORT=1521))
    (ADDRESS=(PROTOCOL=TCP)(HOST=exa10db02.us.oracle.com)(PORT=1521))
    (CONNECT_DATA=
      (SERVICE_NAME=GL)
    )
  )
```

Similarly, you can create a service for SCP with the primary node being the second RAC node. When you connect using the GL service, you will see that you are connected to the first node, and when you connect using the SCP service, you are connected to the second RAC node.

```
SQL> connect system/manager@GL
Connected.
SQL> select instance_name from v$instance;

INSTANCE_NAME
----------------
imdbrac1
```

When you connect using this service, all activities happening at the IMCU are limited to this particular node. It is important to note that, in this case, you would be preventing inter-node parallelism, since nothing is going outside the node. Therefore, you need to set the parameter that facilitates this. Set the initialization parameter **PARALLEL_FORCE_LOCAL** to **TRUE**. By setting this parameter to **TRUE**, you ensure that the parallel server processes can execute only on the same Oracle RAC node where the SQL statement was started.

Along with this, you also need to specify another initialization parameter, **PARALLEL_INSTANCE_GROUP**, which restricts parallel query operations to the instances supported by the service name or specified by the **INSTANCE_ GROUP** parameter on the instance where it is set.

In our example, let's define **PARALLEL_INSTANCE_GROUP = GL** in the first node and **PARALLEL_INSTANCE_GROUP = SCP** on the second node. This will allow population of the GL to the IMCS of the first node and population of the SCP to the IMCS on the second node:

```
SQL> alter system set parallel_instance_group=GL

scope=both sid='imdbrac1';

System altered.

SQL> alter system set parallel_instance_group=SCP

scope=both sid='imdbrac2';

System altered.
```

To populate specific objects in a specific IMCS, the population priority needs to be set to **NONE** for the objects that you want to access in the IMCS. This allows you to completely control the population and make sure that any other incident does not start the population process.

Returning to our discussion on distribution of data using a service—there are four options available under this scenario:

- **NAME** Specifies the service name and the object populated in IMCS where the service is active. If the service name changes or the service is relocated to a different RAC node, the object is removed from the old node and repopulated on the new nodes. Whatever priority settings you have for population of data, it honors that setting.

- **ALL** Specifies that the object is populated on all the RAC instances that have a non-zero–sized IMCS. Whatever priority settings you have for population of data, it honors that setting.

- **NONE** Removes the object from the old service IMCS. The data is not populated until a new service is specified. Though the object is retained from the old service IMCS, all the in-memory attributes are retained for future use.

- **DEFAULT** Populates the data across all the RAC nodes based on whether **PRIORITY** is chosen. If the **ON DEMAND** option is chosen, it will populate the data to all instances mapped by the issuing query's service.

When a particular service is stopped, all the objects are removed from the service's IMCS. All the in-memory attributes are retained for future use.

Multitenant and IMDB

In a traditional Oracle Database architecture, whenever we create a new database we allocate memory structures and background processes associated with the database. If we create 10 databases on the same server, then we need to start 10 sets of memory structures and background processes. Since the server has finite resources, the number of databases that can be created on a particular server is constrained by the number of resources available.

Oracle Database 12c introduces the new Multitenant feature, which changes the way a traditional database is installed. It is an optional feature that includes PDBs. With this architecture, you create a single multitenant CDB and then plug multiple PDBs into it. When this is done, only one set of background processes and memory structures are allocated for the CDB. No matter how many PDBs you plug in to the CDB, only one set of memory structure and background processes is allocated at the CDB level.

Because the background processes and the SGA are being shared, the Multitenant feature provides the following benefits:

- It helps in reducing the capital expenditure, since more databases can be consolidated.

- The operation costs are also lower, because fewer databases need to be managed.

- It is much easier to manage all the pluggable databases, since now only the root database (CDB) needs to be managed.

- Patching and upgrading need to occur only at the CDB level, resulting in upgrading of all the PDBs.

- Only one backup is needed, and only at the CDB level, although you can recover the database at the individual PDB level.

The Multitenant option is fully certified with Database In-Memory. When you implement the Multitenant option, it frees a lot of memory, since only one CDB is required instead of multiple databases. As a result, you can use the freed memory for the In-Memory option. When you implement the In-Memory option along with Multitenant, the In-Memory Area is specified at the CDB level.

Because the In-Memory Area is allocated at the CDB, it is shared by all the PDBs. But that does not mean that you cannot perform granular control. Consider an example: Suppose you have allocated 100GB for the In-Memory Area at the CDB level. You have three databases: Finance, Order Management, and Data-Warehouse. Using inter-database resource management, you can control how much memory you want to specify at the PDB level. For example, out of the 100GB, you can allocate 50GB to Financial, 30GB to Order Management, and 20GB to Data-Warehouse. Since you are controlling the allocation of memory using an intra-database resource plan, you can also overprovision the memory, which means you can allocate 30GB to Data-Warehouse.

Tip & Technique
Creating a database resource plan using the Oracle Enterprise Manager is much simpler than writing complex queries.

Summary

In this chapter you have studied how Database In-Memory works with RAC and the Multitenant option.

Oracle RAC allows multiple instances of a database to run across multiple clustered servers. The database files are stored in a file system that is shared across all the nodes of the cluster. Some of the advantages RAC provides are high availability and horizontal scalability, and it allows online patching and load balancing. You have also learned how a parallel query works and what the significance of degree of parallelism is in case of a parallel query.

When you are using RAC and Database In-Memory, you should set the **PARALLEL_DEGREE_POLICY** parameter to **AUTO** to ensure optimal performance. When the data is populated in RAC, by default, it is populated across all the RAC nodes.

The architecture of the new Multitenant feature of Oracle Database allows you to create a single Multitenant CDB and then plug multiple PDBs into it. When this is done, only one set of background processes and memory structures are allocated for the CDB. No matter how many PDBs you plug in to the CDB, only one set of memory structure and background processes is allocated at the CDB level. Multitenant reduces capital expenditure, lowers operational cost, and provides easier management of all pluggable databases.

Because the In-Memory Area is allocated at the CDB, it is shared by all PDBs. Using inter-database resource management, you can control how much memory you want to specify at the PDB level.

CHAPTER
5

Database
In-Memory Advisor

With more than a few thousand objects in your database, it sometimes becomes very confusing to determine what to keep in memory. The In-Memory Advisor can help by evaluating your workload and job patterns over a period of time and recommending how much benefit you will get by keeping certain objects in memory. The In-Memory Advisor looks at the various metrics obtained from Automated Workload Repository (AWR) reports, SQL plan cardinalities, and the Active Session History (ASH).

The tool also takes the following factors into account to estimate the gains:

- Object statistics

- Compression factor (compression and decompression costs versus gains)

- Various waits events (I/O waits, cluster waits, buffer cache, CPU waits, and so on)

- Optimizer statistics (SQL plan chosen, number of rows fetched, and so on)

Once run, the In-Memory Advisor displays the results in a very easy-to-read HTML format. It lists the objects and describes the benefits you will gain by keeping objects in the IMCS. The In-Memory Advisor also creates a SQL script that can be used to place the recommended objects into memory.

Installing the In-Memory Advisor

The Oracle Database In-Memory Advisor can be downloaded from the Oracle Support web site (support.oracle.com) from Note 1965343.1. The script can also be downloaded from the code provided for this chapter. Oracle Note 1965343.1 contains a zip file, imadvisor.zip. When the file is unzipped, you will find scripts in the imadvisor directory for performing the installation. The In-Memory Advisor can be installed in Oracle Database versions 11.2.0.3 and later. Though the In-Memory Advisor option is available in Oracle Database version 12.1.0.2, installing the Advisor in an earlier version also helps you to identify the objects even before upgrading to version 12*c*.

The In-Memory Advisor can also be installed in a multitenant database. If you are installing in a multitenant database, the Advisor can be installed in the root, CDB$ROOT, or in a pluggable database (PDB). When you are installing the Advisor in PDB, the installation will create a user called IMADVISOR for storing the objects; when you are installing in the root of the multitenant database, a user named C##IMADVISOR will be created.

Unzip the imadvisor.zip file that you downloaded from support.oracle.com. Log in as sys to the database where you want to install the In-Memory Advisor and run the script in the file instimadv.sql.

In this example, we'll install the In-Memory Advisor on a Database version 11.2.0.4 to identify the objects we will benefit from the most after implementing the In-Memory Advisor option:

```
[oracle@host11 imadvisor]$ sqlplus '/ as sysdba '
SQL*Plus: Release 11.2.0.4.0 Production on Sun Aug 7 12:05:27 2016
Copyright (c) 1982, 2013, Oracle.  All rights reserved.
Connected to:
Oracle Database 11g Enterprise Edition Release 11.2.0.4.0 - 64bit Production
With the Partitioning, OLAP, Data Mining and Real Application Testing options

SQL> @instimadv
Welcome to the Oracle Database In-Memory Advisor (DBMS_INMEMORY_ADVISOR)
installation.DBMS_INMEMORY_ADVISOR uses Active Session History (ASH),
Automatic Workload Repository (AWR) and optionally SQL Tuning Sets (STS) to
determine which tables, partitions and subpartitions to place In Memory for
optimized analytics processing performance.  DBMS_INMEMORY_ADVISOR produces a
recommendation report and a SQLPlus script to implement its recommendations.

This installation script will create user IMADVISOR and add objectdefinitions
to the schema including the DBMS_INMEMORY_ADVISOR package.  This installation
script creates user IMADVISOR using the IDENTIFIED BY password method. If you
prefer to use either the IDENTIFIED EXTERNALLY or IDENTIFIED GLOBALLY method,
abort this installation by pressing ^C. Then create user IMADVISOR using your
preferred method.  Add no objects to the IMADVISOR schema.  Then run this
installation script again. These actions will be taken on the database to which
you are currently connected.
```

First the script prompts for the name of the database:

```
Please enter the connection ID for the current database?
prod11
```

Then the script creates a new user called IMADVISOR, and it prompts you for the password for the IMADVISOR user:

```
This installation script creates a new Oracle database user and schema
named IMADVISOR for the operation of DBMS_INMEMORY_ADVISOR...
<enter password>
Please enter the password for user IMADVISOR?
<enter password>
For confirmation, please re-enter the password for user IMADVISOR?
```

Once you enter the password, the script prompts you for the default and temporary tablespaces for the IMADVISOR user:

```
Available tablespaces:

TABLESPACE_NAME
-----------------------------
EXAMPLE
SYSAUX
SYSTEM
TEMP
UNDOTBS1
USERS
Please enter the default, permanent tablespace name for user IMADVISOR?
SYSTEM
Please enter the temporary tablespace name for user IMADVISOR?
TEMP
```

The script then prompts you for the path name of the directory where the imadvisor objects will be stored. It displays the default directory path. Press ENTER if you want to keep the default directory location. If you want to change the path, enter the full directory path:

```
The In-Memory Advisor uses the Oracle directory object IMADVISOR_DIRECTORY
by default.Oracle directory object IMADVISOR_DIRECTORY already exists and is
definedwith directory path=/u01/app/oracle/admin/prod11/imadvisor_directory
If you wish to redefine IMADVISOR_DIRECTORY, please enter an OS host
directory path for the redefinition.
If not, please press ENTER to continue.

Connecting to IMADVISOR @ prod11..
Enter password:
Connected.
No errors.
No errors.
No errors.
No errors.
No errors.
No errors.
No errors.
No errors.
No errors.
No errors.
No errors.
No errors.
No errors.
No errors.
No errors.

DBMS_INMEMORY_ADVISOR installation successful.
```

The script then prompts you for the name of the users who can execute In-Memory Advisor. In this example, I have given the access to the imadv user.

```
Users who will use the DBMS_INMEMORY_ADVISOR package must be GRANTED
EXECUTE on the DBMS_INMEMORY_ADVISOR package.

Please enter a comma separated list of Oracle Database users to whom
you wish EXECUTE on the DBMS_INMEMORY_ADVISOR package to be GRANTED?

GRANT EXECUTE ON dbms_inmemory_advisor TO imadv

While logged in as IMADVISOR or with sufficient privileges, you can
GRANT EXECUTE ON DBMS_INMEMORY_ADVISOR to additional users as needed.

DBMS_INMEMORY_ADVISOR installation and setup complete.

Disconnected from Oracle Database 11g Enterprise Edition Release 11.2.0.4.0 -
64bit Production
With the Partitioning, OLAP, Data Mining and Real Application Testing options
[oracle@host11 imadvisor]$
```

If you want to provide access to another user at a later time, you can do this by running the following command:

```
[oracle@host11 imadvisor]$ sqlplus '/ as sysdba'

SQL*Plus: Release 11.2.0.4.0 Production on Sun Aug 7 12:14:36 2016
Copyright (c) 1982, 2013, Oracle.  All rights reserved.
Connected to:
Oracle Database 11g Enterprise Edition Release 11.2.0.4.0 - 64bit Production
With the Partitioning, OLAP, Data Mining and Real Application Testing options

SQL> GRANT EXECUTE ON dbms_inmemory_advisor TO joyjeet ;

Grant succeeded.
```

After the installation, you are ready to analyze your workload to determine the best candidates to keep in memory.

NOTE
If you want to uninstall the In-Memory Advisor, run the script catnoimadv.sql, which is included in the downloaded scripts.

Running the In-Memory Advisor

You can run the In-Memory Advisor in various ways—against AWR snapshots, against the SQL Performance Analyzer, running the recommendation script directly against a running database, against a container database (CDB) and PDB, and so on. In this section, we'll cover the most popular options.

Example 1: Comparing Against AWR Snapshots In this example database, I'll create two AWR snapshots and then run the In-Memory Advisor against them.

1. I create a snapshot by executing the following command:

```
SQL> execute dbms_workload_repository.create_snapshot

PL/SQL procedure successfully completed.
```

2. I query for the snapshot details by running the following command:

```
SQL> SET LINESIZE 2000
SET PAGESIZE 10000
SET SERVEROUTPUT ON
select snap_id, end_interval_time
from dba_hist_snapshot
where end_interval_time > trunc(sysdate-1)
order by snap_id desc;

SNAP_ID END_INTERVAL_TIME
---------- ----------------------------------------------------------------
        39 07-AUG-16 12.14.27.873 PM
```

This is the only snapshot I have in my database since I have deleted all the older snapshots. Before I generate a new snapshot, I will generate some workload to get some meaningful data to compare the two snapshots. Once I am done generating the workload, I'll run this command again to create additional snapshots for the comparison. When queried, this time I have multiple snapshots.

```
SNAP_ID END_INTERVAL_TIME
---------- ----------------------------------------------------------------
        41 07-AUG-16 12.41.45.908 PM
        40 07-AUG-16 12.25.55.730 PM
        39 07-AUG-16 12.14.27.873 PM
```

Now let's create an In-Memory Advisor task. For this, we need to run a PL/SQL procedure, as shown next. We also need to provide the task name and description of the task.

```
SQL> EXEC dbms_inmemory_advisor.create_task

('IMAdvTask','In memory advisor for book ');
PL/SQL procedure successfully completed.
```

Once I have created the In-Memory Advisor task, my next step is to add statistics between the two snapshots. I need the timestamp for the two chosen snapshots for comparing the statistics. I'll choose the snapshots with IDs 39 and 41. You can use any two snapshots for comparison; they don't have to be consecutive snapshots. Note the time for both the snapshots, because when the system prompts, we need to provide the time as input. In the following example, the input for the value for 1 is the timestamp for the first snapshot and the input for the value for 2 is the timestamp for the second snapshot:

```
SQL> exec dbms_inmemory_advisor.add_statistics
  ('IMAdvTask',to_timestamp('&1', 'DD-Mon-RR HH24.MI.SS.FF'),
to_timestamp('&2', 'DD-Mon-RR HH24.MI.SS.FF'));
Enter value for 1: 07-AUG-16 12.14.27.873
Enter value for 2: 07-AUG-16 12.41.45.908

PL/SQL procedure successfully completed.
```

Once statistics are added, our next step is to execute the In-Memory Advisor task. We need to run the PL/SQL block, as shown in next. We need to provide the same task name we created previously.

```
SQL> exec dbms_inmemory_advisor.execute_task ('IMAdvTask')

PL/SQL procedure successfully completed.
```

The final step is to generate the In-Memory Advisor recommendations. Run the following PL/SQL block. Provide the task name, directory name (we already defined the directory name during the In-Memory Advisor installation), and the planned memory size:

```
SQL> exec DBMS_INMEMORY_ADVISOR.GENERATE_RECOMMENDATIONS
(task_name =>'IMAdvTask', directory_name => ' IMADVISOR_DIRECTORY ',
 inmemory_size => '2147483648')

PL/SQL procedure successfully completed.
```

Once complete, the PL/SQL procedure will generate the recommendation in the IMADVISOR_DIRECTORY, which in our example is /u01/app/oracle/admin/prod11/imadvisor_directory. Let's go to this directory and list the contents:

```
cd /u01/app/oracle/admin/prod11/imadvisor_directory
$ ls -ltr
-rw-r--r--. 1 oracle oinstall 141347 Aug  8 01:16 imadvisor_sql_IMAdvTask.html
-rw-r--r--. 1 oracle oinstall  32356 Aug  8 01:16 imadvisor_IMAdvTask.html
-rw-r--r--. 1 oracle oinstall   8951 Aug  8 01:16 imadvisor_object_IMAdvTask.html
-rw-r--r--. 1 oracle oinstall    269 Aug  8 01:16 imadvisor_IMAdvTask.sql
-rw-r--r--. 1 oracle oinstall  10176 Aug  8 01:16 imadvisor_auxiliary_IMAdvTask.html
$
```

The HTML file imadvisor_IMAdvTask.html shows the recommendations. The output is shown in Figure 5-1.

Oracle Database In-Memory Advisor

In-Memory Advisor Objectives

The In-Memory database feature can be employed to improve the performance of a variety of database operations, the greatest of which is analytics processing.

The objective of the In-Memory Advisor is to produce recommendations to optimize analytics processing. As with SQL optimizer cost estimates, estimates for In-Memory sizes and performance benefits need not be precise in order to produce optimal In-Memory configurations.

Workload Database Usage

Total Database Time (Seconds)	Analytics Processing Time (Seconds)	Analytics Processing Percentage
4495	1979	44%

FIGURE 5-1. *HTML output of the recommendation (continued)*

In-Memory Sizes

Up to an application-specific limit, larger In-Memory sizes will result in greater analytics processing performance improvements.

The In-Memory Advisor first produces a list of In-Memory sizes and estimated analytics processing performance improvement factors. These estimates are based on statistics captured from your database while your application was running. For this report, you selected an In-Memory size of 2GB.

Percentage of Maximum Recommended In-Memory Size	Percentage of Current SGA Size (732MB)	In-Memory Size	Estimated Analytics Processing Time Reduction (Seconds)	Estimated Analytics Processing Performance Improvement Factor
231%	**280%**	**2GB**	**1634**	**5.7X**
100%	121%	887MB	1634	5.7X
95%	115%	843MB	1254	2.7X
90%	109%	799MB	1254	2.7X
85%	103%	754MB	1254	2.7X
80%	97%	710MB	1254	2.7X
75%	91%	665MB	1254	2.7X
70%	85%	621MB	1254	2.7X
65%	79%	577MB	20	1.0X
60%	73%	532MB	20	1.0X
55%	67%	488MB	20	1.0X
50%	61%	444MB	20	1.0X
45%	55%	399MB	20	1.0X
40%	48%	355MB	20	1.0X
35%	42%	311MB	20	1.0X
30%	36%	266MB	20	1.0X
25%	30%	222MB	20	1.0X
20%	24%	177MB	20	1.0X

FIGURE 5-1. *HTML output of the recommendation (continued)*

Percentage of Maximum Recommended In-Memory Size	Percentage of Current SGA Size (732MB)	In-Memory Size	Estimated Analytics Processing Time Reduction (Seconds)	Estimated Analytics Processing Performance Improvement Factor
15%	18%	133MB	20	1.0X
10%	12%	89MB	20	1.0X
5%	6%	44MB	20	1.0X

The following recommendations are designed to optimize your database application's analytics processing with the 2GB In-Memory size that you selected.

With 2GB, Top 10 SQL Statements with Analytics Processing Benefit

SQL Id	Analytics Processing Time Used (Seconds)	Estimated Analytics Processing Time Improvement (Seconds) With Unlimited Memory	Estimated Analytics Processing Performance Improvement Factor With Unlimited Memory	Estimated Analytics Processing Time Improvement (Seconds) With 2GB	Estimated Analytics Processing Performance Improvement Factor With 2GB
2zxackt5ztp08	26	23	9.0X	23	9.0X
475wh0bf089ms	24	21	9.0X	21	9.0X
9syr7zgkkbrfa	24	21	9.0X	21	9.0X
8cb9gbwnatrmt	22	20	9.0X	20	9.0X
d8kgkz03jbdpw	23	20	9.0X	20	9.0X
8f08jqav6g7xv	21	19	9.0X	19	9.0X
95dqjd3j4n2xv	21	19	9.0X	19	9.0X
3nurj9t58q02d	20	18	9.0X	18	9.0X
5b7xs33gs9t99	20	18	9.0X	18	9.0X
6sx2amnwzyp5z	20	18	9.0X	18	9.0X

Click here to view all 285 SQL statements that are estimated to have a performance improvement factor with In-Memory size = 2GB.

FIGURE 5-1. *HTML output of the recommendation (continued)*

With 2GB, All 3 Objects Recommended to Place In-Memory for Analytics Processing

Object Type	Object	Compression Type	Estimated In-Memory Size	Analytics Processing Seconds	Estimated Reduced Analytics Processing Seconds	Estimated Analytics Processing Performance Improvement Factor	Benefit/ Cost Ratio (Reduced Analytics Processing/ In-Memory Size)
TABLE	IMADV .TIMES	Memory compress for query low	1MB	30	20	3.0X	87:1
TABLE	IMADV .SALES	Memory compress for query low	516MB	1390	1234	9.0X	1:1
TABLE	IMADV .CUSTOMERS	Memory compress for query low	222MB	433	380	8.3X	1:1

Click here to view a rationale summary for the previously described recommendations.

Database on Which the In-Memory Advisor Was Run

Oracle Database Name	PROD11
Oracle Database Identifier	4014020257
Oracle Database Creation Date	04-FEB-16
Oracle Database Instance Name	prod11
Oracle Database Instance Number	1
Oracle Database Instance Version	Oracle Database 11g Enterprise Edition Release 11.2.0.4.0 - 64-bit Production
SGA Maximum Size	732MB
In-Memory Size	Not Applicable
Unused In-Memory Space	0B

FIGURE 5-1. *HTML output of the recommendation (continued)*

Oracle Database In-Memory Advisor	Version 1.0.0.0.1 Build #540 Build date 2015-JUL-10 16:56:04 Installation date 2016-AUG-07 12:11:42
Capture Start Time	2016-AUG-07 12:14:28
Capture End Time	2016-AUG-07 12:41:38
Report Date	2016-AUG-08 01:16:34

Click here to view the DDL script that implements the previously described recommendations.

In-Memory Advisor Methods

The In-Memory Advisor differentiates Analytics Processing from other database activity based upon the SQL plan cardinality, the Active Session History (ASH) state, employment of parallel query, and other data and statistics.

The In-Memory Advisor estimates the In-Memory size of objects based upon statistics and heuristic compression factors and, optionally, the DBMS_COMPRESSION package.

The In-Memory Advisor estimates Analytic Processing performance improvement factors based upon the following:

■ Elimination of user I/O waits, cluster transfer waits, buffer cache latch waits, etc.

■ Certain query-processing advantages related to specific compression types

■ Decompression cost heuristics per specific compression types

■ SQL plan selectivity, number of columns in the result set, etc.

FIGURE 5-1. *HTML output of the recommendation*

The HTML file also provides the DDL script for implementing the recommendation. When you click the "Click here" link in the HTML file, the DDL file opens. In the example shown in Figure 5-2, it has generated three commands.

```
Rem Copyright (c) 2014, 2015, Oracle and/or its affiliates.  All rights reserved.
ALTER TABLE " IMADV "."SALES" INMEMORY MEMCOMPRESS FOR QUERY LOW;
ALTER TABLE " IMADV "."CUSTOMERS" INMEMORY MEMCOMPRESS FOR QUERY LOW;
ALTER TABLE " IMADV "."TIMES" INMEMORY MEMCOMPRESS FOR QUERY LOW;
```

FIGURE 5-2. *DDL command generated by the script*

Example 2: Running the In-Memory Advisor Against a Live Database   You can run the In-Memory Advisor against a live database as well. In this example, we will run it against an Oracle Database 12c database. When the In-Memory Advisor is run against a live database, it queries all the AWR data as per the AWR retention period. You also have the option to run the Advisor for any time period during your AWR retention period. If your AWR retention period is short and you want to run the In-Memory Advisor for a longer duration, you can increase the AWR retention period.

Tip & Technique
You can also run the In-Memory Advisor against the AWR warehouse if you retain all the archived AWR reports. In that case, you need to run the In-Memory Advisor against the warehouse environment. Running that will be very useful, because you would be running the In-Memory Advisor on a larger data set.

To run the In-Memory Advisor script against a live database, connect as system or sys or with any user who has been granted the ADVISOR privilege. Run the imadvisor_recommendations.sql included in the code for this chapter.

```
$ sqlplus / as sysdba
SQL*Plus: Release 12.1.0.2.0 Production on Mon Aug 8 21:13:25 2016
Copyright (c) 1982, 2014, Oracle. All rights reserved. Connected to:
Oracle Database 12c Enterprise Edition Release 12.1.0.2.0 -
64bit Production With the Partitioning, OLAP, Advanced Analytics
 and Real Application Testing options

SQL> @imadvisor_recommendations
This script creates and runs an In-Memory Advisor task that
 analyzes your workload to determine an optimal In-Memory configuration.
This script then generates an HTML recommendation report file
 in the current working directory: imadvisor_<task_name>.html
This script also generates a sqlplus DDL script to implement
the recommendations: imadvisor_<task_name>.sql
```

When the In-Memory Advisor is run against the live database, the output is created in an HTML file. In addition to the HTML file, an SQL file containing all the DDLs is created.

```
NOTE: You may specify one of your existing tasks if you wish to optimize for
a different In-Memory size.

Using an existing, executed task is faster than a new task since a
 new task requires statistics gathering and analysis.

But if you wish to analyze a different workload or use a different statistics
capture window or add a SQLSET, you must specify a new task.
The following is a list of your existing tasks:

TASK_NAME                           DATE_CREATED
--------------------------------  --------------------
im_advisor_task_20160804001319        2016-AUG-04 00:13:19

Default task_name (new task): im_advisor_task_20160809002015
Enter value for task_name: LIVE_WORKLOAD

Advisor task name specified: LIVE_WORKLOAD

New Advisor task will be named: LIVE_WORKLOAD...

By default, the Advisor runs against a live workload on this database.
This database also has imported, augmented AWR workloads. Press ENTER
or respond NO to run against a live workload.

Respond YES to run against an augmented AWR workload.
```

Since we are going to run the Advisor against a live database, we type **NO**. If we had the Multitenant option enabled, at this time the system would prompts us for the PDB name. Also if we had multiple RAC instances, the script would prompt us for the RAC instance number.

We can also use the same script for running the report against the AWR data. In the previous example, we used PL/SQL blocks for running the report; the same can be done in an interactive way using this script. To do that, we'd type **YES** at the prompt. The system would display the augmented AWR import DBID in the next screen. Then we'd choose the value of DBID against which we wanted to run the In-Memory Advisor.

```
Analyzing and reporting on a live workload on this database (DBID=2135561901)...

The In-Memory Advisor optimizes the In-Memory configuration for a specific
In-Memory size that you choose.
```

```
After analysis, the In-Memory Advisor can provide you a list of
performance benefit estimates for a range of In-Memory sizes.  You may
then choose the In-Memory size for which you wish to optimize.

If you already know the specific In-Memory size you wish, please enter
the value now.  Format: nnnnnnn[KB|MB|GB|TB]

Or press <ENTER> to get performance estimates first.
Enter value for inmemory_size
```

At this step we can input the desired memory size to identify the benefits. If we don't input any value, the system calculates the performance benefit associated with memory increase. Let's not enter any value to find out what the system comes up with:

```
The In-Memory Advisor will display performance benefit estimates after
analysis.

Enter begin time for report:

--     Valid input formats:
--        To specify absolute begin time:
--           [MM/DD[/YY]] HH24:MI[:SS]
--           Examples: 02/23/03 14:30:15
--                     02/23 14:30:15
--                     14:30:15
--                     14:30
--        To specify relative begin time: (start with '-' sign)
--           -[HH24:]MI
--           Examples: -1:15   (SYSDATE - 1 Hr 15 Mins)
--                     -25     (SYSDATE - 25 Mins)
Default begin time: 08/09/16 00:14:25
Enter value for begin_time: 60
Report begin time specified:60

Enter duration in minutes starting from begin time:

(defaults to <latest-snapshot-end-time> - begin_time)
Enter value for duration: 60
Report duration specified:60

Using 2016-AUG-09 00:15:34.000000000 as report begin time
Using 2016-AUG-09 01:15:33.000000000 as report end time

In-Memory Advisor: Adding statistics...
```

```
In-Memory Advisor: Finished adding statistics. In-Memory Advisor: Analyzing
statistics...
In-Memory Advisor: Finished analyzing statistics
```

IN-MEMORY SIZE	PERCENTAGE OF MAXIMUM SGA SIZE	ESTIMATED ANALYTICS PROCESSING TIME REDUCTION (SECONDS)*	ESTIMATED ANALYTICS PROCESSING PERFORMANCE IMPROVEMENT FACTOR*
19.11GB	1911	653954	6.9X
18.09GB	1809	31001	1.0X
17.26GB	1726	31001	1.0X
16.12GB	1612	31001	1.0X
15.19GB	1519	31001	1.0X
13.95GB	1395	31001	1.0X
12.18GB	1218	31001	1.0X
11.01GB	1101	31001	1.0X
10.34GB	1034	31001	1.0X
9.103	910	31001	1.0X
8.111GB	811	31001	1.0X
7.324GB	732	31001	1.0X
6.877GB	687	31001	1.0X
5.789GB	578	31001	1.0X
5.005GB	500	31001	1.0X
4.212GB	421	31001	1.0X
3.351GB	335	31001	1.0X
2.414GB	241	31001	1.0X
1.813GB	181	31001	1.0X
851.5MB	85	31001	1.0X

```
 *Estimates: The In-Memory Advisor's estimates are useful for making
  In-Memory decisions.  But they are not precise.  Due to performance
  variations caused by workload diversity, the Advisor's performance
  estimates are conservatively limited to no more than 10.0X
  faster.
```

```
Choose the In-Memory size you wish for optimization (default= 19.11GB):
Enter value for inmemory_size: <ENTER>

The In-Memory Advisor is optimizing for an In-Memory size of 19.11GB...
(You can re-run this task with this script and specify a different an In-
Memory size.  Re-running a task to optimize for a different
In-Memory size is faster than creating and running a new task from scratch.)
```

```
Fetching recommendation files for task: LIVE_WORKLOAD

Placing recommendation files in: the current working directory

Fetched file: imadvisor_LIVE_WORKLOAD.html
Purpose:        recommendation report primary html page

Fetched file: imadvisor_LIVE_WORKLOAD.sql
Purpose:        recommendation DDL sqlplus script
```

This example has created the HTML file imadvisor_LIVE_WORKLOAD
.html and the DDL file LIVE_WORKLOAD.sql. The HTML file contains detailed
recommendations, similar to those shown in Figure 5-1, and the DDL file
contains SQL script similar to Figure 5-2.

Implementing Advisor Recommendations and Comparing Results

When the In-Memory Advisor was run using AWR snapshots and against a
live database, the Advisor provided information about how much benefit we
would get by putting certain objects in the IMCS. The next step is to validate
the Advisor's recommendations by taking the following steps.

We start by taking three preliminary steps before implementing In-Memory:

1. Take an AWR snapshot before running any workload and make a note
   of the snap ID.

2. Run a workload in the system that simulates our workload. We can
   use tools such as Real Application Testing to capture and replay our
   production workload. Ideally we would try to capture the workload
   during the peak time. The goal is to run the workload as close to
   the production environment as possible. The more accurate the
   workload, the better will be the recommendations.

3. Take an AWR snapshot after running the workload. Make a note of
   the snap ID. Now we have two snapshots—one before and another
   after running the benchmark.

Now let's implement the In-Memory option:

1. Put all the tables in the memory according to the recommendation of the In-Memory Advisor. The DDLs generated in the SQL file can be run directly in the database to put the tables in memory with compression, if any.

2. Take an AWR snapshot and make a note of the snap ID.

3. Run the workload exactly like it was done in the previous step 2.

4. Take an AWR snapshot after running the workload and make a note of the snap ID.

5. You will four different snap IDs: two obtained after the preliminary three steps and two obtained in step 4.

6. Log in as sysdba to the database. Run the script awrddrpt.sql, located at $ORACLE_HOME/rdbms/admin directory:

```
$ sqlplus '/ as sysdba'

SQL*Plus: Release 12.1.0.2.0 Production on Wed Aug 10 23:37:46 2016

Copyright (c) 1982, 2014, Oracle.  All rights reserved.


Connected to:
Oracle Database 12c Enterprise Edition Release 12.1.0.2.0 - 64bit Production
With the Partitioning, OLAP, Advanced Analytics and Real Application Testing options

SQL> @awrddrpt.sql

Current Instance
~~~~~~~~~~~~~~~~

   DB Id       DB Id     DB Name      Inst Num Inst Num Instance
----------- ----------- ------------ -------- -------- ------------
 1382119978  1382119978 ORCL                1        1 orcl


Specify the Report Type
~~~~~~~~~~~~~~~~~~~~~~~~~
Would you like an HTML report, or a plain text report?
Enter 'html' for an HTML report, or 'text' for plain text
Defaults to 'html'
Enter value for report_type: html
```

```
Type Specified:  html


Instances in this Workload Repository schema
~~~~~~~~~~~~~~~~~~~~~~~~~~~~~~~~~~~~~~~~~~~~~~~

   DB Id      Inst Num DB Name      Instance     Host
------------ -------- ------------ ------------ ------------
* 1382119978        1 ORCL         orcl         em12c.locald
                                                omain

Database Id and Instance Number for the First Pair of Snapshots
~~~~~~~~~~~~~~~~~~~~~~~~~~~~~~~~~~~~~~~~~~~~~~~~~~~~~~~~~~~~~~~~~~
Using 1382119978 for Database Id for the first pair of snapshots
Using           1 for Instance Number for the first pair of snapshots


Specify the number of days of snapshots to choose from
~~~~~~~~~~~~~~~~~~~~~~~~~~~~~~~~~~~~~~~~~~~~~~~~~~~~~~~~
Entering the number of days (n) will result in the most recent
(n) days of snapshots being listed.  Pressing <return> without
specifying a number lists all completed snapshots.


Enter value for num_days: 2

Listing the last 2 days of Completed Snapshots

                                                   Snap
Instance     DB Name       Snap Id  Snap Started   Level
------------ ------------ --------- ------------------ -----
orcl         ORCL             323 09 Aug 2016 00:00     2
                             324 09 Aug 2016 01:02     2
                             326 10 Aug 2016 22:56     2
                             327 10 Aug 2016 23:47     2


Specify the First Pair of Begin and End Snapshot Ids
~~~~~~~~~~~~~~~~~~~~~~~~~~~~~~~~~~~~~~~~~~~~~~~~~~~~~~~
Enter value for begin_snap: 323
First Begin Snapshot Id specified: 323

Enter value for end_snap: 324
First End   Snapshot Id specified: 324
```

Here we have given the snap IDs before implementing the In-Memory
option. The snap ID before running the workload is 323, and the snap ID
after running the workload is 324.

The snap IDs after implementing the In-Memory option are 326 and 327. The script is going to ask for these now:

```
Instances in this Workload Repository schema
~~~~~~~~~~~~~~~~~~~~~~~~~~~~~~~~~~~~~~~~~~~~~~

  DB Id     Inst Num DB Name      Instance     Host
----------- -------- ------------ ------------ ------------
* 1382119978       1 ORCL         orcl         em12c.locald
                                               omain



Database Id and Instance Number for the Second Pair of Snapshots
~~~~~~~~~~~~~~~~~~~~~~~~~~~~~~~~~~~~~~~~~~~~~~~~~~~~~~~~~~~~~~~~~~~~

Using 1382119978 for Database Id for the second pair of snapshots
Using          1 for Instance Number for the second pair of snapshots


Specify the number of days of snapshots to choose from
~~~~~~~~~~~~~~~~~~~~~~~~~~~~~~~~~~~~~~~~~~~~~~~~~~~~~~~~~
Entering the number of days (n) will result in the most recent
(n) days of snapshots being listed.  Pressing <return> without
specifying a number lists all completed snapshots.


Enter value for num_days2: 2

Listing the last 2 days of Completed Snapshots

                                                 Snap
Instance      DB Name       Snap Id  Snap Started  Level
------------ ------------- --------- ------------------- -----
orcl         ORCL              323 09 Aug 2016 00:00    2
                               324 09 Aug 2016 01:02    2
                               326 10 Aug 2016 22:56    2
                               327 10 Aug 2016 23:47    2



Specify the Second Pair of Begin and End Snapshot Ids
~~~~~~~~~~~~~~~~~~~~~~~~~~~~~~~~~~~~~~~~~~~~~~~~~~~~~~~~
Enter value for begin_snap2: 326
Second Begin Snapshot Id specified: 326

Enter value for end_snap2: 327
```

```
Specify the Report Name
~~~~~~~~~~~~~~~~~~~~~~~~~
The default report file name is awrdiff_1_323_1_326.html  To use this name,
press <return> to continue, otherwise enter an alternative.

Enter value for report_name: AWR_IN_MEMORY_BENCHMARK.html

Using the report name AWR_IN_MEMORY_BENCHMARK.html

Report written to AWR_IN_MEMORY_BENCHMARK.html
SQL>
```

The script shows a default HTML filename for writing the report. You can change it to any name you want. In this example, I have used AWR_IN_MEMORY_BENCHMARK.html. The HTML file will be saved in the $ORACLE_HOME/rdbms/admin directory.

Let's open the HTML file and look at some of the key metrics. Since it is a huge file, we are going to cover only the relevant section, as shown in Figures 5-3 and 5-4.

The first snapshot is the workload run before implementing In-Memory; the second snapshot is the workload run after implementing the In-Memory option. You can see that after implementing the In-Memory option, the same workload took less time and there was a savings of around 28.7 percent in total DB timings.

WORKLOAD REPOSITORY COMPARE PERIOD REPORT

Report Summary

Snapshot Set	DB Name	DB Id	Instance	Inst num	Release	Cluster	Host	Std Block Size
First (1st)	ORCL	1382119978	orcl	1	12.1.0.2.0	NO	em12c.localdomain	8192
Second (2nd)	ORCL	1382119978	orcl	1	12.1.0.2.0	NO	em12c.localdomain	8192

Snapshot Set	Begin Snap Id	Begin Snap Time	End Snap Id	End Snap Time	Avg Active Users	Elapsed Time (min)	DB time (min)
1st	323	09-Aug-16 00:00:24 (Tue)	324	09-Aug-16 01:02:25 (Tue)	5.0	60.4	302
2nd	326	10-Aug-16 22:56:15 (Wed)	327	10-Aug-16 23:47:23 (Wed)	5.6	51.1	286.16
%Diff					0	-4.5	-28.712

FIGURE 5-3. *Workload repository compare period report*

Load Profile

	1st per sec	2nd per sec	%Diff	1st per txn	2nd per txn	%Diff
CPU time:	8.1	5.3	-13.1	360.14	290.7	20.14
Background CPU time:	0.0	0.0	100.0	.4	.3	-11.5
Redo size (bytes):	5,039.43	9,396.86	95.15	89,360.15	103,397.4	17.27
Logical read (blocks):	3,868.04	45,911.69	1,195.7	68,588.3	505,185.01	700.15
Block changes:	41.03	65.78	66.66	726.55	724.13	-.34
Physical read (blocks):	2,701.27	37.51	-97.21	44,219.0	351.8	-98.87
Physical write (blocks):	18.2	12.3	-24.3	321.9	148.3	51.8
Read IO requests:	70.2	12.9	-81.8	1,301.2	128.0	-88.3
Write IO requests:	1.2	1.5	15.2	30.4	150.3	-31.3
Read IO (MB):	20.1	.4	-98.1	350.1	3.1	-99.3
Write IO (MB):	0.2	0.2	-51.0	3.4	1.1	-61.9
IM scan rows:	0.0	0.0	0.0	0.0	455,212,010.5	100.0
Session Logical Read IM:						
User calls:	1.3	1.6	23.0	21.4	18.0	-22.9
Parses (SQL):	4.1	17.4	315..7	95.8	189.6	98.1
Hard parses (SQL):	0.0	0.7	6,700.0	11.6	2.7	-76.7
SQL Work Area (MB):	0.0	0.4	100.0	2.0	1.6	100.0
Logons:	0.1	0.1	100.0	2.4	0.3	-87.2
Executes (SQL):	4.3	23.5	418.7	76.3	253.7	221.7
Transactions:	0.0	0.3	100.0			

	1st	2nd	Diff
% Blocks changed per Read:	1.4	.3	-1.1
Recursive Call %:	98.3	99.3	1.3
Rollback per transaction %:	0.0	0.4	0.4
Rows per Sort:	1,238.4	2,108.8	1,000.5
Avg DB time per Call (sec):	4.1	2.8	-1.7

FIGURE 5-4. *Workload repository compare period report: key metrics*

In Figure 5-4, you can see a lot of interesting statistics. Following are the major stats to notice:

■ The CPU time has gone down, which means the overall CPU needed for processing the data is less; therefore, overall throughput increases.

■ The DB time is reduced, which means the same jobs run faster and more data processing can be done.

■ More executes per transactions were performed in the second run, which shows the direct impact of implementing the In-Memory option.

- The logical reads have gone up and physical reads have gone down, which shows the impact of implementing the In-Memory option. Now more data is being read from the IMCS rather than from the hard drive.

Since AWR reports have more than 25 sections, and each section has various subsections, it is not possible to cover each section in detail here. Following are the key benefits you will notice by browsing each section. (Again, these observations apply in the context of the In-Memory option only and may not necessarily be applicable to the database as a whole.)

- When the data is stored in memory, the instance is CPU-bound only.

- In the wait events section, if there is any I/O wait, it is substantially reduced. The In-Memory option gets rid of the unwanted I/O by fetching the data directly from the IMCS.

- The overall wait events are down.

- The I/O response time is drastically faster.

To summarize, your database can do more work at same time with much faster performance and fewer CPU cycles. This results in manifold benefits.

Summary

In this chapter, you learned how to use In-Memory Advisor to determine what to keep in memory. This tool evaluates your workload and the job patterns over a period of time and recommends how much benefit you will gain by storing certain objects in the memory. This tool looks at the various metrics obtained from AWR reports, SQL plan cardinalities, and ASH. It lists the objects and the benefits you will gain by keeping them in the IMCS. In addition to showing the benefits, the script creates an SQL script that can be used to place the recommended objects into memory.

The In-Memory Advisor can be installed by running the script instimadv .sql as the system or sys database user. This script can be downloaded from the Oracle Support web site. If you want to uninstall the In-Memory Advisor, you can run the script catnoimadv.sql.

The In-Memory Advisor can be run in various ways, against the AWR snapshots, against SQL Performance Analyzer, or running the recommendation script directly against a running database.

When you run the In-Memory Advisor against AWR snapshots or against a live database, it provides recommendations in an HTML file that shows the benefit that will be obtained by implementing the In-Memory option. Along with the recommendations, the tool creates an SQL file with the DDL of all the objects that can be stored in memory.

After implementing the In-Memory option, you can validate the In-Memory Advisor recommendation by running the script awrddrpt.sql and comparing the workload before and after implementing the In-Memory option.

CHAPTER
6

Optimizing Database
In-Memory Queries

Y ou can optimize Database In-Memory queries to gain maximum performance benefits in several ways: by using join groups, In-Memory expressions, and In-Memory aggregations. This chapter shows you how to get the most from these operations.

Using Join Groups

A *join group* is a dictionary object created by a user that lists or provides details about two columns that can be joined. Join groups are conceptually similar to the materialized views used by the optimizer for query rewrite. A join group is created by a user, which implies that it is not a system object, but something you are going to create to optimize your queries. When you run a query that involves joining two tables, using join groups provides tremendous performance benefits, because join groups bypass the overhead of decompressing and hashing column values.

In any data-warehouse environment, a join is an integral part of day-to-day queries. Almost all queries use some kind of join to create meaningful reports; for example, if you want to find the total sales per product, you make a join between sales and product tables. If the sales and product tables are stored in memory, the performance of the joins will be much faster.

The following example scenarios are greatly benefited by running a join in memory:

- A query that involves a simple join or complex multiple table joins

- Any query that takes advantage of Bloom filters

- A join of a fact table with multiple small dimension tables

- A join of two tables with a primary key and foreign key relationship

NOTE
A Bloom filter is a data structure designed to tell you, rapidly and memory efficiently, whether an element is present in a set.

You can create a join group by specifying a set of columns of the tables you frequently join. The columns in a join group can be in the same table or in different tables.

Consider our sales table and product table example. When you run the following query to determine the average amount sold per product, a join occurs between the two tables at two columns:

```
SQL> SELECT prod_category, AVG(amount_sold)
FROM sales s, products p
WHERE p.prod_id = s.prod_id
GROUP BY prod_category;
```

If you frequently join these two columns, you can create a join group for **(sales(prod_id),products(prod_id)**, which will provide a huge performance boost. When you create a join group, if the tables referenced by the join group already exist in memory, the database invalidates the current In-Memory contents. When the repopulation happens after creation of the join groups, the database re-encodes the join group objects in memory. So if you are planning to create a join group, it is recommended that you create the join group first before populating the data of the tables.

NOTE
If a column is a part of a join group, it cannot be a part of other join groups. A column can be part of only one join group at a time.

Let's look at how a query works with and without a join group using the sales and product tables. Assume that both tables are part of the data warehouse in star schema format, sales being a fact table and product being a dimension table.

When the query is executed without the join group, the execution plan will use a hash join, as follows (see Figure 6-1):

1. The database scans the product table and decompresses the rows as per the predicate and sends the rows to the hash join.

2. The hash table is built in the Program Global Area (PGA) according to the rows decompressed.

3. The sales table is scanned according to the predicate.

4. The matching rows are decompressed; hash them and then send them to the hash join.

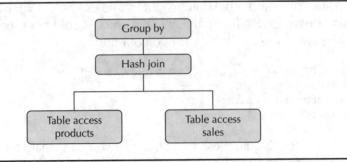

FIGURE 6-1. *Execution plan without a join group*

5. The hash table is probed using the join column, in this case prod_id, to find matching rows.

6. The final rows are filtered using the group by function.

From the execution plan, we can see that the database spends a major chunk of time in two steps:

- Decompression
- Filtering

Supposing we can eliminate both steps while executing this query, how fast will the query run? No doubt when major steps are eliminated, the query will be executed much faster, and this is exactly what a join group does.

Suppose a join group exists on **(sales(prod_id),products(prod_id)**, and the database eliminates the decompression and filtering overhead. The database would work with the compressed data set itself. When the database operates on the compressed data set, the amount of data that needs to be scanned is reduced, and as a result, scans are much faster, resulting in faster performance of the query.

In addition, when a join group is used in a hash join, the database uses an array instead of building a hash table.

Tip & Technique
In some cases, when it is not possible to use a Bloom filter, a query can be optimized using a join group.

Every join column value for a join group has a unique code that is stored in a common dictionary. A *common dictionary* is a segment-level, instance-specific set of master dictionary codes created from local dictionaries. A *local dictionary* is a sorted list of dictionary codes specific to a column compression unit (CU). These dictionary codes have a fixed length and are dense, which makes them space efficient. The advantage of storing code is that when the join happens, the database joins on the codes and not the actual column value. As a result, the overhead of copying row sources is totally eliminated, saving a lot of time and thereby improving query performance.

The common dictionary performs the following functions:

- It helps the optimizer choose all the statistics such as cost, cardinality, distribution of column values, and so on.

- Internally, it encodes the values in the local dictionary with codes from the common dictionary. It provides mapping between the local and common dictionary, and, as a result, the cache efficiency and compression benefits are obtained in an In-Memory Compression Unit (IMCU).

- It helps the joins use the dictionary code to construct and probe the data structures used during hash joins. The real optimization comes when the join happens on common dictionary code instead of column values. By doing this, the dictionary eliminates the use of a hash table for the join.

When the query is executed with the join group, the execution of the query will be different. Here's the execution path with join groups:

1. The product table is scanned, and the dictionary code (not the original column values) is sent to a hash join. When the scan happens, the product table is scanned in compressed format.

2. An array of common distinct dictionary code is built in the Program Global Area (PGA) for a unique product.

3. The sales table is scanned and filters are applied.

4. The matching rows are sent to the join in compressed format.

5. The corresponding values are looked up in the array rather than probing a hash table, thus avoiding the need to compute a hash function on the join key columns.

6. The final rows are filtered using the group by function.

Tip & Technique
The common dictionary is automatically created in the IM Column Store (IMCS) when a join group is defined on the underlying columns. You don't have to create the common dictionary manually.

Creating a Join Group

A join group can be created using the **CREATE INMEMORY JOIN GROUP** statement:

```
CREATE INMEMORY JOIN GROUP join_group_name ( table1(col1), (table2(col2) );
```

For our example, we can create the join group by running the following command:

```
SQL> CREATE INMEMORY JOIN GROUP
example_joingrp (sales(prod_id), products(prod_id));
```

Now let's put the underlying tables in memory:

```
SQL> ALTER TABLE SALES INMEMORY;

SQL> ALTER TABLE PRODUCTS INMEMORY;
```

Let's run a query to populate the data into the memory:

```
SQL> SELECT  COUNT(*) FROM SALES;

SQL> SELECT  COUNT(*) FROM PRODUCTS;
```

After the data has been populated, to view the definition of the join group, query DBA_JOINGROUPS:

```
SQL> SELECT JOINGROUP_NAME, TABLE_NAME, COLUMN_NAME, GD_ADDRESS
FROM DBA_JOINGROUPS;

JOINGROUP_NAME     TABLE_NA     COLUMN_    GD_ADDRESS
----------------   --------     -------    --------------
example_joingrp    SALES        PROD_ID    00B123A14005N
example_joingrp    PRODUCTS     PROD_ID    00B123A14005N
```

If you observe carefully, you will notice that for the example_joingrp join group, the column GD_ADDRESS has the same value, which shows that the join group joins on the same common dictionary address.

When you run the command to create a join group, the metadata for the join group is immediately visible in the data dictionary. The construct for the common dictionary is not created immediately. It is created when the table referenced in the join group is populated or repopulated in the IMCS.

As discussed previously, when you create a join group that references a table, and if the table already exists in the memory, the database invalidates the table. Similarly, modifying or dropping also invalidates the tables referenced within the join group.

Using IM Expressions

As discussed in Chapter 2, an expression is a combination of one or more values, operators, and SQL functions that evaluates to a value. When In-Memory expressions optimization is enabled, the database automatically calculates and caches results of frequently evaluated expressions.

The procedure **DBMS_INMEMORY_ADMIN.IME_CAPTURE_ EXPRESSIONS** not only identifies but also populates the hot expressions. This populated hot expression is called an *In-Memory expression*. The DBMS_INMEMORY_ADMIN package is the central point for managing all the IM expressions. In addition to DBMS_INMEMORY_ADMIN, the DBMS_ INMEMORY package can be used to drop IM expressions. Table 6-1 provides the package names and the related PLSQL procedures and their main tasks.

Using the DBMS_INMEMORY_ADMIN package, you can capture, drop, or repopulate; whereas by using DBMS_INMEMORY, you can only drop SYS_IME columns. As discussed in Chapter 2, the IM expression is materialized as a hidden virtual column but is accessed in the same way as a nonvirtual column.

Package	Procedure	Procedure Description
DBMS_INMEMORY_ ADMIN	**IME_CAPTURE_ EXPRESSIONS**	Captures and populates the 20 most frequently accessed (hottest) expressions in the database in the specified time range
DBMS_INMEMORY_ ADMIN	**IME_DROP_ALL_ EXPRESSIONS**	Drops all SYS_IME virtual columns in the database
DBMS_INMEMORY_ ADMIN	**IME_POPULATE_ EXPRESSIONS**	Forces the population of IM expressions captured in the latest invocation of the **IME_CAPTURE_EXPRESSIONS** procedure
DBMS_INMEMORY	**IME_DROP_ EXPRESSIONS**	Drops a specified set of SYS_IME virtual columns from a table

TABLE 6-1. *Packages and Procedures Related to IM Expressions*

For example, if you want to populate IM expressions (forcefully) immediately, you would use

```
DBMS_INMEMORY_ADMIN.IME_POPULATE_EXPRESSIONS
```

The populating and computation of the results of the IM expression are done using the IM expression infrastructure. This infrastructure is also responsible for populating into IM virtual columns and any other computations that happen in the IMCS. The IM infrastructure supports both static (binary JSON columns) and dynamic (virtual columns and IM expressions) expressions. With the release of Oracle Database 12.2, the IMCS also supports the binary JSON format. The IM expression infrastructure is used to load a binary representation of JSON text columns as virtual columns.

When you don't invoke **DBMS_INMEMORY_ADMIN.IME_POPULATE_ EXPRESSIONS** to populate the database, it populates SYS_IME columns when their corresponding parent IMCUs are repopulated. And if the parent IMCUs are not populated (when the table is not populated), the SYS_IME columns are not at all populated and are captured by **IME_CAPTURE_EXPRESSIONS**. Of course, you can solve this problem by forcefully populating using **POPULATE_ EXPRESSIONS**. When you run the **IME_POPULATE_EXPRESSIONS**, it calls **DBMS_INMEMORY.REPOPULATE** for all tables that have SYS_IME columns with the **INMEMORY** attribute. If you want to populate the SYS_IME columns in a specified subset of tables, use **DBMS_INMEMORY.REPOPULATE** rather than **DBMS_INMEMORY_ADMIN.IME_POPULATE_EXPRESSIONS**.

Whenever you run **DBMS_INMEMORY_ADMIN.IME_CAPTURE_ EXPRESSIONS**, the database accesses the Expression Statistics Store (ESS) and identifies the top 20 most recently used expressions during the specified time range. The database considers expressions only for those tables that are fully or partially populated in either the past 24 hours or since the database creation. The nonpopulated tables are not taken into consideration. Once it identifies the 20 hottest expressions, the database adds these expressions to their respective tables as hidden SYS_IME virtual columns. While adding these expressions, it also applies the default In-Memory compression clause. For a table, the maximum number of SYS_IME columns is 50. If you reach this limit and want to add more, you can do that only by deleting SYS_IME columns using either **DBMS_INMEMORY_ADMIN.IME_DROP_ALL_EXPRESSIONS** or **DBMS_INMEMORY.IME_DROP_EXPRESSIONS**.

Tip & Technique

As you are probably aware, there is a 1000-column limit on a table. Both SYS_IME virtual columns and user-defined virtual columns count toward this limit.

As you learned in Chapter 2, the In-Memory Coordinator (IMCO) process and Space Management Slave (W*nnn*) background process load the IM expressions into the In-Memory Expression Units (IMEUs) automatically. The following steps run in the background to achieve this:

1. The expression values are created.

2. The newly created values are converted into columnar format and compressed to IMEUs.

3. Each IMEU is linked to the IMCU associated with it. (Just to recap, the physical columns reside in the IMCU and the associated virtual columns reside in the IMEU.)

The type of IM expression is controlled by the initialization parameter **INMEMORY_EXPRESSIONS_USAGE**. This parameter has the following values:

- **ENABLE**   When the parameter is set to **ENABLE**, the database populates both static and dynamic IM expressions. This is the default value for the parameter **INMEMORY_EXPRESSIONS_USAGE**. For some tables, setting this value increases the In-Memory footprint.

- **STATIC_ONLY**   This enables the IMCS to cache OSON (binary JSON) columns, which are marked with an **IS_JSON** check constraint. The OSON is actually a hidden virtual column internally marked as **SYS_IME_OSON**.

- **DYNAMIC_ONLY**   Setting this parameter enables the IMCS to populate only the hot, or frequently used, expressions that have been added to the table as **SYS_IME** hidden virtual columns. For some tables, setting this value increases the In-Memory footprint.

- **DISABLE**   Specifies setting **INMEMORY_EXPRESSIONS_USAGE** to **DISABLE** to stop populating any IM expression. No matter which type of IM expression it is—simple or dynamic—it is not populated.

Tip & Technique

Note that changing the initialization parameter *INMEMORY_EXPRESSIONS_USAGE* to a different setting does not immediately impact the IM expressions currently populated. Suppose, for example, that the current setting is *STATIC_ONLY* and you have changed the initialization parameter to *DISABLE*. The changes will be reflected only the next time repopulation occurs, and at that time the IM expressions will be removed.

You can run an **ALTER SYSTEM** command to configure the IM expression usage, as shown next. You must have the appropriate privileges to run this command.

```
SQL> ALTER SYSTEM SET INMEMORY_EXPRESSIONS_USAGE='ENABLE';

SYSTEM ALTERED
```

```
SQL> ALTER SYSTEM SET INMEMORY_EXPRESSIONS_USAGE='STATIC_ONLY';

SYSTEM ALTERED

SQL> ALTER SYSTEM SET INMEMORY_EXPRESSIONS_USAGE='DYNAMIC_ONLY';

SYSTEM ALTERED

SQL> ALTER SYSTEM SET INMEMORY_EXPRESSIONS_USAGE='DISABLE';

SYSTEM ALTERED
```

Use the following steps to enable the database to capture IM expressions:

1. Set the value of the initialization parameter **INMEMORY_EXPRESSIONS_USAGE** to a value other than **DISABLE** (use **ENABLE**, **STATIC_ONLY**, or **DYNAMIC_ONLY**).

2. Set the initialization parameter **INMEMORY_SIZE** to a value greater than zero.

3. Set the compatibility of the database to 12.2.0 or higher.

4. Execute the **DBMS_INMEMORY_ADMIN.IME_CAPTURE_EXPRESSIONS** with either of the following parameters:

   - **CUMULATIVE**   The database considers all expression statistics since the creation of the database.

   - **CURRENT**   The database considers only expression statistics from the past 24 hours (for example, **EXEC DBMS_INMEMORY_ADMIN.IME_CAPTURE_EXPRESSIONS('CURRENT');**).

5. If you want the population to start immediately, run **DBMS_INMEMORY_ADMIN.IME_POPULATE_EXPRESSIONS**.

If you want to query the IM expressions, run the following query against the view **DBA_IM_EXPRESSIONS**:

```
SQL> select table_name , column_name , sql_expression from dba_im_expressions;
```

If you want to drop the IM expressions, it's pretty simple: Execute the **DBMS_INMEMORY_ADMIN.IME_DROP_ALL_EXPRESSIONS**. It drops all the SYS_IME virtual columns from the database. To drop only a few columns, use **DBMS_INMEMORY.IME_DROP_EXPRESSIONS** to drop a specified set of columns from SYS_IME virtual columns.

Use the following steps to drop the database and capture the IM expressions:

1. Set the value of the initialization parameter **INMEMORY_EXPRESSIONS_USAGE** to a value other than **DISABLE** (use **ENABLE**, **STATIC_ONLY**, or **DYNAMIC_ONLY**).

2. Set the initialization parameter **INMEMORY_SIZE** to a value greater than zero.

3. Set the compatibility of the database to 12.2.0 or higher.

4. Execute **DBMS_INMEMORY_ADMIN.IME_DROP_ALL_EXPRESSIONS** to drop everything.

If you don't want to drop everything and want to drop in a selective manner, execute **DBMS_INMEMORY_ADMIN.IME_DROP_EXPRESSIONS**. In this case, you need to provide additional parameters to specify which schema, table, and column name you want to drop:

- **SCHEMA_NAME**   The database schema containing the In-Memory table.

- **TABLE_NAME**   The actual table name.

- **COLUMN_NAME**   The name of the SYS_IME column. By default, this value is null, which specifies all SYS_IME columns in this table.

```
SQL> EXEC DBMS_INMEMORY.IME_DROP_EXPRESSIONS('SH', 'SALES');
```

Using In-Memory Aggregations

An In-Memory aggregation (IMA) optimizes certain types of joins and aggregations. IMA is designed to optimize queries that join relatively small tables or dimension tables to relatively large fact tables and aggregate data.

IMA introduces three new SQL operations:

- **KEY VECTOR CREATE**
- **KEY VECTOR USE**
- **VECTOR GROUP BY**

These SQL operations enable operations to occur simultaneously. For example, the **VECTOR JOIN** and **GROUP BY** operations occur in parallel with the scan of a large table. As a result, these operations aggregate as they scan, so they don't have to wait for table scans and join operations to complete. So, for example, a database could create a report outline dynamically and gradually fill in the report details when scanning the fact table.

IMA is most effective with difficult queries—those that aggregate more fact rows, join more dimensions, select more attribute columns, and involve more concurrent users. It provides the biggest benefit when a query joins relatively small tables to a relatively large fact table and aggregates data in the fact table. It usually happens in a data warehouse star schema or snowflake query.

NOTE
The only criterion for using IMA is that the size of the In-Memory Area should be greater than zero.

For executing the new three SQL operations, no application change is needed. The optimizer will choose IMA based on the cost of the plan. When the optimizer chooses IMA, the operations process queries faster and uses less CPU and memory. IMA also provides the following advantages:

- Leverages the fast scan speeds of in-memory tables
- Uses efficient array-based in-memory data structures
- Minimizes the amount of data that needs to be carried from one SQL operation to the next

IMA may not be beneficial in the following use cases:

- If you try to join two large tables, this defeats the purpose of IMA. The optimizer won't choose the **VECTOR GROUP BY** transformation clause. IMA is most beneficial when you want to join a small table with a large fact table.

- When the dimension table contains more than 2 billion rows.

- If you don't have enough resources in the system. IMA is a memory-intensive feature, and if you don't have enough memory, this feature won't kick in.

NOTE
The tables do not need to be populated to use IMA.

IMA works in a three-step process:

1. Joins between dimension tables and fast tables are transformed into fast in-memory scans of the fact table.

2. Aggregated fact (measure) data is accumulated into new in-memory array structures.

3. Aggregated fact data is joined to attribute data from the dimension tables.

Take a look at an SQL query of a data-warehouse environment:

```
SELECT /*+ no_parallel */
    a1.calendar_year_name,
    a1.calendar_quarter_name,
    a3.region_name,
    SUM(f.sales),
    SUM(f.units)
FROM time_dim a1,
    customer_dim a3,
    units_fact f
WHERE a1.day_id = f.day_id
AND a3.customer_id = f.customer_id
AND a1.calendar_year_name ='2015'
```

```
GROUP BY a1.calendar_year_name,
  a1.calendar_quarter_name,
  a3.region_name;
```

This is a classic star schema query in which the time and customer dimension tables are joined with the units fact table and the sales and units measures are aggregated in the fact table.

Now let's look at the execution plan:

```
-----------------------------------------------------------------------
| Id  | Operation                      | Name                          |
-----------------------------------------------------------------------
|   0 | SELECT STATEMENT               |                               |
|   1 |  TEMP TABLE TRANSFORMATION     |                               |
|   2 |   LOAD AS SELECT               | SYS_TEMP_A233KMN_DD231A       |
|   3 |    VECTOR GROUP BY             |                               |
|   4 |     KEY VECTOR CREATE BUFFERED | :KV0000                       |
|   5 |      PARTITION RANGE ALL       |                               |
|   6 |       TABLE ACCESS INMEMORY FULL | TIME_DIM                    |
|   7 |   LOAD AS SELECT               | SYS_TEMP_A233KMN_DD231A       |
|   8 |    VECTOR GROUP BY             |                               |
|   9 |     KEY VECTOR CREATE BUFFERED | :KV0001                       |
|  10 |      TABLE ACCESS INMEMORY FULL | CUSTOMER_DIM_500M_10        |
|  11 |   HASH GROUP BY                |                               |
|  12 |    HASH JOIN                   |                               |
|  13 |     HASH JOIN                  |                               |
|  14 |      TABLE ACCESS FULL         | SYS_TEMP_A233KMN_DD231A       |
|  15 |      VIEW                      | VW_VT_AF278325                |
|  16 |       VECTOR GROUP BY          |                               |
|  17 |        HASH GROUP BY           |                               |
|  18 |         KEY VECTOR USE         | :KV0001                       |
|  19 |          KEY VECTOR USE        | :KV0000                       |
|  20 |           PARTITION RANGE SUBQUERY |                           |
|  21 |            TABLE ACCESS INMEMORY FULL| UNITS_FACT_500M_10      |
|  22 |     TABLE ACCESS FULL          | SYS_TEMP_A233KMN_DD231A       |
-----------------------------------------------------------------------
```

The execution plan uses the *vector transformation plan,* which is another name for IMA. A query is eligible for a vector transformation plan when

■ One or more relatively small tables are joined to a large table using equijoins

■ One or more measures are aggregated from the large table using an aggregation operator such as SUM, MIN, MAX, or AVERAGE

■ GROUP BY grouping syntax is used (group by cube, rollup, and grouping sets are not yet supported)

From the SQL execution plan, notice that the following vector transformation operations take place (and are highlighted in boldface):

- **TEMP TABLE TRANSFORMATION**
- **VECTOR GROUP BY**
- **KEY VECTOR CREATE**
- **KEY VECTOR USE**

The **VECTOR GROUP BY** operates by combining the work of various phases, converting joins to filters, and aggregating while scanning the fact table. The work is divided into multiple stages known as data flow operators (DFAs).

The vector transformation plan (IMA) starts with the creation of some in-memory objects known as *key vectors*. A key vector enables fast lookups. There will be one **KEY VECTOR CREATE** for each dimension or attribute table.

KEY VECTOR CREATE creates a memory data structure that contains a mapping between the join keys and a surrogate key known as the *dense grouping key*. A dense key is a numeric key that is stored as a native integer and has a range of values. A *dense join key* represents all join keys whose join columns come from a fact table or dimension. A dense grouping key represents all grouping keys whose grouping columns come from a particular fact table or dimension.

The structure of the key vector varies depending on the joins and the data types. The key vector object mapping serves two purposes:

- The fact table is scanned using the join keys.
- The dense grouping key is used to index the aggregate accumulating.

Once the key vector is created, temporary tables are created to store the filtered values from the dimension or attribute tables. The temporary tables will contain only the selected columns, plus the dense grouping key and the rows after applying the filter.

Saving this data to the side allows the intermediate operations to use only the dense grouping keys, minimizing the amount of data that needs to be carried through the SQL execution plan. Aggregate data from the fact table will be joined back to attribute data using the dense grouping keys very late in the execution plan. The actual definition of the temporary table will vary depending on the query.

Next, the fact table is processed using the **KEY VECTOR USE** and **VECTOR GROUP BY** operations. In this step, the fact table is scanned (that is, filtered) and data is aggregated in a single pass of the fact table. The table is scanned using the **KEY VECTOR USE** operation, comparing the join key values in the key vector object with the values in the fact table using the fast scanning capabilities of the In-Memory table. The database uses very fast array lookups into the key vector, avoiding the relativity high costs of computing hash values that would occur with a hash join.

As the fact table is scanned, aggregated measures are accumulated into an array-based aggregate accumulator. At first, aggregated data is stored into empty cells of the accumulator. As new fact rows are found during the scan of the fact table, existing aggregated values are replaced with new aggregate values. This strategy eliminates the need to gather all the rows in the fact table that meet the filter conditions and then aggregate those values in a separate step. This is a good example of how the vector transformation plan minimizes the amount of data that needs to be carried throughout the SQL execution plan.

Depending on the data returned by the query, it is possible that the array-based aggregate accumulator might grow too large, because the size of that array is the Cartesian product of the dense grouping keys. When the database detects this condition, it switches over to **HASH GROUP BY**. This use of **HASH GROUP BY** is still more efficient in most cases because it uses the dense grouping keys.

Now that we have the filtered dimension data and the aggregated fact data, it's time to put the final result set together. This is done by joining the array-based aggregate accumulator with the **HASH GROUP BY** accumulator (if it exists) and then joining that result back to the temporary tables with filtered attribute data.

The use of the array-based accumulator and late materialization minimizes the amount of data that needs to be carried through the intermediate operations of this plan. The fast array-based lookups into the key vector object and fast scan speeds of In-Memory optimize the joins.

This is how the optimizer handles the vector transformation. It compares the vector transformation to alternative plans for each hash join, Bloom filter, and **HASH GROUP BY**.

Typically, the **KEY VECTOR CREATE** operation and creation of the temporary tables add some up-front costs to the query, with the expectation that **KEY VECTOR USE** and **VECTOR GROUP BY** will be more efficient than alternative operations. The expense of **KEY VECTOR CREATE** is proportional to the size of the dimension/attribute tables, with larger tables having a higher cost. The benefits of **KEY VECTOR USE** and **VECTOR GROUP BY** are proportional to the number of joins (more joins, more benefit) and the number of rows aggregated.

In practice, the optimizer costs of the vector transformation plan and alternative plans—typically those using Bloom filters—are close enough that the vector transformation plan is not chosen as often as it should be.

If you don't get the vector transformation plan, it's easy to force it using the **VECTOR_TRANSFORM** hint. With this hint, the database will use the vector transformation plan if the query is eligible for it, regardless of costing. You can compare plans using **VECTOR_TRANSFORM** and **NO_VECTOR_TRANFORM** hints.

Summary

In this chapter, you have learned different ways to optimize In-Memory queries: using join groups, using In-Memory expressions, and using In-Memory aggregations.

A join group is a dictionary object, created by a user, which lists or has details of the two columns that can be joined. When you run a query that involves joining two tables, using join groups provides tremendous performance benefits, since it bypasses the overhead of decompressing and hashing column values. You can create a join group by specifying a set of columns of the tables you join frequently. The columns in a join group can be in the same table or different tables.

A join group can be created using the **CREATE INMEMORY JOIN GROUP** statement.

The procedure **DBMS_INMEMORY_ADMIN.IME_CAPTURE_EXPRESSIONS** not only identifies but also populates the hot expressions. This populated hot expression is called an In-Memory expression. The **DBMS_INMEMORY_ADMIN** package is the central point for managing all the IM expressions. In addition to **DBMS_INMEMORY_ADMIN**, the **DBMS_INMEMORY** package can be used to drop IM expressions.

In-Memory aggregation optimizes certain types of joins and aggregations. In-Memory aggregation is designed to optimize queries that join relatively small table attributes or dimension tables to relatively large fact tables and aggregate data.

In-Memory aggregation introduces three new SQL operations:

- **KEY VECTOR CREATE**

- **KEY VECTOR USE**

- **VECTOR GROUP BY**

In-Memory aggregation provides the following advantages:

- Leverages the fast scan speeds of in-memory tables

- Uses efficient array-based in-memory data structures

- Minimizes the amount of data that needs to be carried from one SQL operation to the next

CHAPTER
7

In-Memory and
Engineering Systems

As the fastest growing product in Oracle's history, Oracle Exadata Database Machine provides extreme performance for both data warehousing and Online Transaction Processing (OLTP) applications, making it the ideal platform for consolidating onto grids or private clouds. It is a complete package of servers, storage, networking, and software that is massively scalable, secure, and redundant. With Exadata Database Machine, customers can reduce IT costs through consolidation, manage more data on multiple compression tiers, improve performance of all applications, and make better business decisions in real time. Today Exadata is being used everywhere for data warehousing, OLTP, database consolidation, RAC, and even enterprise resource planning (ERP) systems like Oracle E-Business Suite and Siebel.

Exadata is optimized to achieve enterprise performance levels that are unmatched in the industry. Faster time to production is achieved by implementing pre-engineered and preassembled hardware and software bundles. With an inclusive "cloud-in-a-box" strategy, Oracle's Exadata system combines best-of-breed hardware and software components with game-changing technical innovations. Designed, engineered, and tested to work best together, Exadata can power the cloud or streamline data center operations to make traditional deployments even more efficient.

Exadata is preassembled for targeted functionality and then—as a complete system—optimized for extreme performance. By taking the guesswork out of these high-availability, purpose-built solutions, Oracle delivers a sophisticated simplicity that's completely integrated throughout every layer of the technology stack—a simplicity that translates into less risk and lower costs for the business.

In this chapter, we'll study the advantages of Exadata, its unique architecture, the benefits it provides for running Database In-Memory, and how to get the most out of Exadata.

Advantages of Exadata

Let's look at some of the advantage that Exadata provides for running Oracle Database.

- **Time to market** Typically, an application implementation cycle takes from 6 months to a few years to complete. During the cycle, there is always a need to provision environments very quickly during the development, conference room pilot (CRP), user acceptance testing (UAT), and testing cycles. If an environment cannot be provided on time, it causes the project costs to go up, since all the developers and testers sit idle while waiting for the application. Even after go-live, new functionalities are often added to application, and thus the development cycle is always ongoing. Exadata is ready for use in any application implementation cycle beginning with day one because it comes with a preconfigured database, RAC, and storage.

- **RAC ready**   Application migration to a RAC environment is usually a two- or three-month project. For any new RAC implementation, all the components need to be assembled and configured, from storage and networking, to installing the operating system and clusterware. Exadata comes prebuilt with RAC databases, and applications can be migrated to Exadata the day it is installed. This easily saves two or three months and a lot of consulting money.

- **Proactive maintenance**   All customers running Exadata use the same configuration. All patches in Exadata are applied via Exadata bundle patches, which take care of patching the DB nodes, storage cells, and InfiniBand switches. The Exadata bundle patches are released periodically, and all customers' upgrades to the bundle are patched at around the same time. Oracle monitors customers' Exadata boxes, and if a customer faces any issue, Oracle immediately is alerted and provides a fix. Any other customer who is running a similar configuration is alerted immediately with the fix, even before they encounter the issue. Because all database machines are the same, each customer does not need to diagnose and resolve unique issues that occur only on their configuration. Performance tuning and stress testing performed at Oracle are done on the exact same configuration that the customer has, ensuring better performance and higher quality. In addition, service requests for Oracle Support are about half as much for Exadata compared to other legacy environments, and resolution time is 30 percent faster.

- **Redundant at all levels**   All components in Exadata are redundant. Each database server, storage server, and InfiniBand switch has redundant, hot-swappable power supplies. Disk drives and fans are also hot-swappable. Automatic Storage Management (ASM) provides protections against storage server failures, and RAC provides protection against database server failures. There are two or three InfiniBand switches in every Exadata machine, depending on the configuration, and this provides redundancy for the InfiniBand network and high resilience. The machine can tolerate loss of an entire switch or connections without affecting performance. There are two redundant power distribution units (PDUs) for rack-level power. Exadata uses up to six power cables, which are connected to redundant data center power sources to eliminate single points of failure.

- **Simpler administration** Exadata simplifies the administration of database, storage, networking, and disks. From a single console, all the Exadata components can be managed easily. More importantly, Exadata reduces the number of "working parts" and redundant administration. For example, storage is administered once by the DBA without having to involve a separate storage administrator.

- **Single vendor** All the layers, starting from disks to the database server, are provided by a single vendor, which makes support for Exadata very easy. Customers don't have to follow up with multiple vendors, avoiding vendor finger-pointing and conflicts.

- **Auto Service Request (ASR)** ASR is a secure, scalable, customer-installable software solution available as a feature with Exadata. The ASR software helps to resolve problems faster by using auto-case generation when specific hardware faults occur. ASR automatically opens service requests (SRs) with Oracle Support when specific hardware faults occur either in the Exadata storage servers or database servers. ASR is currently applicable only for hardware faults detected on the following server components: CPUs, disk controllers, disks, flash cards, flash modules, InfiniBand cards, memory modules, system boards, power supplied, and fans.

Exadata Architecture

Figure 7-1 shows the components of Exadata. As you can see in the figure, Exadata comprises the following building blocks:

- Database servers or compute nodes
- Exadata storage cells or Exadata storage servers
- InfiniBand

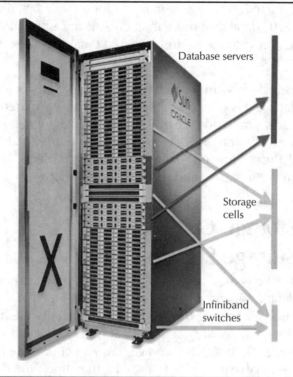

FIGURE 7-1.   *Exadata components*

Database Servers or Compute Nodes

An Exadata machine consists of from one to eight database servers, depending on the configuration. The database server runs the following components in addition to the Oracle Database:

- **Operating system**   Exadata comes installed with the Linux operating system. The current generation of Exadata X6 comes with Oracle Enterprise Linux 6.

- **Grid infrastructure**   The Oracle Grid Infrastructure is the software that runs Oracle Clusterware and ASM. Oracle Clusterware provides the foundation for running RAC, whereas ASM provides volume management capabilities.

- **RAC**   Oracle RAC is the foundation for the Exadata machines. In Oracle RAC database, more than one instance concurrently runs and executes transactions against a shared database. (RAC was discussed in Chapter 4.)

- **Database File System (optional)**   The Oracle DBFS is not a feature of Exadata, but is often installed in Exadata as a shared network file system. It is similar to NFS and is used for staging temporary files such as event trace log (ETL) files, temporary files, flat files, and so on. DBFS uses Oracle Database to store the objects. The DBFS is stored in the database and has its own instance.

Exadata Storage Cells or Exadata Storage Servers

Traditionally, storage is used only for storing data and does not play any role in processing data. Disk arrays run CPUs, but they are typically low-power CPUs that are used for serving blocks of data. It's usually the database server that does the processing of the data. Exadata is very unique in this aspect, however: In an Exadata machine, storage plays an equal role in processing the data, like the database servers. In Exadata machines, the data is stored in an Exadata storage server, or storage cell. An Exadata storage server has comparatively high-powered CPUs (compared to traditional disk arrays), and that horsepower is used to perform Oracle database processing. The Exadata storage server runs a portion of the Oracle DBMS processing logic within the storage layer. This storage server executes a portion of the SQL processing, which frees a portion of the database tier CPU. In addition, the storage server processes a lot of data itself and returns only the relevant results, rather than sending all results to the database node for query processing, which frees up a large amount of I/O bandwidth.

When a query is executed in Exadata, the optimizer determines that an Exadata Storage Cell is attached to it and immediately offloads the query to the storage cells, so the storage cells take care of the query. Most of the data is filtered and sorted in the storage cells, and only relevant results are shipped to the database compute nodes. With a non-Exadata system, all data is sent from storage to the database buffer cache, where the query processing occurs.

Exadata Storage Server also runs on Oracle Enterprise Linux operating system. Exadata uses the Intelligence Database Protocol (iDB) for all communications between database servers and storage servers. Whenever a query is run and the database kernel determines that the underlying storage is Exadata, it constructs an iDB command for sending the SQL and metadata information about the SQL to the storage cell and getting the data blocks from the cell. The iDB is built on Reliable Datagram Sockets (RDS), which in turn runs on the InfiniBand protocol. RDS is a high-performance, low-latency, reliable, connectionless protocol for delivering datagrams. It was developed by Oracle. RDS also supports Remote Direct Memory Access (RDMA), in which the memory of a computer is accessed from another without involving both the operating systems. This mode doesn't need any CPU cycles, so it's very useful in a parallel processing environment. Exadata Storage Server uses RDMA for sending and receiving data. With RDMA and RDS, high-bandwidth and low-latency communication to storage within Exadata is achieved. Most of the Exadata-specific features such as query offload and resource management are leveraged by Oracle Database and ASM using iDB.

Exadata Storage Server runs the following core processes:

- **Cell server (CELLSRV)**   The cell server takes care of handling all the iDB requests that come from the database server. It deals with all the storage offload, I/O requests, predicate filtering at the cell level, and so on. This multi-threaded process does most of the heavy lifting in the storage server and takes the maximum amount of CPU cycles. CELLSRV can operate in block server mode as well.

- **Management server (MS)**   The management server facilitates the management of the storage cell. It works in conjunction with the cell control command-line interface (CellCLI) to manage the standalone storage cell. The CellCLI utility provides a CLI to the cell management functions, such as cell initial configuration, cell disk and grid disk creation, and performance monitoring. The CellCLI utility runs on the storage cell and is accessible from a client computer that has network access to the Exadata storage server or is directly connected to the cell.

- **Restart server (RS)**   The restart server is responsible for monitoring the storage server and MS and restarts them whenever needed.

InfiniBand

The database nodes and the storage cells are connected via InfiniBand, which provides a massive speed of 40Gb/sec in each direction. The interconnect across the RAC database node also uses InfiniBand for connectivity. InfiniBand uses zero-copy reservation, wherein the data is transferred by bypassing the buffer copies in various layers of the network. InfiniBand also uses buffer reservation so that hardware knows well ahead of time where to place the buffers.

Exadata uses the Zero-copy Datagram Protocol (ZDP), also developed by Oracle. ZDP has a very low CPU overhead. It's based on Reliable Datagram Sockets (RDS) OpenFabrics Enterprise Distribution (OFED), a high-performance, low-latency, reliable, connectionless protocol for delivering datagrams.

Database In-Memory running on Exadata uses InfiniBand for messaging between the In-Memory Column Store (IMCS). It uses InfiniBand for data population and duplication of the data across multiple RAC nodes. The massive bandwidth provided by InfiniBand ensures that the IMCSs are transactionally consistent and in sync with each other.

Exadata Hardware Configurations

Exadata comes in two formats: X*n*-2 and X*n*-8, where *n* is the generation number, and the number following the hyphen is the number of CPU sockets on the database servers. The X*n*-2 format includes four configurations: one-eighth, one-quarter, half, and full rack. The X*n*-8 format includes two configurations: full and half rack. The current generation of Exadata at the time of writing this book is X6; thus, the formats are X6-2 and X6-8.

A full-rack Exadata X6-2 has eight database compute nodes, fourteen storage cells, three InfiniBand switches, and one Ethernet switch. A half-rack X6-2 consists of four database nodes, seven storage servers, three InfiniBand switches, and one Ethernet switch. A quarter-rack X6-2 consists of two database nodes, three storage cells, two InfiniBand switches, and one Ethernet switch. An eighth-rack X6-2 is exactly the same as the quarter-rack X6-2, except 50 percent of the resources (CPU memory and storage) remain disabled.

Each database server in X6-2 has two 22-core Xeon E5 2699 v4 processors. The default memory is 256GB, which can be upgraded to 786GB. Each storage cell or storage server comes with two 10-core Xeon

E5-2630 v4 processors for processing SQL. The memory in the storage cell is 128GB. Customers can choose Extreme Flash (EF), which is 100 percent flash storage, or a mix of magnetic- and flash-based high capacity (HC) drives that provide the capacity of tiered storage. Exadata Flash in an HC storage server can be used directly as flash disks, but it is almost always configured as a flash cache (Exadata Smart Flash Cache) in front of disk storage, since caching provides flash-level performance with much more data than fits directly into flash.

A full-rack Exadata X6-8 has two database compute nodes, fourteen storage cells, two InfiniBand switches, and one Ethernet switch. A half-rack X6-2 consists of two database nodes, three storage cells, two InfiniBand switches, and one Ethernet switch. Each database compute node contains eight 18-core Xeon E7-8895 v3 processors (2.6 GHz), with 2TB memory, which can be expandable up to 6TB. The storage cells used in the X6-8 are the same as those used in the X6-2.

Exadata is also available in an Elastic Configuration. Refer to the Exadata datasheet for more details.

Exadata Features

Let's look at the features that make Exadata so unique and how you can use these features to make Database In-Memory perform wonders.

Hybrid Columnar Compression

Compressing data can provide a dramatic reduction in the storage consumed for large databases. Exadata provides an advanced compression capability, *Hybrid Columnar Compression* (HCC), which enables the highest levels of data compression and provides enterprises with tremendous cost-savings and performance improvements due to reduced I/O.

The "hybrid" part of the name indicates that it is not pure columnar compression, in which grouping is done at the columnar level; for example, all the values for column 1 for all the rows will be stored together, all the values for column 2 for all the rows will be stored together, and so on. In HCC, a subset of a row is chosen, and for that subset, each column is stored separately. It's also "hybrid" because we place updated rows into uncompressed blocks.

HCC is a second-generation columnar technology that combines the best of row and column formats to provide the best compression matching full columnar, excellent scan time as good as full columnar, and good single-row lookup.

The subset of rows into which the physical data is organized are *compression units* (CUs). Within a CU, the data is organized by column instead of by row, and then the data is compressed. Organizing the data by column brings similar values close to each other and thus enhances compression. Figure 7-2 shows a CU.

Let's look at how the HCC works. Table 7-1 shows the inventory of three major components in three different stores of a company.

The rows from the inventory table will be stored as a one unit. HCC will store each unique value from the column Store_Code with metadata that maps the values to the rows. Thus, the compressed value after implementing HCC will look like this:

 `CALIFORNIA001CALIFORNIA002CALIFORNIA003`

The database then compresses the repeated word "CALIFORNIA" in this value by storing it once and replacing each occurrence with a reference. If the reference is smaller than the original word, the database achieves compression. The compression benefit is particularly evident for the Date column, which contains only one unique value.

A CU can span multiple data blocks. The values for a particular column may or may not span multiple blocks. Figure 7-3 shows a CU spanning four data blocks.

These CUs are larger than the database blocks and are usually 32K in size. The type of compression algorithm chosen governs the size of the CU.

Any operation of work, such as loading, reading, inserting, updating, deleting, and so on, can occur in a CU. It is possible to access a particular

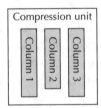

FIGURE 7-2. *A three-column compression unit*

Store_Code	Item_Code	Date	Quantity
CALIFORNIA001	5350	26-Apr-04	982218
CALIFORNIA002	5350	26-Apr-04	88182
CALIFORNIA003	5350	26-Apr-04	199010
CALIFORNIA001	2296	26-Apr-04	399299
CALIFORNIA002	2296	26-Apr-04	290300
CALIFORNIA003	2296	26-Apr-04	923012
CALIFORNIA001	3109	26-Apr-04	22112
CALIFORNIA002	3109	26-Apr-04	23940
CALIFORNIA003	3109	26-Apr-04	33491

TABLE 7-1. *Inventory of Three Components in Three Different Stores*

row within a CU, but for that we first need to read the CU and then fetch
that particular row from the CU. So it's an abstraction at a higher level than
a block. A CU is a self-contained unit of one or more rows. Thus, a CU has
information about all the rows contained in it. There is no need to look for the
information about those rows anywhere outside the CU.

The CU looks like a very long row, or like a chained row. Suppose, for
example, that the size of the CU is 32K and the block size is 8K. The CU
is stored as a single column across multiple blocks. The row head has an
appropriate header already, so there is no need to change it for HCC. A flag

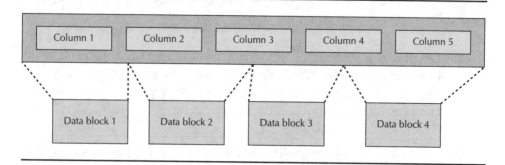

FIGURE 7-3. *Compression unit spanning four data blocks*

in the row head indicates whether a single column does not fit in a block and it goes over to the next block. In HCC, the flag is reused.

Given a small set of rows, the creation of the CU involves the following steps:

1. Buffer the subset of rows.

2. Divide them column-wise.

3. Choose a column for this set of rows and compress them using an algorithm.

4. The next column is chosen, and the values of the next column—say, column 2—are chosen from the set of rows and compressed using a compression algorithm. The compression algorithm used in the second column can be different from the algorithm used in the first column.

5. The same steps are repeated until all the columns of the CU are stored.

When all the columns are compressed, the top-level compression unit (CU header) and the offsets to the column CU pointing to each column are updated, and both are stored uncompressed. The offsets of the column CUs are used for the random access of data. If the data is requested only for one or two columns, then during data fetch, the offsets are used to obtain the information, and a data scan happens only for these column CUs instead of scanning all the column CUs.

For each column, an initial transformation to the data is applied, followed by a standard compression algorithm. Depending on the data, transformation or compression may not be applied at all.

Provided next are the transformations typically applied to the data before the compression algorithm is implemented. Transformation of data helps to increase the compression ratio for a standard algorithm.

- **Length/value** Separation of length and value may not by itself result in any compression. Since the length could be the same or could be in a small range, by storing all the lengths together, the standard compression algorithm can do a much better job. This is a standard Oracle column format.

- **Length separated** The length of each column is stored separately, and the value of each column is stored separately. Thus, there will be a length vector for each column and there will be a value vector corresponding to it. If the length is constant for a large run, then the length is stored just once, thereby providing very good compression.

■ **Run-length encoded**   If a single value is repeated multiple times, the value is stored only once, making a note of the occurrence (run) of that value. This provides a very good compression ratio when the runs are very large, and at the same time gives very good decompress results as well.

■ **Delta**   Delta does not give compression by itself, since the number of bytes stored does not change, but it helps to improve the efficiency of the compression algorithm. The delta used in transformation is a byte-wise delta and not number-wise.

■ **Length-separated delta**   In length delta, the length and the value are stored separately, and then the delta is applied on each individually.

HCC uses these three compression algorithms internally:

■ **LZO**   LZO (for creators Lempel-Ziv-Oberhumer) is a portable lossless data compression library written in ANSI C. LZO offers pretty fast compression and extremely fast decompression. Decompression requires no memory. LZO provides lower compression ratios compared to other compression algorithms. LZO algorithms and implementations are distributed under the GNU General Public License. (More information about LZO can be obtained from www.oberhumer.com/opensource/lzo/.)

■ **ZLIB**   The ZLIB compression library provides in-memory compression and decompression functions, including integrity checks of the uncompressed data. The compression speed of ZLIB is lower than that of LZO but higher than BZ2, and the compression ratio is better than LZO but lesser than BZ2. (For more information, see www.zlib.net.)

■ **BZ2**   BZ2 compresses files using the Burrows-Wheeler block-sorting text compression algorithm and Huffman coding. It provides slower compression and decompression speeds compared to ZLIB and LZO, but it gives the highest compression ratios compared to LZO. (For more information about the BZ2 compression, see www.bzip.org.)

HCC can be implemented at the table level, partition level, and tablespace level. While data in HCC tables can be modified using conventional Data Manipulation Language (DML) operations (Insert, Update, Delete), performing such operations could result in a reduction of the HCC compression ratio. It is recommended that HCC be enabled on tables or partitions with no or infrequent DML operations. If frequent DML operations are planned on a table or partition, the Oracle Advanced Compression Option is better suited for such data.

Exadata offers two types of compression depending on your requirements and the type of applications you will be running: warehouse compression and online archival compression.

Warehouse compression, also known as query compression, is optimized for query performance and is intended for data warehouse applications. This mode is known as query mode. **COMPRESS FOR QUERY** is useful in data warehousing environments. Valid values are **LOW** and **HIGH**, with **HIGH** providing a higher compression ratio. The default is **HIGH**.

Archive compression (**COMPRESS FOR ARCHIVE**) uses higher compression ratios than query compression and is useful for compressing data that will be stored for long periods of time. Valid values are **LOW** and **HIGH**, with **HIGH** providing the highest possible compression ratio. The default is **LOW**. In contrast to warehouse compression, archive compression is a pure storage-saving technology. Tables or partitions using archive compression will typically experience a decrease in performance—a factor of the compression algorithm being optimized for maximum storage savings. Therefore, archive compression is intended for tables or partitions that store data that is rarely accessed. It benefits any application with data retention requirements and is the best approach for information lifecycle management (ILM) and data archival.

Advantages of HCC and Database In-Memory

The main goal of HCC is to compress the data, so when HCC was invented, its main goal was not to get maximum performance, but rather to compress as much data as possible—and at the same time, scan the tables with decent speed. HCC also reduces the I/O, since the data is compressed and thus lots of unproductive I/Os are avoided. When you populate the IMCS data in Exadata, since the data is already compressed, it can be read very fast—and the faster the data is read, the quicker you can populate the data. Since the

Exadata storage servers have immense horsepower, the CPUs and extreme I/O capabilities make data population lightning fast. Similarly, when you need to repopulate the stale data, this occurs at impressive speeds.

Smart Scans vs. Traditional Architecture

In traditional architecture, database servers are connected to a SAN infrastructure, where the Oracle Database files are stored. The SAN, or the storage, is used to keep the data and does not play any role in processing the data. Storage simply keeps the data, and the storage layer has no intelligence about the data—that is, the conventional storage array does not understand the Oracle data format and hence cannot perform any intelligent operations, such as predicate evaluation, in the storage layer itself.

The pipe between the storage arrays and the database tends to be small and can limit the I/O bandwidth. Because resources are fixed, finite resources can lead to oversubscription, which in turn causes performance bottlenecks. In modern computer systems, the I/O is a source of bottlenecks that result from oversubscription.

Traditional storage arrays lack scale-out architecture. If the storage consumed in the array reaches the maximum capacity of the array, it is not very easy to plug in additional components and scale out incrementally.

With Exadata, storage plays a role in processing the data. Each storage cell is equipped with CPUs and memory, which helps in processing the data. Exadata Smart Scan, a feature of the Exadata Database Machine, offloads the data search and retrieval processing to the storage cell. Smart Scan is designed to reduce the amount of data that flows from storage devices to the database server. It not only reduces the I/O bottleneck problem from the storage devices to the CPU, but it also reduces the amount of processing that has to be done by the database node, resulting in performance improvements based on the reduced demand for computing resources.

Let's look at the differences between processing traditional storage and storage with Smart Scan.

To appreciate the benefit of Smart Scan, let's first look at a traditional scan processing of the following SQL statement:

```
select customer_name from customers where customer number IN  ('6500 ,7500' );
```

In traditional architecture, the statement requests records from a 1TB table, though we don't need all the records from the 1TB table. With traditional processing, the SQL statement is parsed and the execution plan is prepared. The next step is to request the extents from the table, which will be required to process this SQL statement. The storage system receives this request and proceeds to execute the I/Os required to retrieve 1TB of data, which is then returned to the DB server. The entire 1TB of data is sent back to the DB server. The DB server goes through that data in the buffer cache and selects the 1000 customer names, which are formed into a result set and returned to the client. Thus, for only 1000 records, the entire 1TB of data was shipped from storage to the DB servers; it used a lot of resources to send a lot of unnecessary data over the network, serving lots of I/O requests with limited bandwidth. Though the client needs only 1000 records, in this case, all 1TB of data has to travel from storage to DB server, wasting a lot of resources.

Let's take a look at the steps in a bit more detail:

1. The client issues the SQL statement with a predicate to filter a table and return only the rows of interest to the user. In this case, the predicate is an **IN** clause and the rows of interest to the user are customer numbers between 6000 and 7000. Thus, the user is interested in looking at information for only 1000 customers.

2. The database kernel maps this request and identifies the extents for *all* of the data blocks belonging to the table.

3. The database kernel issues the I/O and requests all the table blocks from the storage.

4. All the blocks for the table are fetched from storage into the memory of the database server. During this step, actual data movement happens from the storage to the database server.

5. SQL processing occurs against those data blocks in the database buffer cache, searching for only those rows that satisfy the predicate: customer numbers between 6000 and 7000.

6. The rows that satisfy the predicate clause are sent to the end user. The data stays in the database buffer cache and is wiped out based on the LRU algorithm.

Now let's look at the same process with Exadata Smart Scan. As soon as the query is parsed, the optimizer knows that an Exadata storage cell is attached to it. The request for the table extent is sent to the storage system along with the metadata about that SQL statement. This metadata is used to implement Smart Scan processing—for instance, some of that metadata could be the selection criteria—and Smart Scan will use that to identify the rows that could be part of the result set, eliminating the need to send all the useless rows back to the database node for processing. Metadata also includes information such as what columns are requested so the amount of information returned to the database nodes is limited only to those columns required to process the query, eliminating even more data from the I/O being sent back to the database node. The net result of the Smart Scan processing is that, instead of sending back 1TB of data for processing to the database node, only 100MB of data is sent. The database server uses this result to create the result set to return it to the client. This process is much faster and is much less resource intensive, because it involves less data and much less work for the DB node to perform.

Let's take a detailed look at the steps involved:

1. The client issues the SQL statement with a predicate to filter a table and return only the rows of interest to the user. In this case, the predicate is an **IN** clause and the rows of interest to the user are customer numbers between 6000 and 7000. Thus, the user is interested in looking at the information for only 1000 customers.

2. The database kernel identifies that data is stored in Exadata storage cells, so it constructs an iDB command and sends it to the Exadata storage cells. The iDB command contains an SQL *fragment*, or a portion of the original SQL statement. Each step in the data flow operator (DFO) tree is expressed as an SQL statement, or fragment.

3. Exadata Storage Server gets into action and starts scanning the data blocks, extracting only the relevant rows and columns that match the SQL query fragment.

4. Once the data scan is completed, the Exadata storage cell returns the database server iDB messages containing the requested data. Exadata does row and column projection, so it returns only the requested rows and columns at this step. The data is set from the Exadata storage cells to the database server. Exadata also returns data in row-source format, not data block format. A row-source is a part of the DFO tree processing. Only the relevant 100MB of data will be sent.

5. The database server consolidates the results from all the Exadata storage cells.

6. The client is returned the requested data.

The query is offloaded to the storage cells, and this is what Smart Scan is all about.

Smart Scan does smart I/O, not block I/O. With block I/O, the data is shipped to the location where it can be processed—the RDBMS or the database server; with smart I/O, some of the processing is shipped to where data resides—Exadata Storage Server. Results from the storage layer may be further processed in the RDBMS.

Smart Scan uses direct reads, which involve reading the data into Program Global Area (PGA) buffers as opposed to the buffer cache used for caching data blocks. Direct read is useful when the ratio of cache-to-data to be read is very small.

Smart Scan provides a lot of advantages, including the following:

- *It eliminates a lot of unproductive I/Os.* For any application, the biggest bottleneck is I/O. Smart Scan eliminates the bottleneck, reducing the network I/Os and disk I/Os by filtering the data using smart I/O operations offloaded to the storage layer.

- *The DB server has to spend fewer CPU cycles in processing the I/Os.* When the I/O is reduced, the DB server CPU cycle is freed up, reducing the processing burden on the host. The freed CPU cycles can be used for serving other requests.

- *Data blocks are transferred from the Exadata storage cells to the DB server via InfiniBand.* This provides 40Gb/sec connectivity and a much bigger pipe compared to 4GFC or 8GFC (Fibre Channel). If a customer is running on a 8GFC, they need five Fibre Channel cards to deliver 40Gb/sec. Exadata also runs in active/active configuration, so it delivers an 80Gb/sec signaling rate.

- *Smart Scans correctly handle complex cases.* These include uncommitted data, locked rows and chained rows, compressed tables, national language processing, date arithmetic, regular expression searches, and partitioned tables.

- *Smart Scan can perform specialized operations.* These include predicate filtering, column filtering, join processing, scans on encrypted data, scans on compressed data, data mining, creating/ extending tablespaces, and RMAN operations.

- *Smart Scans are transparent to the application.* No application or SQL changes are required, and returned data is fully consistent and transactional.

- *Smart Scans provide both horizontal and vertical parallelism.* Horizontal parallelism is achieved by concurrent processing of the smart I/O requests by many Exadata storage servers and concurrent processing of smart I/O requests from a single database process by many threads within a single Exadata storage server. Vertical parallelism is obtained as Exadata storage servers process more results while the database is consuming results already returned.

Tip & Technique
If you want to leverage Smart Scan for a homegrown application, you may want to try disabling the database index for Smart Scan to kick in.

When you run Database In-Memory in Exadata, the In-Memory optimization can be offloaded to Exadata storage cells. As discussed in previous chapters, In-Memory aggregation (IMA) provides the vector group-by feature, which enhances performance. IMA ensures that a minimum amount of data flows through the execution plan by using a vector transformation plan. It uses **KEY VECTOR USE** and **VECTOR GROUP** operations to get the vector transformation plan. As a result, the **VECTOR GROUP BY** transform joins to a **KEY VECTOR** filter and a dimension table in a warehouse, making it an extremely fast operation and requiring minimal CPU overhead.

If the table is not available in the IMCS, IMA can offload **KEY VECTOR** use to Exadata storage servers as well. As a result of storage offload, the processing becomes extremely fast with minimum CPU overhead and minimizes the data that needs to be returned to the compute nodes or the database server.

Storage Index

The Exadata storage cell maintains a *storage index* that contains the summary of the distribution of the data in the hard drives. The storage index is very different from the database index. It is not maintained by the database, but is maintained automatically and cannot be created or altered manually, unlike indexes in the database objects. The storage index is very transparent to the Oracle Database.

An *RDBMS index* is a data structure that finds data quickly. The Exadata storage index is a data structure that helps to filter out data very efficiently. Thus, a storage index is a negative index, or anti-index, as opposed to database indexes that use B-tree or bitmap types of data structures in their implementations. An Exadata storage index is an array of structures that are stored in the physical memory of Exadata storage cells. Each individual structure of the array is known as a region index (RIDX), and each RIDX stores summaries for up to eight columns. There is one RIDX for each 1MB of disk space.

The decision to store which columns in the RIDX is independent of that of other region indexes, making RIDX highly scalable, so no latch contention occurs. Let's look at an example to see how the storage index works.

As shown in Figure 7-4, column B of the index stores the values 1–9. Our query requests the following:

```
select * from table where B=3
```

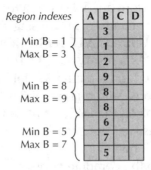

FIGURE 7-4. *Three regions of an RIDX*

The Exadata storage cell divides the table into equal-sized logical portions, or regions. The first set of three rows is the first region, the second set of the three rows is the second region, and so on. The minimum and maximum range of the column is stored in each region. So, for the preceding query, the value of the predicate B = 3 lies in the first logical region, so the storage index will eliminate the second and the third regions when fetching the data. Storage indexes minimize the disk I/Os by using the minimum and maximum values to eliminate the unnecessary I/Os.

Queries using the following comparisons benefit the most by the Exadata storage index:

- Equality (=)

- Inequality (<, !=, or >)

- Less than or equal (<=)

- Greater than or equal (>=)

- IS NULL

- IS NOT NULL

The Exadata storage index works in conjunction with Smart Scan and reduces the overall disk I/Os. Smart Scan helps in reducing the overall network I/Os. When Smart Scan and storage indexes work together, both disk I/Os and network I/Os are reduced. Exadata storage indexes avoid scanning unnecessary partitions of the table and provide improvement in join performance since table joins can skip unnecessary I/O operations.

The benefits obtained from the Exadata storage index can be obtained by querying the V$MYSTAT view, which shows the details of the I/Os that can be reduced. This view has many metrics, but the main one that provides the details related to storage indexes shows the impact of storage index in saving I/Os and tells us how many bytes of I/O elimination occurred using the storage index:

```
SQL>  select name, value from v$sysstat where name like '%storage%';
NAME                                                             VALUE
------------------------------------------------------- -----
cell physical IO bytes saved by storage index                  754098176
```

The storage index helps avoid unnecessary I/Os. When the data is populated in the IMCS on Exadata, the storage index plays a very important role by providing the information about where the actual data is stored. Imagine a situation with no storage index: You have bought one of the largest systems with huge memory—your RAM is 2TB and you are planning to put 1.8TB of data in IMCS. Without a storage index, the operation for populating the data will go for hours. Also, if the memory card fails, your entire IMCS will be lost since the data is not duplicated.

Only Exadata enables you to duplicate the data in the IMCS across multiple nodes. In addition, when the data is not available in IMCS and disk read needs to be done, a storage index helps in quickly retrieving the data.

Exadata Smart Flash Cache

Today's multicore, multisocket application server designs are increasingly held back by slow storage. When requesting data, the server spends most of its time waiting for storage. Hard disk drives, even the fastest 15K RPM, cannot feed the servers fast enough. These drives are much slower than what today's servers are capable of, so they spend most of their time waiting for data after a request. Application performance remains sluggish, regardless of the server CPU horsepower.

Exadata Smart Flash Cache bridges this gap by sitting in between the server and spinning hard disks. The flash cards are directly placed in the Exadata Storage Server. This enables applications to get the fast response time they require from flash while storing infrequently used data on slower HDD technology. The Exadata Smart Flash Cache enables frequently accessed data to be kept in very fast flash storage, while most of the data is kept in very regular spinning disks. This happens automatically without the user having to take any action. The Exadata flash cache is called Smart Flash Cache because it monitors the data usage and keeps only the frequently used data in the flash cache. If the data is not reused frequently, then Exadata Smart Flash Cache avoids caching that data.

NOTE
Exadata Smart Flash Cache is available only with the high capacity (HC) drives. Extreme Flash (EF) drives come with 100 percent flash storage and there are no spinning disks. Extreme Flash provides unprecedented I/O capabilities.

In addition to spinning disks, HC storage servers have four PCI flash cards, each with 3.2TB (raw) Exadata Smart Flash Cache, whereas EF storage servers have an all-flash configuration with eight PCI flash drives, each with 3.2TB (raw) storage capacity.

The flash is based on Flash Accelerator F320 NVMe PCIe cards with a total raw capacity of 12.8TB of flash memory. These flash cards are also based on innovative 3D Vertical NAND (V-NAND) technology. This low-latency, solid-state flash storage is packaged on a PCI card.

NOTE
The flash cards used in the Exadata storage cells are not flash disks. These cards are placed directly in the PCI slots, which are connected directly to the bus; hence, the performance of the flash cards are not bottlenecked by slow disk controllers, and the bandwidth or input/output operations per second (IOPS) are not compromised.

Exadata Smart Flash Cache has two behaviors: write-through and write-back. With write-through, frequently accessed data is cached into the Exadata Smart Flash Cache. In write-back cache, the Exadata Smart Flash Cache also caches database block writes. Write caching eliminates disk bottlenecks in large-scale OLTP and batch workloads. The Exadata write cache is transparent, persistent, and fully redundant. The default behavior of the Exadata machines is write-through cache. The write-back cache needs to be manually enabled.

Exadata and Database In-Memory provide a complete solution to tiered storage. The hottest data can reside in the IMCS in the physical RAM, the hot data can reside in the Exadata Smart Flash Cache, and cold data can reside on the spinning disk. In addition, when the data resides in so many locations (IMCS, database buffer cache, Exadata Smart Flash Cache, and spinning hard drives), there is no maintenance overhead, and you don't have to track or chase manually which data is residing at which storage. The Oracle Database and Exadata do it automatically for you. The database is aware of the data and can seamlessly access the data without any bottleneck.

If the data resides in the Exadata Smart Flash Cache or in Extreme Flash storage, population of the data will be even faster.

Tip & Technique
*You can pin important objects in Exadata Smart
Flash Cache so that they stay there permanently
and are not aged out.*

Database In-Memory Fault Tolerance for Exadata

Exadata provides another important feature: fault-tolerant capabilities that are available exclusively to Exadata. When this feature is enabled, the data populated in the IMCS is mirrored across a different compute node. The duplication of the data in the IMCS can be enabled at the table/partition or subpartition level. Therefore, each IMCU will be available across different nodes of the RAC cluster, providing data high availability. In case one of the RAC nodes goes down, IMCS is available at a surviving node.

The duplication of data can be enabled with the **DUPLICATE** clause. It specifies how many copies of each In-Memory Compression Unit (IMCU) of the tables in the IMCS will be spread across all the Oracle RAC instances. The **DUPLICATE** clause has three settings:

- **NO DUPLICATE**   Data is not duplicated across Oracle RAC instances. This is the default.

- **DUPLICATE**   Data is duplicated on another Oracle RAC instance, resulting in data existing on a total of two Oracle RAC instances.

- **DUPLICATE ALL**   Data is duplicated across all Oracle RAC instances. The database also uses the **DISTRIBUTE AUTO** setting, regardless of whether or how you specify the distribute clause:

```
SQL > ALTER TABLE inventory INMEMORY DUPLICATE;
SQL> ALTER TABLE COSTS INMEMORY DISTRIBUTE AUTO DUPLICATE ALL;
SQL> ALTER  SYSTEM SET INMEMORY_CLAUSE_DEFAULT='INMEMORY

MEMCOMPRESS FOR QUERY DISTRIBUTE AUTO DUPLICATE ALL' SCOPE=BOTH;
```

The duplication of the IMCS also provides a performance benefit: whenever a query is run, it can read the data either from the primary IMCS or from the backup IMCS copy. It also helps to co-locate the joins between the large distributed fact tables and the small dimension tables. As a result of duplication of the data, IMCS can be found locally. Thus, data required for a join operation can be obtained locally instead of fetching it from a remote node.

Summary

In this chapter you have learned how to use Oracle Exadata Database Machine and the Database In-Memory option. Oracle Exadata Database Machine provides extreme performance for both data warehousing and Online Transaction Processing (OLTP) applications, making it the ideal platform for consolidating onto grids or private clouds. When combined with the Database In-Memory option, the benefits are exponential.

Exadata comprises the following building blocks:

■ Database servers or compute nodes

■ Exadata storage cells or Exadata storage servers

■ InfiniBand

We studied several helpful Exadata features in this chapter. Hybrid Columnar Compression enables the highest levels of data compression and provides enterprises with tremendous cost-savings and performance improvements due to reduced I/O. Smart Scan, a feature of the Exadata Database Machine, offloads data search and retrieval processing to the storage cell. Exadata storage cell maintains the summary of the distribution of the data in the hard drives known as Storage Index. Exadata Smart Flash Cache enables frequently accessed data to be kept in very fast flash storage, while most of the data is kept in very regular spinning disks.

Exadata provides fault-tolerant capabilities to Database In-Memory. These capabilities are available exclusively to Exadata. With fault-tolerant capabilities, the data populated in the IMCS is mirrored across a different compute node. The duplication of the data in the IMCS can be enabled at the table/partition or subpartition level. Therefore, each IMCU will be available across different nodes of the RAC cluster, providing data with high availability. In case one of the RAC nodes goes down, IMCS is available at a surviving node.

CHAPTER

8

In-Memory Lab

I n this chapter, you'll get to play with several In-Memory features. The chapter includes examples and queries and lets you use several important In-Memory features. The goal of the chapter is to provide you with some practical experience.

After finishing this chapter, you will have ample exposure to In-Memory and you should be able to implement it at your workplace without any problem. For demonstrating the In-Memory examples, I have installed Oracle Database 12cR2 in a server with enough memory. As you know, when Oracle Database is installed, the In-Memory option is not enabled by default, so you need to enable it manually.

You may have seen a few similar examples in previous chapters, but I have provided some of them again to maintain the flow of this chapter. To work with the examples in this chapter, you need the following:

- Oracle Database with In-Memory option

- Oracle Enterprise Manager

- SwingBench, the Java-based load generator for Oracle

You can download Oracle Enterprise Manager (EM) from oracle.com/technetwork/oem/enterprise-manager/downloads/index.html. EM installation is simple and intuitive and does not take more than two hours. Once EM is installed, let it discover the database that you installed plus the In-Memory option. After EM discovery is done, you are all set.

After the Oracle Database is installed and you have hooked it up with EM for monitoring, the database has no data in it. Next, you need to generate/populate data in the database to get working with the Database In-Memory option. To do this, you'll use SwingBench, a tool created by Dominic Giles (dominicgiles.com/swingbench.html). Using this tool, you should be able to generate the data you need. I'll cover how to generate data using SwingBench in the relevant section.

View the Server Memory Specification

First, let's look at the server's memory specification in which I have installed the database. I have installed the Oracle Database in Red Hat Enterprise Linux 7.

```
$ cat /proc/meminfo
MemTotal:        125467636 kB
MemFree:          51826896 kB
```

```
MemAvailable:     84566912 kB
Buffers:               884 kB
Cached:           69631780 kB
SwapCached:              0 kB
Active:           16198252 kB
Inactive:         55236952 kB
Active(anon):      2780760 kB
Inactive(anon):   36788048 kB
Active(file):     13417492 kB
Inactive(file):   18448904 kB
Unevictable:             0 kB
Mlocked:                 0 kB
SwapTotal:               0 kB
SwapFree:                0 kB
Dirty:              113820 kB
Writeback:               0 kB
AnonPages:         1802608 kB
Mapped:            2695192 kB
Shmem:            37766256 kB
Slab:              1260768 kB
SReclaimable:      1127036 kB
SUnreclaim:         133732 kB
KernelStack:         16272 kB
PageTables:         123992 kB
NFS_Unstable:            0 kB
Bounce:                  0 kB
WritebackTmp:            0 kB
CommitLimit:      62733816 kB
Committed_AS:     42131948 kB
VmallocTotal:   34359738367 kB
VmallocUsed:        231184 kB
VmallocChunk:   34359500540 kB
HardwareCorrupted:       0 kB
AnonHugePages:     1032192 kB
HugePages_Total:         0
HugePages_Free:          0
HugePages_Rsvd:          0
HugePages_Surp:          0
Hugepagesize:         2048 kB
DirectMap4k:        106496 kB
DirectMap2M:     127893504 kB
```

As you can see, the server has close to 120GB of RAM, which is pretty large. Since the database has just been installed, even if we query the In-Memory Area, it won't show anything (because the database is empty).

```
SQL> show sga

Total System Global Area 3.8655E+10 bytes
```

```
Fixed Size               19247304 bytes
Variable Size          5368713016 bytes
Database Buffers       3.3152E+10 bytes
Redo Buffers            114966528 bytes
SQL>
```

Notice that the total size of SGA is close to 36GB, which includes the buffer cache as well. The size of SGA has been allocated by the installer. When Oracle Database is installed, it also installs a lighter version of EM called EM Express, by default. Now if you look at the SGA using EM Express, you'll notice that it shows the breakdown of all the components of the SGA and corresponding sizes allocated to it, as shown in Figure 8-1.

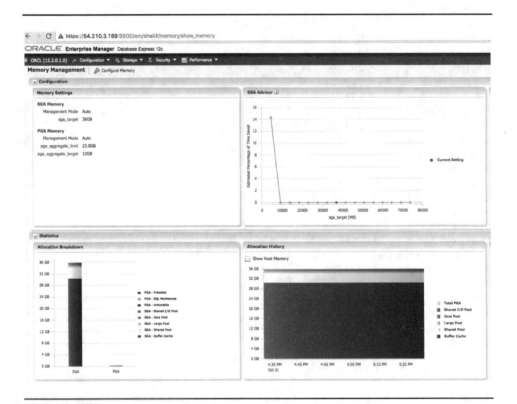

FIGURE 8-1. *Enterprise Manager Express showing SGA*

Alternatively, if you want to query the SGA size and details about In-Memory, you can run the following two queries:

```
SQL> show parameter sga
NAME                                    TYPE                VALUE
------------------------------------    ----------------    ----------
allow_group_access_to_sga               boolean             FALSE
lock_sga                                boolean             FALSE
pre_page_sga                            boolean             TRUE
sga_max_size                            big integer         36G
sga_min_size                            big integer         0
sga_target                              big integer         36G
unified_audit_sga_queue_size            integer             1048576
```

```
SQL> show parameter inmemory

NAME                                    TYPE            VALUE
------------------------------------    -----------     ----------
inmemory_adg_enabled                    boolean         TRUE
inmemory_clause_default                 string
inmemory_expressions_usage              string          ENABLE
inmemory_force                          string          DEFAULT
inmemory_max_populate_servers           integer         0
inmemory_query                          string          ENABLE
inmemory_size                           big integer     0
inmemory_trickle_repopulate_servers_    integer         1
percent
inmemory_virtual_columns                string          MANUAL
optimizer_inmemory_aware                boolean         TRUE
```

As seen from the output of the previous query, the size of In-Memory is set to 0, which means the In-Memory area is not allocated yet. The following command sets the In-Memory size to 50G:

```
SQL> alter system set inmemory_size=50G scope=spfile;

System altered.
```

Let's also increase the SGA:

```
SQL> alter system set SGA_TARGET=85G scope=spfile;

System altered.
```

Now restart the database to propagate the changes in the system:

```
SQL> shutdown immediate ;
Database closed.
Database dismounted.
ORACLE instance shut down.
SQL> startup
ORACLE instance started.

Total System Global Area 9.1268E+10 bytes
Fixed Size                  19249808 bytes
Variable Size             4831839600 bytes
Database Buffers          3.2481E+10 bytes
Redo Buffers               249184256 bytes
In-Memory Area            5.3687E+10 bytes
Database mounted.
Database opened.
SQL>
```

Go to EM and verify the changes. Select the database where you have enabled the In-Memory option. Choose Administration | In-Memory Central, as shown in Figure 8-2. Enterprise Manager will prompt you for a username and password. Log in as a user with sysdba credentials. You can log in with system or sys user.

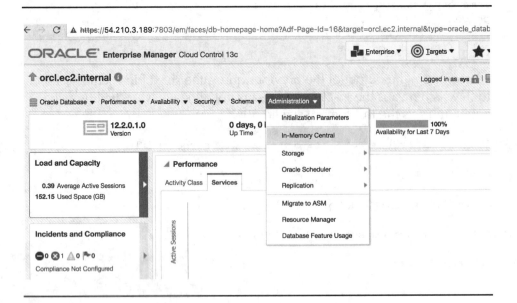

FIGURE 8-2. *Selecting In-Memory Central from EM*

FIGURE 8-3.   *In-Memory Central home page from EM*

Once selected, the home page of In-Memory Central shows the memory that has been allocated to the In-Memory Area and objects that are populated in the In-Memory Area and details of the same.

On the left side of Figure 8-3, you can see the details of space allocated for In-Memory and other parameters and their corresponding values for In-Memory, which is enabled for this database. On the right side, you see "No Data," because although we have enabled the database for In-Memory, we haven't populated any objects in the In-Memory Column Store.

Load Data Using SwingBench

Because our database doesn't have any data in it, let's load some data into the database using SwingBench. The examples in this chapter used version 2.5.971 of SwingBench. Download SwingBench from dominicgiles .com/swingbench.html and extract the swingbench.zip file.

NOTE
Make sure you have Java installed on the server before you run this tool.

Once it's extracted, the tool is ready to go. Using SwingBench, you can generate OLTP as well as data warehouse data.

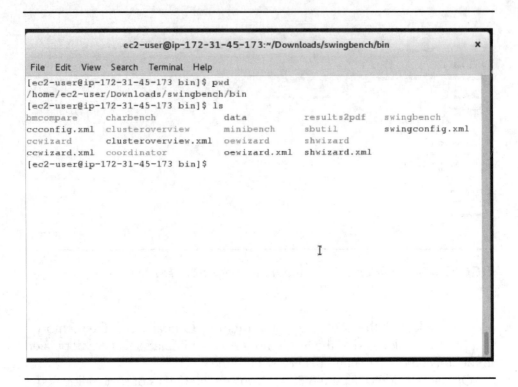

```
                    ec2-user@ip-172-31-45-173:~/Downloads/swingbench/bin              ✕

 File  Edit  View  Search  Terminal  Help
[ec2-user@ip-172-31-45-173 bin]$ pwd
/home/ec2-user/Downloads/swingbench/bin
[ec2-user@ip-172-31-45-173 bin]$ ls
bmcompare        charbench              data              results2pdf    swingbench
ccconfig.xml     clusteroverview       minibench         sbutil         swingconfig.xml
ccwizard         clusteroverview.xml   oewizard          shwizard
ccwizard.xml     coordinator           oewizard.xml      shwizard.xml
[ec2-user@ip-172-31-45-173 bin]$
```

FIGURE 8-4   *Contents of SwingBench bin directory*

Go to the bin directory where you have installed SwingBench, shown in Figure 8-4.

Once inside the bin directory, you will see multiple files. We'll run the oewizard and shwizard wizards to populate order entry and sales data in our database. Let's first run the Order Entry Install wizard, oewizard.

1. At the command prompt at the bottom of the list of files, type **oewizard**, as shown next:

```
[ec2-user@ip-172-31-45-173 bin]$ pwd
/home/ec2-user/Downloads/swingbench/bin
[ec2-user@ip-172-31-45-173 bin]$ ls
bmcompare        charbench              data              results2pdf    swingbench
ccconfig.xml     clusteroverview       minibench         sbutil         swingconfig.xml
ccwizard         clusteroverview.xml   oewizard          shwizard
ccwizard.xml     coordinator           oewizard.xml      shwizard.xml
[ec2-user@ip-172-31-45-173 bin]$ ./oewizard
```

2. On the Order Entry Install wizard home page, shown next, click
   Next to continue.

3. On the next screen, select Version 2, as shown here, and then
   click Next.

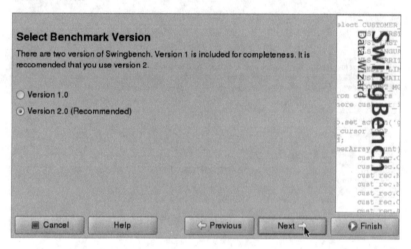

4. When you are prompted to select a task, as shown next, select
   the Create The Order Entry Schema. (If for any reason the data
   generation fails and you want to restart it, you can do the cleanup

by choosing the second option, Drop The Order Entry Schema and then restarting the oewizard.) Click Next.

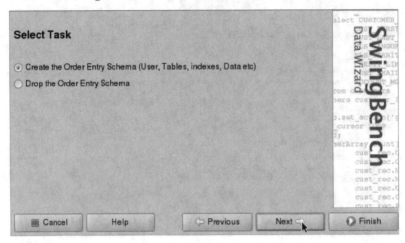

5. The tool will prompt for the database connectivity details. Enter this information as shown in the next illustration:

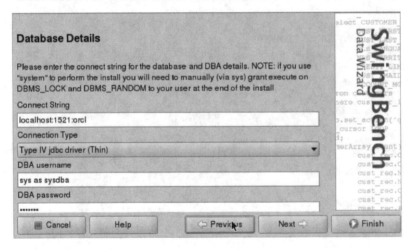

Enter the Connect String, the *hostname:portname:SID/* service of the instance. The tool comes with the JDBC driver installed, so you do not need to install and download it. For DBS Username, you must connect as a user with DBA privileges in the database. In this example, I have logged in as the sys user as sysdba. Click Next.

6. The tool prompts for the Schema Details: Username, Password, Tablespace and Datafile location. Enter all the details, as shown here, and then click Next.

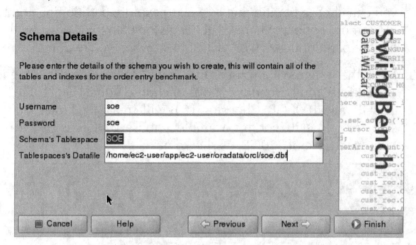

You don't have to create the user or the tablespace, because SwingBench does it for you.

7. The wizard next asks you about some of the Database Options, such as partitioning and type of compression used (see the next illustration). It will ask whether you want to use a bigfile tablespace or a regular tablespace and if you want to enable the indexes.

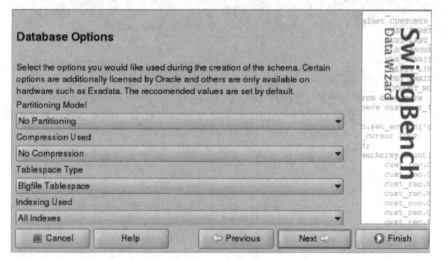

Since this is an OLTP workload, for Partitioning Model, choose Partitioning; for Compression Used, choose Advanced Compression. (Note that when you generate the data for the data warehouse, you can choose partitioning as well to explore partitioning and the In-Memory option. When we generate the data for DW we will choose partitioning as well.) Click Next when you're done.

8. Next, the system will prompt for Sizing Details of the data it's going to generate. You have four options to choose from: 1GB, 10GB, 100GB, and 1000GB. Choosing 1GB will create the tablespace size of 2.5 to 3GB. For this example, choose 100GB to create a tablespace size of 320GB, as shown next:

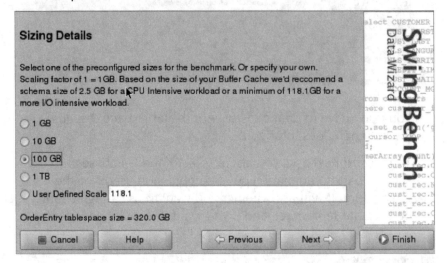

(Note: Depending on how much RAM you have on the server and how much you want to allocate for the In-Memory Area, you can generate the data accordingly. You may want to generate a larger volume of data as well, because in real life, the size of the database will be exponentially larger than the In-Memory Area. That way, you will get an idea about a real-life use case. Once you have generated enough data, you may want to run a few benchmarks and invoke the In-Memory Advisor as well.)

9. Click Next to proceed. The system will prompt for the Level Of Parallelism, as shown next. Choose a value that equals 2 × the number of CPUs for this. Then click Finish.

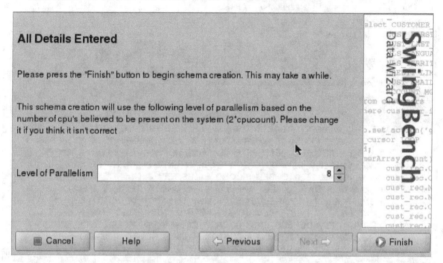

The system will start creating the schema and generate the relevant data, as shown next:

Type	Description	Time
	Clear Events	
ⓘ	Connecting to : jdbc:oracle:thin:@localhost:1521:orcl	03:32:27
ⓘ	Connected	03:32:27
ⓘ	Starting script ../sql/soedgcreatetablespace.sql	03:32:27

10. Once it's finished, a message will pop up saying that the schema creation and data generation are successful (Figure 8-5). Click OK.

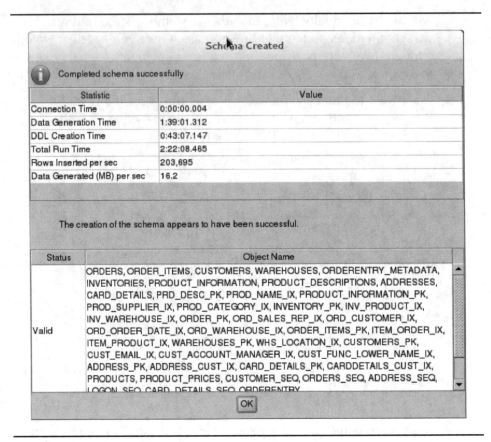

FIGURE 8-5. *Schema creation successful*

Generate Data for Sales History

Now that the data for the OLTP has been generated, let's generate the data for the DW (Sales History data). For that, we need to run the shwizard script:

```
[ec2-user@ip-172-31-45-173 bin]$ ./shwizard
```

The tool will prompt you with the same set of questions used for the order entry wizard, so there's no need to go over each step. Once the wizard is finished, it will create the schema and generate the data.

Now log in to the database and look at the tables created by the order entry wizard:

```
SQL> connect soe/soe;
Connected.
SQL> select tname from tab ;

TNAME
-----------------------------------------------------------------------
ADDRESSES
CARD_DETAILS
CUSTOMERS
INVENTORIES
LOGON
ORDERENTRY_METADATA
ORDERS
ORDER_ITEMS
PRODUCTS
PRODUCT_DESCRIPTIONS
PRODUCT_INFORMATION
PRODUCT_PRICES
WAREHOUSES
```

You can see that SwingBench has created many tables in the soe schema in addition to views, material views, and other objects in the database. SwingBench will create a similar number of objects for the sales history wizard.

Now let's put a CUSTOMERS table in memory. This is very simple and straightforward:

```
SQL> alter table CUSTOMERS inmemory ;

Table altered.

SQL>
```

Check Memory-Related Parameters

Before we start the data population, let's look at the memory-related parameters and make sure we have everything set up correctly.

1. From Enterprise Manager, choose Administration | In-Memory Central and click the Edit button, as shown in Figure 8-6.

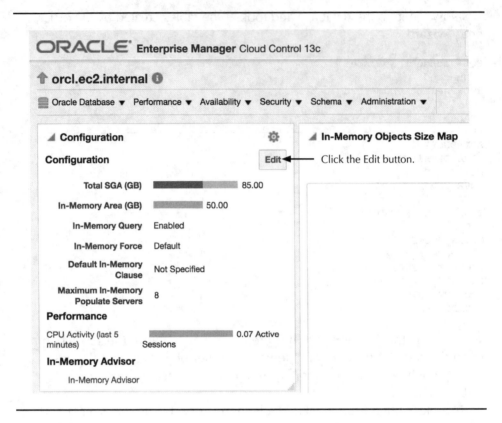

FIGURE 8-6. *Modifying the In-Memory parameters from Enterprise Manager*

   2. As shown in Figure 8-7, the inmemory_max_populate_servers
   parameter is set to 8, and since we have 16 CPUs in the server, we
   can bump it to a higher number. Increase the value to 12, and then
   click Apply in the lower-right corner.

The system will display a message saying the operation has been successful,
as shown next.

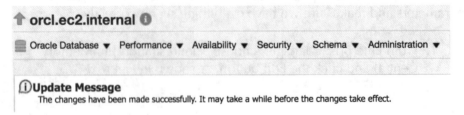

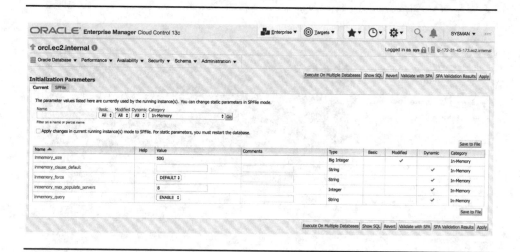

FIGURE 8-7. *Memory related initialization parameters*

Tip & Technique
*You can also issue an **alter system** command as
a sysdba to change the parameter in a traditional
fashion if you don't want to use EM for making
this change.*

Start Data Population

Now let's run a simple **count(*)** from the table to start the data population:

```
SQL> select count(*) from customers ;

  COUNT(*)
----------
 100000000

SQL>
```

Look at the In-Memory Central home page from EM and notice that the
right side of the screen now displays the object that is in memory, as shown
in Figure 8-8.

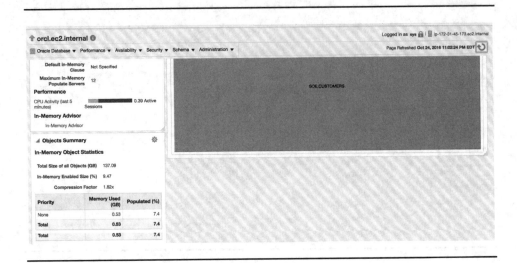

FIGURE 8-8. *EM showing In-Memory object map*

The left side of the screen shows the total size of the object, the compression factor, memory used, and what percentage of the data population has been done. If you scroll farther down, you will see more details about the compression algorithm, compression factor, and so on, as shown in Figure 8-9.

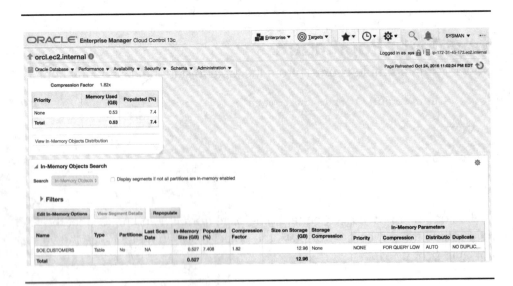

FIGURE 8-9. *More details about the In-Memory object*

Now let's add a few more tables using a different compression algorithm and then examine the behavior.

```
SQL> alter table inventories inmemory ;

Table altered.

SQL> alter table ADDRESSES inmemory memcompress for query high ;

Table altered.

SQL>
```

Run a **count (*)** on these tables to populate the data load:

```
SQL> select count(*) from inventories   ;

  COUNT(*)
----------
    899312

SQL> select count(*) from addresses ;

  COUNT(*)
----------
 150000000

SQL>
```

Check EM to look for progress, as shown in Figure 8-10.
To monitor the population status by running an SQL query, use the following:

```
SQL> select v.segment_name name,v.partition_name,
v.populate_status status, v.bytes_not_populated
from v$im_segments v
Order by 1;

NAME            PARTITION_NAME        STATUS              BYTES_NOT_POPULATED
-------  -----------------  ------------  -------------------------------
ADDRESSES                              COMPLETED           0
CUSTOMERS                              COMPLETED           0
INVENTORIES                            COMPLETED           0
```

BYTES_NOT_POPULATED set to 0 means that all the data has been populated in memory. This means that by the time we checked the EM and ran the query, the data was already populated.

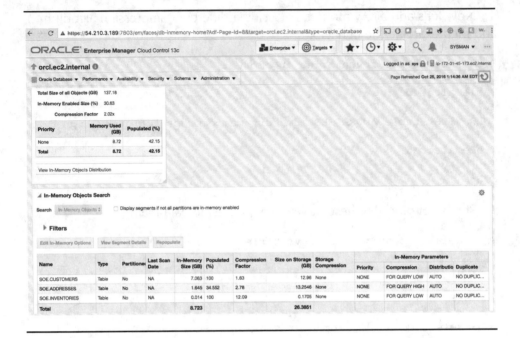

FIGURE 8-10. *Progress of data population*

Similarly, to check the compression ratio from the command line, run the following:

```
SQL> select v.segment_name name,
round(v.bytes/1024/1024,3) orig_size,
round(v.inmemory_size/1024/1024,3) in_mem_size,
ROUND(v.bytes/v.inmemory_size,2) comp_ratio
from v$im_segments v
order by 1  ;
```

NAME	ORIG_SIZE	IN_MEM_SIZE	COMP_RATIO
ADDRESSES	13572.75	2.313	5869.3
CUSTOMERS	13271.047	7232.813	1.83
INVENTORIES	174.555	14.438	12.09

From the screen shown in Figure 8-10 click View In-Memory Objects Distribution to display the In-Memory Objects Distribution window, shown next:

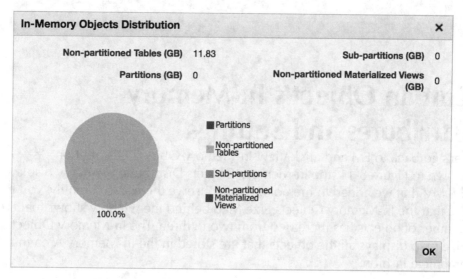

Create a Materialized View

Because we have only populated nonpartitioned tables in memory, the pie chart shows 100 percent for Non-Partitioned Tables. Let's put something other than a table in memory and look at the pie chart again. Let's create a materialized view (MV) and then put that in memory:

```
SQL> create  MATERIALIZED VIEW  CUSTOMERS_MV INMEMORY as select * from CUSTOMERS ;
```

Then run a **count(*)**to populate the data:

```
SQL> select count(*) from CUSTOMERS_MV;
```

Next, run a query to check the In-Memory parameters relating to the MV:

```
SQL> SELECT table_name,
  2  inmemory,
  3  inmemory_priority,
  4  inmemory_compression,
  5  inmemory_duplicate
  6  FROM   user_tables
  7  WHERE  table_name ='CUSTOMERS_MV';
```

TABLE_NAME	INMEMORY	INMEMORY	INMEMORY_COMPRESS	INMEMORY_DUPL
CUSTOMERS_MV	ENABLED	NONE	FOR QUERY LOW	NO DUPLICATE

SQL>

Edit an Object's In-Memory Attributes and Settings

Let's go back to EM and click View In-Memory Objects Distribution. As shown in Figure 8-11, the In-Memory Objects Distribution window displays the MV that we added in memory. If you observe the figure carefully, you'll see that the In-Memory Objects Size Map behind the window shows that the number of objects has increased from two to three. The In-Memory Objects Size map displays all the objects that are stored in the In-Memory Area in a graphical fashion.

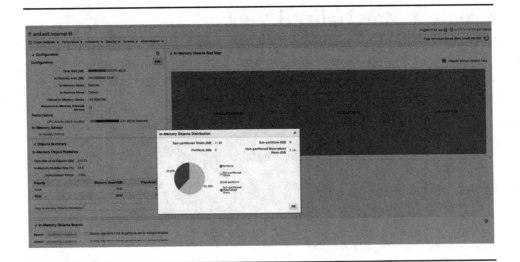

FIGURE 8-11. *In-Memory Objects Distribution showing MV*

Next, we'll use EM to edit an object's In-Memory attributes. Let's start with the table first.

1. Choose Schema | Database Objects | Tables, as shown next:

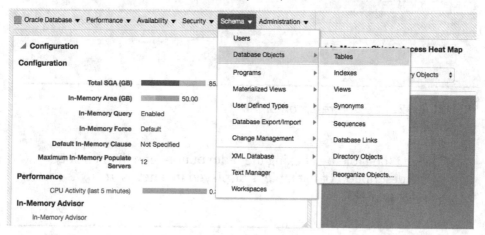

2. In the Tables section, under Search, enter the Schema and Object Name. Then click Go:

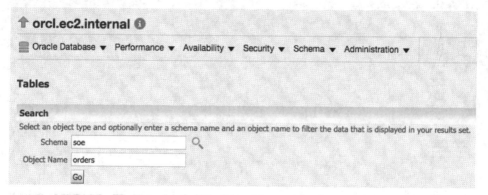

3. The table is displayed in the list at the bottom of the screen, as shown in Figure 8-12.

FIGURE 8-12. *Search result of table*

4. Select the table by clicking the radio button, and then click Edit.
   The description of the table is displayed in a new screen, as shown
   in Figure 8-13.

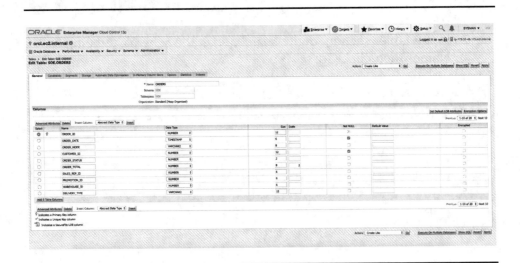

FIGURE 8-13. *Table description*

5. Click the In-Memory-Column Store tab at the top of the screen.
   The In-Memory Column Store and all the columns of the table are
   displayed, as shown in Figure 8-14.

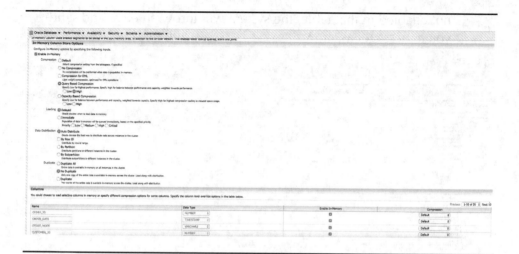

FIGURE 8-14. *IMCS and columns of the table*

Look carefully, and you will realize that all the default options are selected and all the columns are selected to enable In-Memory. From this screen, you can either deselect the columns you don't want to enable In-Memory or change the options for compression, loading, data distribution, and duplicate.

6. Change Loading to Immediate and Priority to High, and leave everything else set to the default values. Then click Apply. A message will pop up saying the operation is successful, as shown next.

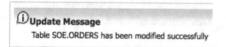

Update Message
Table SOE.ORDERS has been modified successfully

7. From the same screen, in the Data Distribution section, choose By Partition and click Apply to save the changes. Since partitioning is

not enabled in that table, the system will throw an error and send you a message, as shown next:

Now let's edit the In-Memory settings for the tablespace.

1. Choose Administration | Storage | Tablespaces, as shown next:

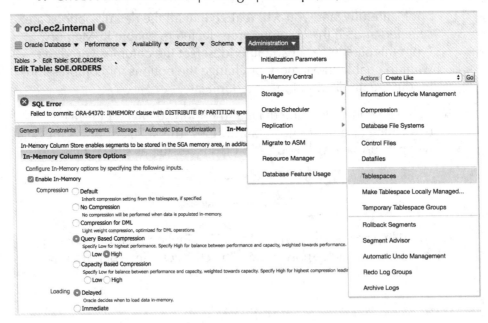

2. On the Tablespaces home page, all the tablespaces are listed, as shown in Figure 8-15. Select the tablespace for which you want to enable the In-Memory option. In this case, choose the SB tablespace, and then click Edit.

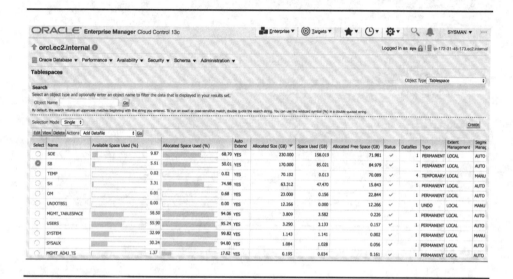

FIGURE 8-15. *Choose the SB tablespace.*

3. Click the In-Memory Column Store tab, shown in Figure 8-16.

4. Select the Enable In-Memory check box at the top of the page. You have the same options available here that are available for a table. Choose the desired Compression, Loading, Data Distribution, and duplication methods and click Apply. You'll see a confirmation, as shown next:

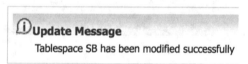

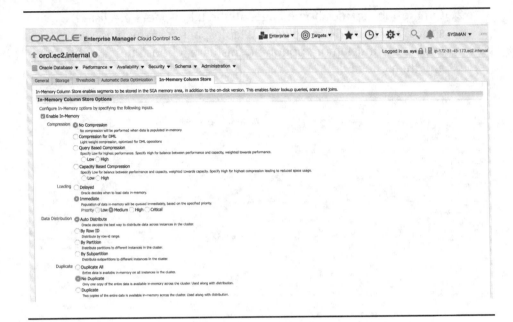

FIGURE 8-16. *Enable In-Memory for a tablespace*

Disabling the In-Memory Option

So far, we have only enabled the In-Memory option. Now let's try disabling the same and observe the behavior. During these hands-on exercises, we have created a materialized view, CUSTOMERS_MV. Now let's examine that MV from Enterprise Manager and disable the In-Memory option.

1. Choose Schema | Materialized Views | Materialized Views, as shown next:

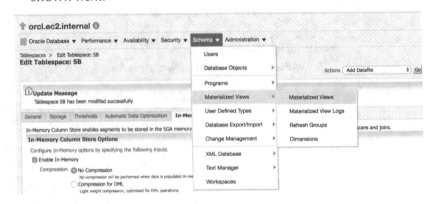

2. Now search for the MV. Enter the schema name and materialized view name and click Go. Then select the MV and click Edit, as shown in Figure 8-17.

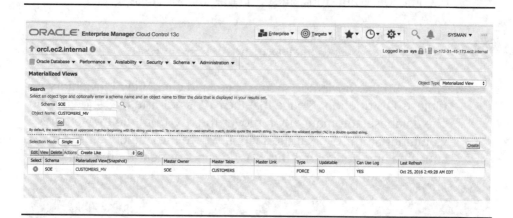

FIGURE 8-17.   *Selecting the MV*

3. Select the In-Memory Column Store tab and notice that In-Memory is already enabled:

Check this button.

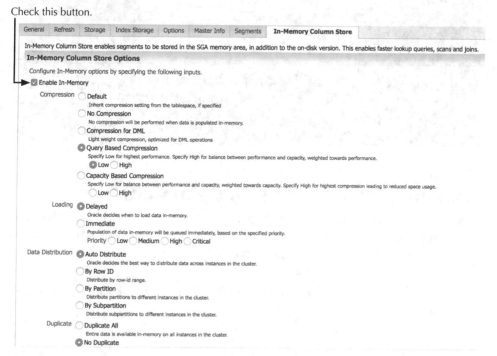

4. Uncheck the button to disable the In-Memory option for this MV. Click Apply. The moment you uncheck the button Enable In-Memory, all the other options are disabled automatically since they now become irrelevant. You will see a confirmation message:

ⓘ **Update Message**
Materialized View SOE.CUSTOMERS_MV has been modified successfully

5. Now go to the In-Memory home page, and click View In-Memory Objects Distribution. Notice that the MV is not listed, as shown next. The database automatically removes the MV from the In-Memory Columnar Store. Look at the section where the object names are specified and notice that this MV does not appear there either.

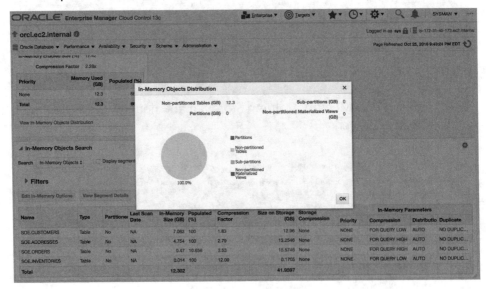

Install the In-Memory Advisor

If you hook up your database with the latest version of EM (which at the time of writing is 13c), EM also enables you to install the In-Memory Advisor from the EM console itself. Let's configure that.

1. Navigate to the In-Memory home page. Select In-Memory Advisor, as shown next:

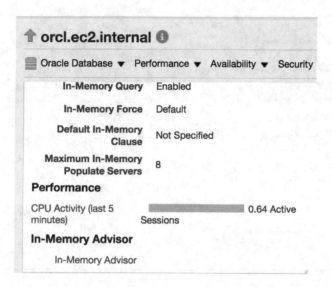

2. The system will show a message saying that In-Memory Advisor is not installed. Click the Install Advisor Job link to install it, as shown next:

ⓘ Information
In-Memory advisor is either not installed (or installed version is less than 1.0.0.0.1) on the target or the DB user does not have access to run the advisor. Run the Install Advisor job to install the advisor.

---

3. In the Create Install IM Advisor Job screen, by default, the General tab is displayed. Enter the job name (for our example, enter **In Memory Advisor**) and select the database where you want the job to be run. You can see the database listed at the bottom of Figure 8-18.

4. The system also prompts for number of Automatic Attempts. Since we are going to install this only once, keep the default setting, <none>. Then click the Parameters tab.

5. Enter four parameters in the screen (shown after the parameter list):

   ■ **Directory** This directory is used by the user imadvisor for storing the data. You also need to create a database directory in the backend. So let's do that in parallel:

   ```
   SQL> create directory imadvisor as '/u01/imadvisor';

   Directory created.
   ```

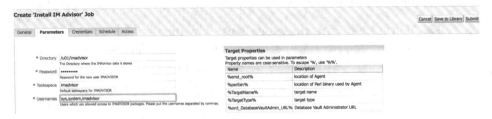

FIGURE 8-18. *Start of the IM Advisor install job*

- **Password for the imadvisor**   Use any password you want. The tool will create the user for you.

- **Tablespace for the imadvisor user**   Create this tablespace before running the tool:

```
SQL> create tablespace imadvisor datafile '/u01/app/ec2-
user/oradata/orcl/imadv.dbf' size 10g autoextend on ;

Tablespace created.
```

- **Usernames**   These users will be allowed to access the Imadvisor package. In this example, enter **sys,system,imadvisor** to indicate three users.

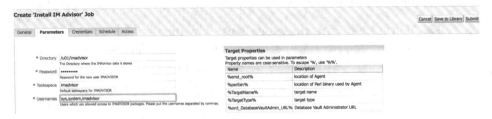

6. Click the Credentials tab. You need to provide the sys credentials here:

7. Click the Schedule tab. Since we want to run this one time and immediately, leave the default setting at One Time (Immediately):

8. Click Submit. Once the job is submitted, the system shows a message displaying the job is submitted successfully.

9. Click the job name. Once the job is successful, the system will show this (Figure 8-19).

FIGURE 8-19. *Successful job execution—installing In-Memory Advisor*

Run a Workload

Now let's run a workload using SwingBench and then run the In-Memory Advisor and see the recommendations.

You can connect to the schemas that you have created previously and run the workload in those schemas. The longer the duration of the workload you run, the more data will be present in the system, so the results will be more accurate.

Go to the directory where you have downloaded SwingBench and navigate to the bin directory. Start the benchmark by running the script shown next:

On the SwingBench home page, you need to connect to the schema for which you want to run the benchmark. As you can see in Figure 8-20, you can tailor the benchmark/workload to run according to the way you want. You can set up the number of users, set the duration for which the benchmark will run, set up the delay between the user logons, and set up the delay between transactions. If you are not familiar with SwingBench, add 5 to 10 users to start the workload and run the benchmark for an hour.

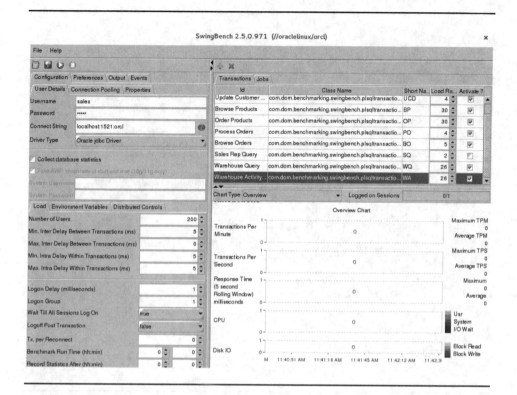

FIGURE 8-20.   *Choosing the scripts for running the benchmark*

On the right side of the screen are the scripts SwingBench will run during the benchmark. You can also specify how many users will run what script. Choose a mix of OLTP and DW and click the Play icon (the right-facing white arrow) to start the workload.

The benchmark will start and the users will start logging on in the system one by one, as shown in Figure 8-21.

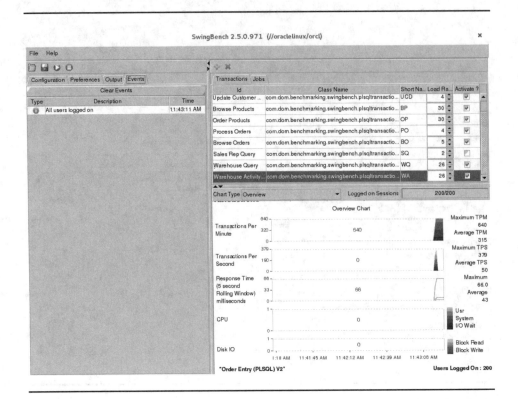

FIGURE 8-21. *Users logged on*

The system will indicate when all the users are logged on. Click the Configuration tab to see what scripts the benchmark is running at the current moment (Figure 8-22).

Once the stipulated time you have defined for the benchmark is completed, the benchmark will finish. Now run In-Memory Advisor to see the results.

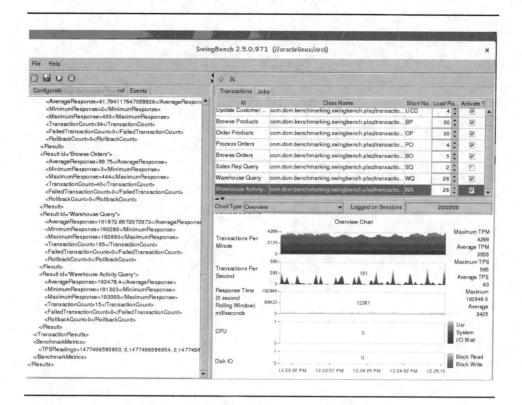

FIGURE 8-22.   *Details of the scripts being run*

Summary

In this chapter, you have worked on some hands-on lab exercises to learn more about the In-Memory option. I hope these exercises have been helpful.

APPENDIX A

Installing the Oracle Database and Enabling In-Memory

In this appendix, you will learn the first steps to using the Oracle Database In-Memory option: installing the Oracle Database and enabling the In-Memory option. If you are already using Oracle Database for an existing application or data warehouse, you can enable the In-Memory option in that database instance. Note, however, that the In-Memory option is supported only on Oracle Database release 12.0.1.0 and later; if your database version is previous to that, you must upgrade to 12cR1 or higher before you can use In-Memory.

Preinstallation Steps

Before you begin the install, you must confirm that the hardware and operating system meet the minimum requirements for Oracle Database and that the system has the necessary accounts and groups created.

For hardware, the following are needed at a minimum:

- The run level of the system should be set to 3 or 5 for Linux and 3 for Solaris.

- The server should have at least a 1024 × 768 display, which Oracle Universal Installer (OUI) requires.

- The server must be connected to a network.

- The minimum RAM required for installing Oracle Database is 1GB, but to enable the In-Memory option, much more memory is needed. To install Oracle Database in a Real Application Cluster (RAC), the minimum memory requirement is 4GB.

NOTE
The minimum RAM requirement is for installing the Oracle Database. Since you are going to run the Oracle Database In-Memory option, you need more RAM. In fact, the more RAM you have, the bigger the In-Memory store will be.

The operating system (OS) must have OpenSSH installed. If OpenSSH is not installed as a part of a default Linux or Solaris OS, you'll need to install OpenSSH manually.

In addition to OpenSSH, the packages listed in Table A-1 must be installed.

Operating System	Package
Oracle Linux 7	Oracle Linux 7 with the Unbreakable Enterprise kernel: 3.8.13-35.3.1.el7uek.x86_64 or later Oracle Linux 7 with the Red Hat Compatible kernel: 3.10.0-123.el7.x86_64 or later
Red Hat Enterprise Linux 7 Oracle Linux 6.4	Red Hat kernel 3.10.0-123.el7.x86_64 or later Unbreakable Enterprise kernel 2: 2.6.39-200.24.1.el6uek.x86_64 or later
Oracle Linux 6	Red Hat Compatible kernel: 2.6.32-358.el6.x86_64 or later
Red Hat Enterprise Linux 6	Red Hat kernel 2.6.32-358.el6.x86_64
SUSE Linux Enterprise Server 12	SUSE Linux kernel 3.12.28-4-default or later
Oracle Solaris 11.2 (SPARC)	SRU 5.5 Oracle Solaris 11.2.5.5.0 or later SRUs and updates
Oracle Solaris 10 Update 11 (SPARC)	Oracle Solaris 10 1/13 s10s_u11wos_24a or later updates
Oracle Solaris 11.2 (x86–6)	SRU 5.5 (Oracle Solaris 11.2.5.5.0) or later SRUs and updates
Oracle Solaris 10 Update 11 (x86–6)	Oracle Solaris 10 1/13 s10x_u11wos_24a or later updates

TABLE A-1. *Minimum OS Version*

NOTE
Oracle Linux users should run an Oracle preinstallation RPM (Red Hat Package Manager) or the Linux release to configure the OS for Oracle Database. This allows downloading and automatically installing the Linux packages required for Oracle installation.

Once the respective packages are installed, confirm that you have proper space in the file system, that you have created proper users and groups, and that you have sized the SWAP space correctly. We'll discuss each step in further detail.

Disk Space in Temporary File System

The temporary file system is where the installer writes all installation log files and keeps temporary files required for installation. Once the installation is done, it is OK to delete all these files. Oracle recommends 2GB or more in the temporary file system, which is often known as /tmp in the UNIX file system. You can set the temp directory by running the following commands:

```
$ TMP=/mount_point/tmp
$ TMPDIR=/mount_point/tmp
$ export TMP TMPDIR
```

SWAP Space Relative to RAM

The SWAP space allocation in the UNIX file system is dependent on the physical RAM of the machine. Oracle provides the following guidelines to size the SWAP file system:

- If the RAM size is 1–2GB, the SWAP file system should be 1.5 times the RAM.

- If the RAM size is 2–16GB, the SWAP file system should be equal to the RAM.

- If the RAM size is more than 16GB, the SWAP file system should be equal to the RAM.

Because you will be running the Oracle Database In-Memory option, your RAM should be much bigger. The server is always provisioned with memory before the installation happens, so you can safely assume that the SWAP size should be 16GB or more.

Oracle Inventory Directory

The inventory directory is where the details of the entire Oracle installation inventory are kept. Most of today's enterprises keep the inventory in a central place. Before the installation, determine whether a central inventory exists or whether inventory is kept locally for each server. If you have a central inventory, make sure the Oracle installer (the account from which you would be installing Oracle Software) has proper permission to access it. The location of the inventory is kept in a file called oraInst.loc. The file is stored either in the /etc directory or in the /var/opt/oracle directory.

The file has the following two entries:

- **inventory_loc**=*central_inventory_location* or *local_inventory_location*

- **inst_group**=*group*

```
# cat /var/opt/oracle/oraInst.loc
inventory_loc=/u01/app/oracle/oraInventory
inst_group=oinstall
```

Users who have the Oracle inventory group as their primary group are granted the OINSTALL privilege to write to the central inventory. The OINSTALL group must be the primary group of all Oracle software installation owners on the server. If the Oracle inventory group does not exist, the installer uses the group of the installation owner as the oraInventory group.

CAUTION
The oraInventory directory should never be kept under the ORACLE_HOME or ORACLE_BASE, because it can cause permission errors for other Oracle installations.

Users and Groups

If you have already installed the server, you will likely have already configured all the users and groups needed for running Oracle software. If you are installing the Oracle software for the first time, you must create the user who is going to own the Oracle software and the group to which it should belong. The operating system that owns the Oracle software is called the Oracle user (oracle). The oracle user is always a part of multiple UNIX groups: dba, oinstall, asmdba, and osoper. The dba group is responsible for all the DBA activities, the oinstall group is responsible for all the Oracle-related installation activities, the asmdba group is responsible for administrating the ASM instance, and the osoper group has the privilege to start and shut down the database. By default, the members of the dba group have the osoper privilege.

If you don't have the groups already created in the system, you can create them using the **groupadd** command, as shown here:

```
# /usr/sbin/groupadd -g 511 dba
```

Once all the groups have been created, create the Oracle user as shown in the following command:

```
# /usr/sbin/useradd -u 510 -g oinstall -G dba, oinstall, asmdba oracle
```

The following command shows to what groups an Oracle user belongs:

```
$ id -a oracle
uid=510(oracle) gid=510(oinstall) groups=510(oinstall),511(dba),512(asmdba)
```

Environmental Variables

If you are already running Oracle on the server where you are going to install the Oracle Database In-Memory option, you must unset all the Oracle-related environment variables before starting the installer. Unset the following environment variables:**$ORACLE_HOME** or **$ORACLE_BASE**, **$ORA_NLS10**, and **$TNS_ADMIN**:

```
$ unset ORACLE_HOME
$ unset ORACLE_BASE
$ unset TNS_ADMIN
$ unset ORA_NLS10
```

Also check the **PATH** variable and make sure there is nothing related to the Oracle environment set.

If you are going to install the Oracle Database with the oracle user, the umask for the oracle user must be set to 022. You can set up the same in the /etc/profile or ~/.bashhrc file:

```
$ vi /etc/profile
```

Or

```
$ vi ~/.bashrc
```

Append/modify the following line to set up a new umask:

```
umask 022
```

Setting the umask to 022 ensures that the oracle user is able to create all the files related to Oracle software with 644 UNIX permissions.

The display must be set for the oracle user to install the software, because the installer needs X server for the installation. You can check the display by running the command

```
$ echo $DISPLAY
```

If the display is not set, run the command:

```
$ export DISPLAY=local_host:0.0
```

> **NOTE**
> *If you are not able to run the installer even after setting the display, check with your system administrator.*

Root Access

During the installation, you will be prompted to run certain files related to installation as root user. Therefore, you must have either root access or sudo access to root user to run these files. If you have neither root access nor sudo access to the root user, you can request that the system administrator run these scripts for you.

Oracle Software Location

The Oracle Database needs approximately 8GB of space at a bare minimum for the ORACLE_HOME. You will need to plan the space requirements for other files such as log files, audit files, dump files, and so on. These files can be stored inside the ORACLE_HOME or in a separate directory, but they need to be accounted for in space planning.

You can install the Oracle software in a local file system or in a shared file system, such as Network File System (NFS). Make sure that you have a mirroring solution such as RAID in either case. The Oracle software installation space does not include the space needed to create the database. If you are planning to create the database during the installation itself, you need to provision that space as well. The database size depends on your requirements. The database files can be stored in the following locations:

- A local file system mounted on the server; it is always recommended that you keep the database files in a file system different from the location of ORACLE_HOME

- A network file system on a network attached storage

- The Oracle Automatic Storage Management (ASM) file system

Depending on your Recovery Time Objective (RTO) and Recovery Point Objective (RPO), you need to set up mirroring for your database. ASM provides double mirroring and triple mirroring for Oracle Database files. If you have very stringent SLAs, triple mirroring is recommended for mission-critical production databases.

Grid Infrastructure (Conditional)

If you are installing the database as a RAC database, the Grid Infrastructure (GI) must exist before you begin the installation. If GI does not exist, you need to install it first before installing the Oracle Database.

In addition, if you want to keep the Oracle Database files in ASM, you must install the GI first. Installing the GI also installs the ASM instance. Discussing the GI installation is beyond the scope of this book.

Staging the Software

You can download the latest version of the database software, Oracle Database 12cR2, from the Oracle Technology Network at oracle.com/ technetwork/database/enterprise-edition/downloads/index.html.

The software is split into two files. Download and unzip both the files to the same directory. You must have an unzip utility already installed in your server. If you do not, you can download one from the software download location.

A media pack is the electronic version of the software available on a CD-ROM or DVD. If you want to download the media pack, you can download it from the Oracle Software Delivery Cloud portal at edelivery .oracle.com/.

You need to complete the export validation process by entering your name, e-mail address, and other details before downloading the software. Once you download the software, make sure the MD5 or SA-1 checksum matches the value listed on the media download page. If it does not match, there is an issue with the download and you need to redownload it.

If you are planning to install the software from a CD-ROM or a DVD-ROM, mount the device in the server before you start the installation. After inserting the disc, run the following command as root user to verify whether it is mounted automatically:

```
# ls /mnt/dvd
```

If the command does not show any output, you have to mount the disc manually. To do this as a root user, run the following command:

```
# mount -t iso9660 /dev/dvd /mnt/dvd
```

It is always advisable to copy the files to the hard drive and then install them from there instead of running the installation from the CD-ROM or DVD-ROM. This will ensure a smooth and fast installation.

Running Oracle Universal Installer

Once you have completed all the preinstallation steps, the next step is to do the actual installation. You need to log in as an Oracle user in the machine and run the Oracle Universal Installer (OUI) utility. Use the runInstaller utility to install the software.

Go to the stage location where you have copied/downloaded the Oracle software and run the following command:

```
$ cd /location_of_oracle_software
$ ./runInstaller
```

As shown in Figure A-1, when the command is run, it shows the location of the OUI log files, and all the log files are being written to the /tmp directory. The log file name also contains the date and time to identify the exact log file of the database installation.

The first screen (Figure A-2) prompts you for your My Oracle Support (MOS) e-mail address. If you provide this optional information, Oracle keeps you updated with security fixes and product updates.

Click Next in the lower-right corner to view the next screen, Select Installation Option, where you will choose installation options. Three options are displayed:

- **Create And Configure A Database**   This option is comprehensive. After installing the Oracle software, it also creates the database for you. If you choose this option, you should be ready to use your database.

```
[jbanerje@slc05aak database]$ ls
install  response  rpm  runInstaller  sshsetup  stage  welcome.html
[jbanerje@slc05aak database]$
Display all 1517 possibilities? (y or n)
[jbanerje@slc05aak database]$
[jbanerje@slc05aak database]$ ./runInstaller
Starting Oracle Universal Installer...

Checking Temp space: must be greater than 500 MB.   Actual 45486 MB    Passed
Checking swap space: must be greater than 150 MB.   Actual 16112 MB    Passed
Checking monitor: must be configured to display at least 256 colors.   Actual 1
6777216    Passed
Preparing to launch Oracle Universal Installer from /tmp/OraInstall2016-01-12_10
-35-56PM. Please wait ...█
```

FIGURE A-1.   *Using the runInstaller to install the OUI*

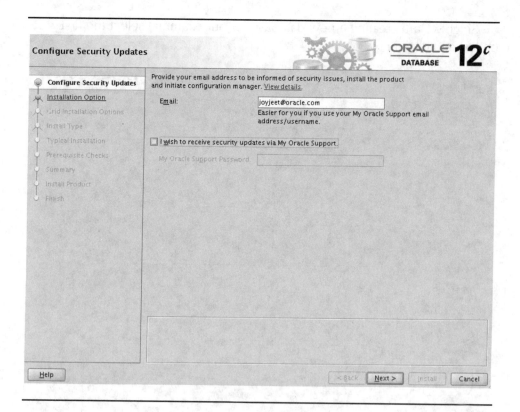

FIGURE A-2. *Configuring security updates*

- **Install Database Software Only**   Installs just the Oracle software—that is, it configures your ORACLE_HOME. Chose this option if you don't want to install the database during installation, if you are going to clone a database into the new ORACLE_HOME, or you are going to install the database at a later time.

- **Upgrade An Existing Database**   Use this if you are planning to upgrade your database to a later version (Oracle Database 11gR2 to Oracle Database 12cR2, for example).

Since we are creating a new database for our example, select the first option and click Next.

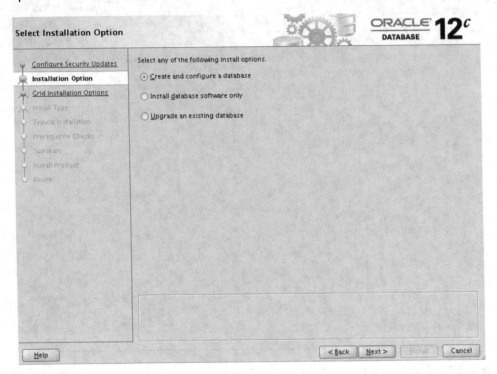

In the next screen, System Class, two options are provided:

- **Desktop Class** Choose this if you want to install the database on a laptop or desktop. This option is mostly used for building demos, testing small scripts, and training purposes. It is not recommended for production databases.

- **Server Class** This option is used when installing the Oracle databases on servers. Any enterprise installation of Oracle Database is done at the server level only. Choose this option if you are deploying the Oracle Database on a server. For our example, select this option and click Next.

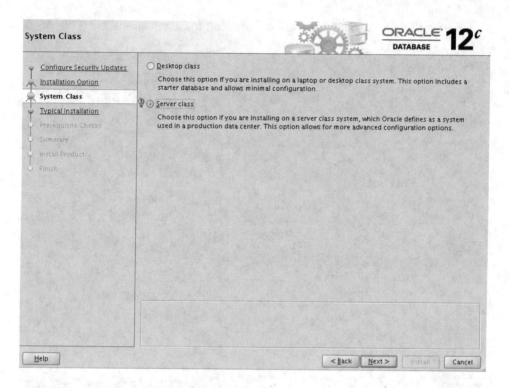

Next, you will select from the various installation options for the Oracle Database. From the Grid Installation Options screen, choose between a single-instance or RAC database:

- **Single Instance Database Installation** Installs the single-instance database. This is the simplest form of Oracle Database installation.

- **Oracle Real Application Clusters Database Installation** Installs the database as an RAC database. If you choose this option, you must have Grid Infrastructure already installed in this server. If GI is not installed, you must install it before choosing this option.

- **Oracle RAC One Node Database Installation** Configures a RAC one-node database. You can select this if you want to install the single-instance database beneath a cluster or if you want to use ASM storage for your single-instance database.

Choose the option Single Instance Database Installation and click Next.

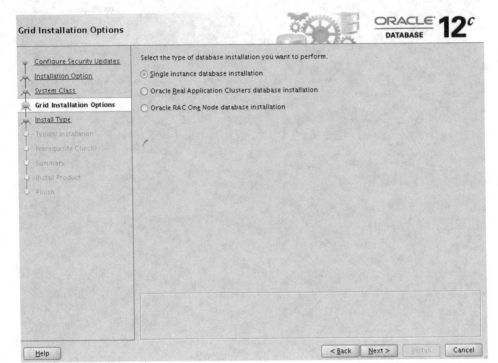

You'll now choose between a typical and an advanced installation in the Select Install Type screen:

■ **Typical Install** Choosing this option installs the database with the most basic configuration. If you choose this option, then in the next screen you provide all the information related to ORACLE_HOME and base, storage type (ASM or file system), database file system location, database name, database edition, dba group, password, and whether you want to configure a container database or not.

■ **Advanced Install** This option provides more flexibility with many more options during the installation itself. In the typical install option, you can provide only one password for all the schemas, whereas the advanced install allows you to provide different passwords for different schemas such as SYS, SYSTEM, and so on.

The Advanced Install option also configures the database in multiple languages, provides the option to choose the character set of the database, configures automatic backups, sets up the FRA (Fast Recovery Area), and provides you the option of configuring the database with Enterprise Manager for monitoring and managing the Oracle Database.

Choose Advanced Install and click Next.

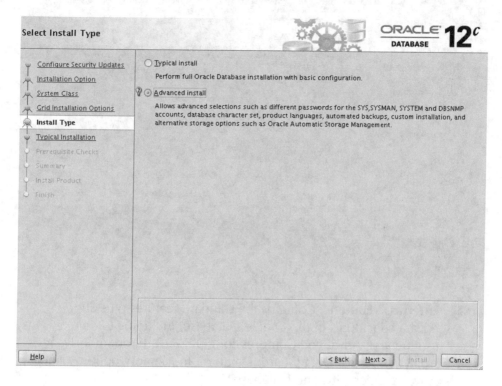

NOTE
If you want to explore all the features of the Standard and Enterprise Editions in more detail, refer to the following link: oracle.com/ au/products/database/enterprise-edition/ comparisons/index.html.

In the Select Database Edition screen, you will choose from two options for the database edition, as shown here. Click Next after you've chosen an option.

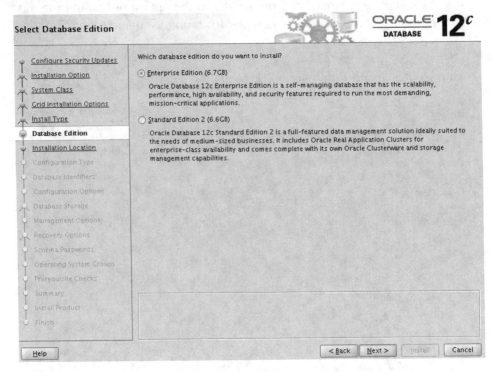

- **Enterprise Edition**   Contains the standard features plus all the advanced features of the Oracle Database, including Oracle Multitenant, Advanced Compression, OLAP, Partitioning, Advanced Analytics, Active Data Guard, Database In-Memory option, Oracle Advanced Security, and Database Vault.

- **Standard Edition**   Contains all the standard database features including Oracle RAC and Oracle Clusterware. It does not have all the advanced features available in the Enterprise Edition.

NOTE
Purchasing the Enterprise Edition does not authorize you to use all options such as In-Memory, Partitioning, and Advanced Compression. You need separate licenses for each option you want to use. If you are not sure what database options you own or have a license for, check with your Oracle sales representative.

The Specify Installation Location screen prompts you for the location to install the database software. Input the location of the ORACLE_BASE for the Oracle Base field and ORACLE_HOME in the Software Location field, as shown here. Click Next after entering the locations.

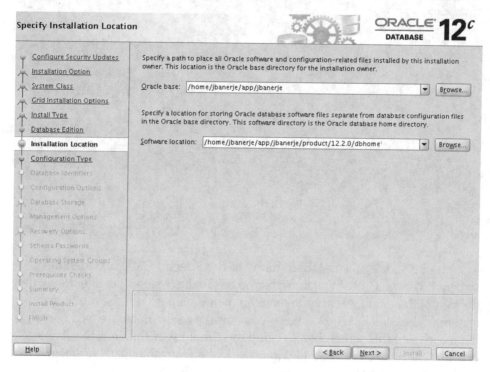

The Select Configuration Type screen prompts you for the type of database to be installed: General Purpose/Transaction Processing or Data Warehousing, as shown next. If you are planning to use Oracle Database for OLTP, choose the first option. If you are planning to use it for database warehousing, choose the second option. Selecting the option best suited for your needs enables the installed database to be optimized for the chosen option.

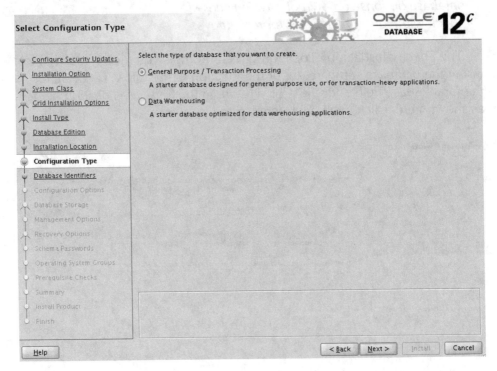

You can specify the database name in the Specify Database Identifiers screen. Enter the Global Database Name or Oracle System Identifier (SID), the domain of the database, from this screen. If you want to use the multitenant feature of the Oracle 12c Database, you can create the database as a container database from this screen by checking the Create As Container Database option. Once selected, you need to provide the Pluggable Database Name that is going to be a part of the container database. Click Next.

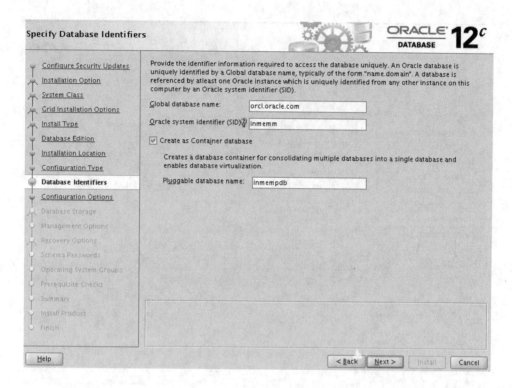

The choices in the Specify Configuration Options screen are related to the database character set and memory management. There are three tabs in the installer window, as shown in Figure A-3.

The installer provides the following options: Use Unicode (AL32UTF8), Use OS Character Set, or Choose From The Following List Of Character Sets in a drop-down list. Choosing the proper character set is very important. Once installed, it's a very painful process to change the character set. You have to export the entire database, change the character set, and reimport the database for converting the character set.

The character set of the database is used for the data stored in SQL character data types such as CHAR, VARCHAR2, and NUM; for identifiers such as table names, column names, and PLSQL variables; and for stored SQL/PLSQL source code.

The default character set for General Purpose or Data Warehouse is Unicode AL32UTF8. Oracle recommends using the default character set unless you need a special character set. Unicode is the universal character set that supports most of the currently spoken languages of the world. It also supports

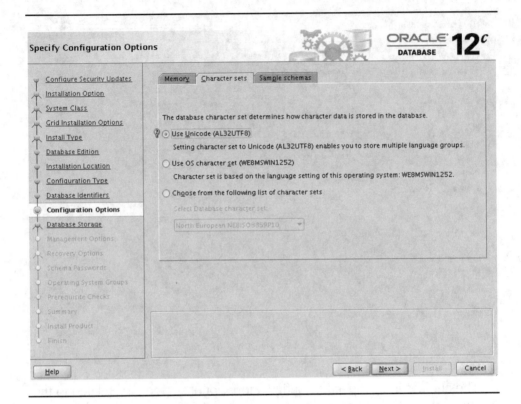

FIGURE A-3. *Database character sets*

many historical scripts (alphabets). Unicode is the native encoding of many technologies, including Java, XML, XHTML, ECMAScript, and LDAP. Unicode is ideally suited for databases supporting the Internet and the global economy.

If you are planning to install the Oracle Database in a language other than English, choose the character set compatible with that language. The database character set to be selected in this case is the character set of most clients connecting to this database.

NOTE
If you are planning to use the Multitenant option as well, ensure that the character set you choose for the CDB is compatible with the database character sets of the databases to be plugged into this CDB.

If you select the Memory tab here, as shown in Figure A-4, you can choose the Enable Automatic Memory Management option. When enabled, the Oracle Database instances automatically manage and tune memory for you. With automatic memory management, you choose a memory target, and the instance automatically distributes memory between the System Global Area (SGA) and the instance Program Global Area (instance PGA). As memory requirements change, the instance dynamically redistributes memory between the SGA and instance PGA.

If you don't want to enable this during installation, you can always enable it later by editing the initialization parameter file and restarting the database.

NOTE
Enabling this option does not automatically manage the memory of the Oracle Database In-Memory option.

Specify Configuration Options

ORACLE **12**ᶜ
DATABASE

- Configure Security Updates
- Installation Option
- System Class
- Grid Installation Options
- Install Type
- Database Edition
- Installation Location
- Configuration Type
- Database Identifiers
- **Configuration Options**
- Database Storage
- Management Options
- Recovery Options
- Schema Passwords
- Operating System Groups
- Prerequisite Checks
- Summary
- Install Product
- Finish

| Memory | Character sets | Sample schemas |

Enabling Automatic Memory Management allows the database to distribute memory automatically between the system global area (SGA) and the program global area (PGA), based on user-specified overall database memory target size. If automatic memory management is not enabled, then the SGA and PGA must be sized manually.

☐ Enable Automatic Memory Management

Allocate memory: 256   6085   15212   6,085 ⏷ 40 %

SGA target: 4563   MB
PGA aggregate target: 1522   MB

Target database memory: 6085   MB

| Help | | < Back | Next > | Install | Cancel |

FIGURE A-4. *Memory tab options*

Because enabling this option does not manage the Oracle Database In-Memory option, we won't enable Automatic Memory Management for our installation.

The third tab is Sample Schemas, where you can install sample schemas along with the installation of the Oracle Database. Sample schemas are used mainly for demos and testing purposes. Click Next to proceed.

From the next screen, Specify Database Storage Options, you specify the location for the database files. If you choose a file system for your database files, specify the location for the Specify Database File Location option, as shown in Figure A-5. If you want to use Oracle ASM to store the database

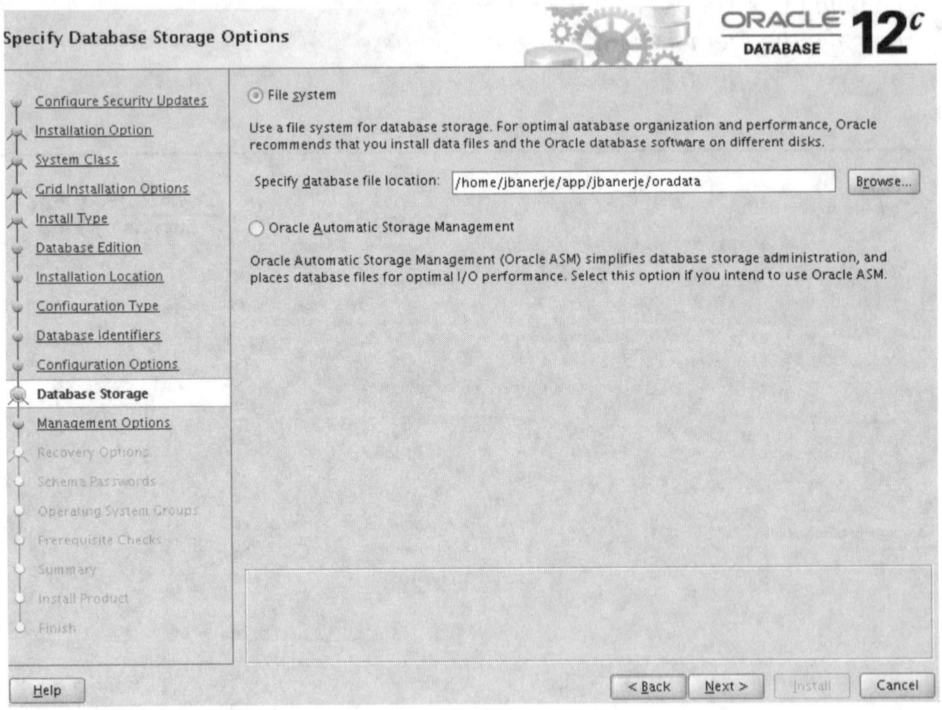

FIGURE A-5. *Setting a database file location*

files, select the ASM option. Since we are going to keep the database files in a file system, select File System, and then click Next to proceed.

From the Specify Management Options screen, you can integrate your database with the central EM if you have one. (If you don't have a centrally managed EM, you can skip this step.) Input the OMS Host name, OMS Port, and EM Admin User Name and Password, as shown next. If you don't want to integrate the database with EM now, you can do it later from the EM admin console. In this example, we are not going to integrate the database with EM, so we will leave the option Register With Enterprise Manager (EM) Cloud Control unchecked.

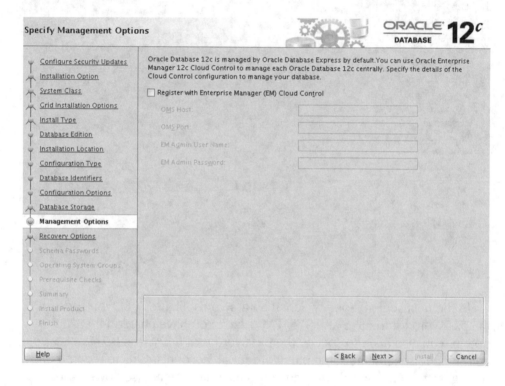

From the Specify Recovery Options screen, you can configure the recovery area either in a file system or inside the ASM storage, as shown next. If you don't want to configure this now, you can configure it later by changing the initialization parameter file. For our example, we won't select this option. Click Next to proceed.

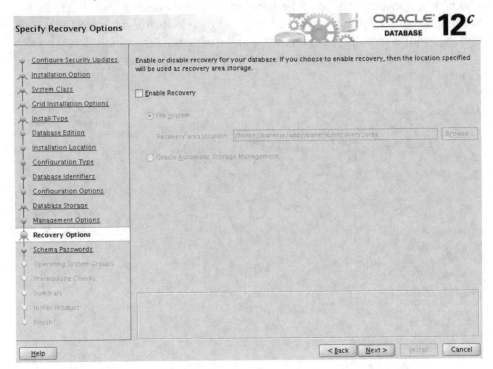

In the next screen, Specify Schema Passwords (Figure A-6), you specify the password for the SYS and SYSTEM user. If you have enabled the CDB option, you also need to specify the password for PDBADMIN. There is also an option to specify the same password for all accounts. Oracle recommends having a strong password with the combination of uppercase, lowercase,

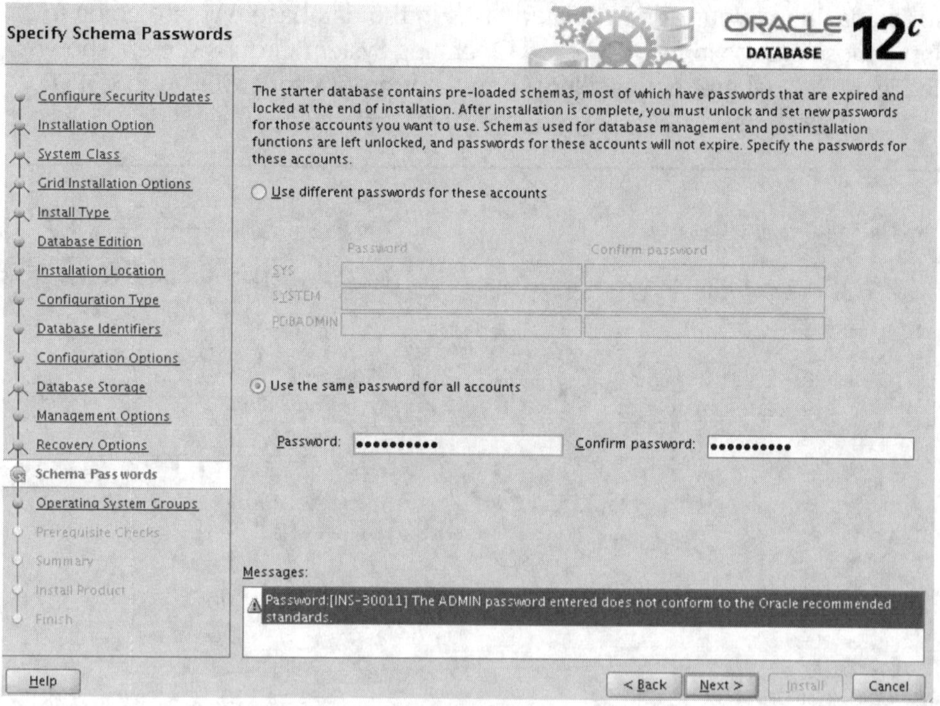

FIGURE A-6. *Setting the schema password*

numbers, and special characters. All the passwords for the preloaded schemas get expired and locked by default. You should manually unlock and reset the password for the schemas that you are going to use.

We'll use the same password for all the schemas. Because we have not chosen an Oracle-recommended strong password, the message at the bottom of the screen is displayed: "The ADMIN password entered does not conform to the Oracle recommended standards."

Recall that before the start of installation, we created multiple UNIX groups for managing various admin-related tasks in the database. We are going to input those groups in the Privileged Operating System Groups screen, shown in Figure A-7, where the installer prompts for groups for OSDBA, OSOPER,

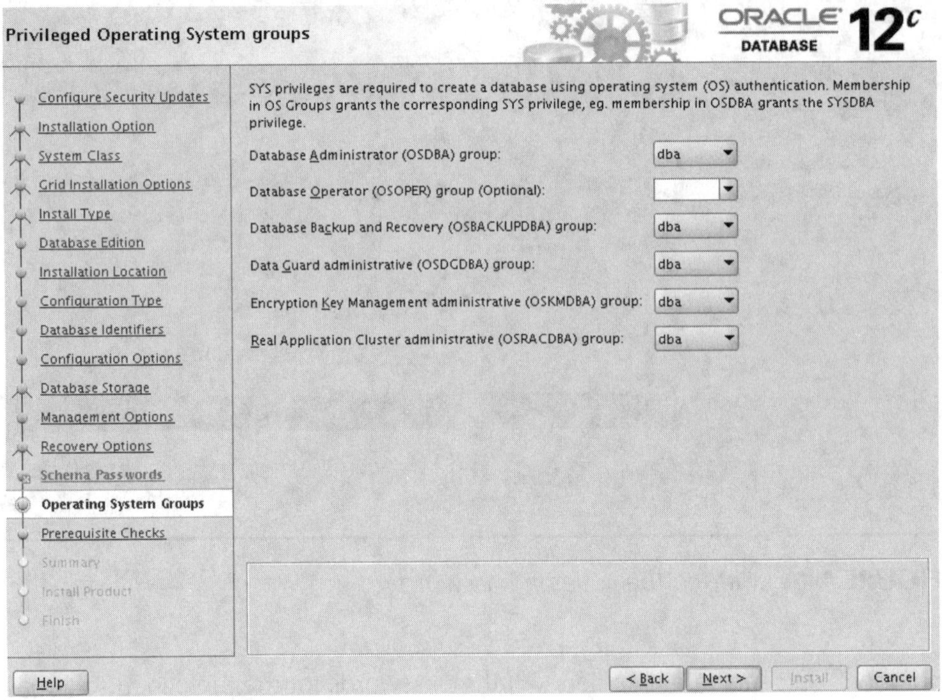

FIGURE A-7. *Operating system groups*

OSBACKUPDBA, OSDGDBA, OSKMDBA, and OSRACDBA. To keep things simple, choose dba as the group for all of the options. Then click Next.

Next, the installer does various checks, as shown in the following illustration, to make sure that all the prerequisites for the installation are met and the installation will be successful. If the installer notices any kind of discrepancies, it notifies you.

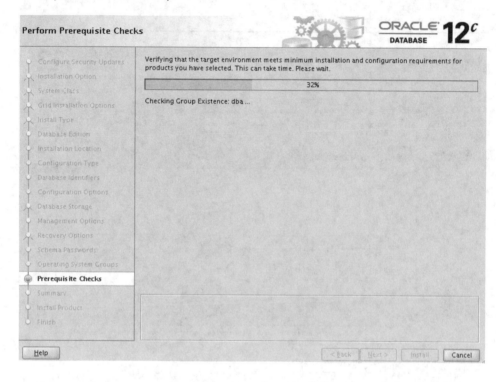

If the prerequisite check is not successful, the installer displays the details of where the check failed and how to fix it. Figure A-8 shows a failed prerequisite check and fix.

If the prerequisite check is successful, the installer summarizes all the components it is going to install and summarizes all the options you have selected/entered during the various prompts, as shown in Figure A-9.

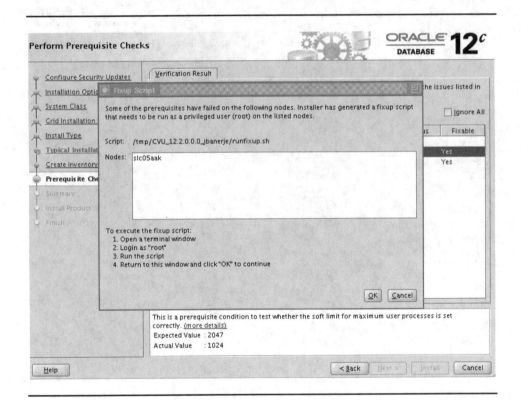

FIGURE A-8. *Failed prerequisite check*

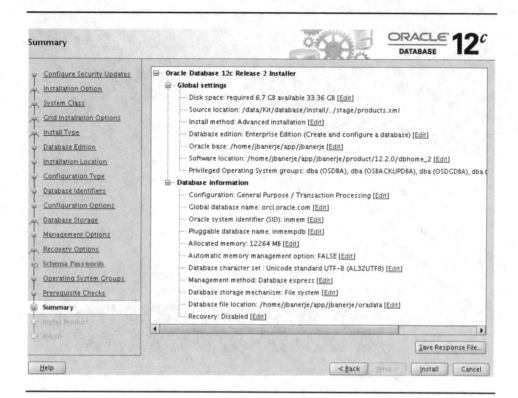

FIGURE A-9.   *Summary screen*

Once the installer finds everything OK, click Next to start the actual installation process, as shown in Figure A-10.

As previously discussed, you will need root access to run certain scripts. At this stage, when the database installation happens, you are required to run certain scripts as root. The installer will prompt you with the details at the terminal. When prompted, open another terminal and run those scripts as root. Figure A-11 shows the script the installer prompts to run as root user.

```
[root@slc05aak oraInventory]# ./orainstRoot.sh
Changing permissions of /home/jbanerje/app/oraInventory.
Adding read,write permissions for group.
Removing read,write,execute permissions for world.
```

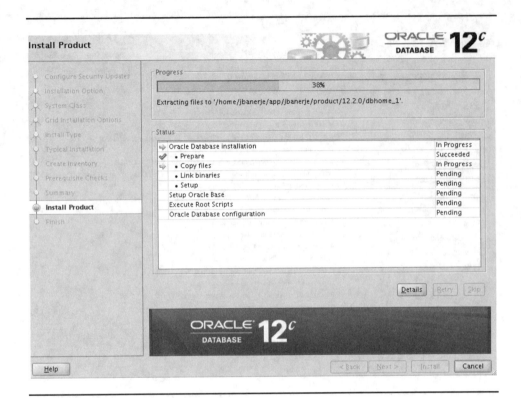

FIGURE A-10. *Database installation progress*

```
Changing groupname of /home/jbanerje/app/oraInventory to dba.
The execution of the script is complete.

[root@slc05aak dbhome_2]# ./root.sh
Performing root user operation.

The following environment variables are set as:
    ORACLE_OWNER= jbanerje
    ORACLE_HOME=  /home/jbanerje/app/jbanerje/product/12.2.0/dbhome_2

Enter the full pathname of the local bin directory: [/usr/local/bin]:
    Copying dbhome to /usr/local/bin ...
    Copying oraenv to /usr/local/bin ...
    Copying coraenv to /usr/local/bin ...
```

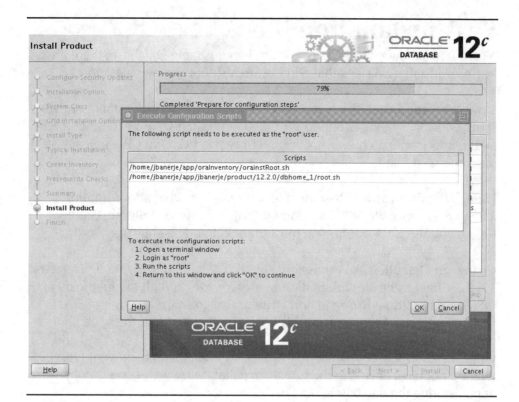

FIGURE A-11. *Scripts to be run as root user*

```
Creating /etc/oratab file...
Entries will be added to the /etc/oratab file as needed by
Database Configuration Assistant when a database is created
Finished running generic part of root script.
Now product-specific root actions will be performed.
Do you want to setup Trace File Analyzer(TFA) now ? yes|[no] :
yes
Installing Trace File Analyzer (TFA).
Log File: /home/jbanerje/app/jbanerje/product/12.2.0/dbhome_2/install/
root_slc05aak.oracle.com_2016-01-12_23-24-43.log
Finished installing Trace File Analyzer (TFA)
[root@slc05aak dbhome_2]#
```

Once you run the scripts as root, click OK and the installer will continue
to complete the database configuration. Once the database is installed
successfully, the Finish screen is displayed.

Post-Installation Steps

Now that you have successfully installed your Oracle Database, there are a few post-installation steps that will ensure a smooth implementation.

Download and Install the Latest Patches   After successful installation, you should check My Oracle Support for the latest patches. You can download all the important patches, bug fixes, security patches, and CPU patches at one time.

Unlock the Passwords   Passwords for all Oracle system administration accounts except SYS, SYSTEM, and DBSMP are revoked after installation. Before you use an account, you must unlock it and reset its password.

Change in Default SGA Permission   In all releases prior to Oracle Database 12cR2, Oracle software installation owner (oracle) and all the members of OSDBA group (dba) had read and write access to shared memory SGA. In Oracle Database 12.2 releases, this behavior changed and the system is more secure. Now only the Oracle software owner (oracle) has read and write access to shared memory. However, this change may prevent DBAs who do not have access to the Oracle installation owner account from administering the database.

Oracle Database 12.2 introduces a new parameter, **ALLOW_GROUP_ ACCESS_TO_SGA**, that determines whether the Oracle Database installation owner account (oracle in Oracle documentation examples) is the only user that can read and write to the database SGA, or if members of the OSDBA group can write to the SGA. The default value for this parameter is FALSE, so that only the Oracle Database installation owner has read and write permissions to the SGA. If you want to set your database to use the previous user and group permissions, you can change the initialization parameter **ALLOW_GROUP_ACCESS_TO_SGA** setting from FALSE to TRUE.

Enabling the In-Memory Option

By default, the In-Memory option is not enabled when the database is installed. You need to enable it manually. Once enabled, the SGA shows an In-Memory Area. You can see that in our newly installed database, the SGA does not have any entry for In-Memory:

```
SQL> show sga ;

Total System Global Area 9663676416 bytes
Fixed Size                  4592552 bytes
Variable Size            1543507032 bytes
Database Buffers         8086618112 bytes
Redo Buffers               28958720 bytes
SQL>
```

Let's check the In-Memory Area to see if the system allocates some area by default:

```
SQL> select * from v$inmemory_area;

POOL                   ALLOC_BYTES     USED_BYTES POPULATE_STATUS           CON_ID
---------------------- ----------- ---------- ------------------------- ----------
1MB POOL                         0          0 OUT OF MEMORY                  1
64KB POOL                        0          0 OUT OF MEMORY                  1
1MB POOL                         0          0 OUT OF MEMORY                  2
64KB POOL                        0          0 OUT OF MEMORY                  2
1MB POOL                         0          0 OUT OF MEMORY                  3
64KB POOL                        0          0 OUT OF MEMORY                  3

6 rows selected.
```

The In-Memory Area also does not show anything being allocated for the In-Memory option, so we need to set the In-Memory Area explicitly after installing the database by running the following query:

```
SQL> ALTER SYSTEM SET INMEMORY_SIZE = 100M SCOPE=SPFILE;

System altered.
```

Restart the database to initialize the IM Column Store. With Oracle Database 12cR2, this parameter is also dynamic, which means that you can set the parameter without restarting the database. To increase the size of the In-Memory Area dynamically, run the following command. Note that you can increase the size dynamically only if the new size is greater than 128MB.

```
SQL> ALTER SYSTEM SET INMEMORY_SIZE = 300M;

System altered.
```

As soon as you change the size of the In-Memory Area, the change is immediately reflected in the v$view:

```
SQL> select * from v$inmemory_area;

POOL        ALLOC_BYTES USED_BYTES POPULATE_STATUS           CON_ID
------ ----------- ---------- ------------------------- ----------
1MB POOL      229638144          0 DONE                           1
64KB POOL      66519040          0 DONE                           1
1MB POOL      229638144          0 DONE                           2
64KB POOL      66519040          0 DONE                           2
1MB POOL      229638144          0 DONE                           3
64KB POOL      66519040          0 DONE                           3

6 rows selected.
```

If you want to disable the In-Memory option, you can set the value of the parameter **INMEMORY_SIZE** to 0.

Once the In-Memory Area is allocated, you are ready to use this new feature.

Summary

You have successfully installed the Oracle Database and enabled the In-Memory option. You learned that in order to use the In-Memory option, the database version must be Oracle Database 12cR1 or later. If you are running a database version previous to 12cR1, you must upgrade to use the In-Memory option.

The latest Oracle Database software can be downloaded from Oracle Technology Network and installed using the Oracle Universal Installer. The Database In-Memory option can be enabled only in the Enterprise Edition, so make sure you choose this option while running the installer.

Once the database is installed successfully, you need to edit the parameter **INMEMORY_SIZE** to define the size of your In-Memory footprint. You can increase the size dynamically only if the new size is greater than 128MB.

Index

Join the Largest Tech Community in the World

 Download the latest software, tools, and developer templates

 Get exclusive access to hands-on trainings and workshops

 Grow your professional network through the Oracle ACE Program

 Publish your technical articles – and get paid to share your expertise

Join the Oracle Technology Network
Membership is free. Visit community.oracle.com

🐦 @OracleOTN f facebook.com/OracleTechnologyNetwork

Climb the Career Ladder

Think about it—97 percent of the Fortune 500 companies run Oracle solutions. Why wouldn't you choose Oracle certification to secure your future? With certification through Oracle, your resume gets noticed, your chances of landing your dream job improve, you become more marketable, and you earn more money. It's simple. Oracle certification helps you get hired and get paid for your skills.

93%
Hiring managers who say IT certifications are beneficial and provide value to the company[1]

7%
Salary growth for Oracle Certified professionals[5]

70%
Believe that Oracle certification improved their earning power[2]

90%
Say that Oracle certification gives them credibility when looking for a new job[2]

68%
Think that certification has made them more in demand[3]

6x
Increased LinkedIn profile views for people with certifications, boosting their visibility and career opportunities[4]

Take the next step
http://education.oracle.com/certification/press

[1] "Value of IT Certifications," CompTIA, October 14, 2014, [2] Oracle Certification Survey, [3] "Certification: It's a Journey Not a Destination," Certification Magazine 2015 Salary Edition, [4] "The Future Value of Certifications: Insights from LinkedIn's Data Trove," ATP 2015 Innovations in Testing, [5] Certification Magazine 2015 Annual Salary Survey

ORACLE®

Push a Button
Move Your Java Apps to the Oracle Cloud

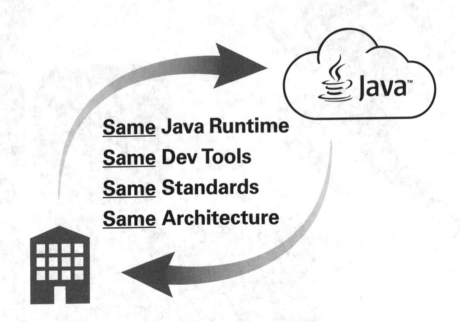

Same Java Runtime
Same Dev Tools
Same Standards
Same Architecture

... or Back to Your Data Center

cloud.oracle.com/java

Reach More than 640,000 Oracle Customers with Oracle Publishing Group

Connect with the Audience that Matters Most to Your Business

Oracle Magazine
The Largest IT Publication in the World
Circulation: 325,000
Audience: IT Managers, DBAs, Programmers, and Developers

Profit
Business Insight for Enterprise-Class Business Leaders to Help Them Build a Better Business Using Oracle Technology

Circulation: 90,000
Audience: Top Executives and Line of Business Managers

Java Magazine
The Essential Source on Java Technology, the Java Programming Language, and Java-Based Applications

Circulation: 225,00 and Growing Steady
Audience: Corporate and Independent Java Developers, Programmers, and Architects

For more information or to sign up for a FREE subscription: Scan the QR code to visit Oracle Publishing online.

Beta Test Oracle Software

Get a first look at our newest products—and help perfect them. You must meet the following criteria:

✔ **Licensed Oracle customer or Oracle PartnerNetwork member**

✔ **Oracle software expert**

✔ **Early adopter of Oracle products**

Please apply at: pdpm.oracle.com/BPO/userprofile

If your interests match upcoming activities, we'll contact you. Profiles are kept on file for 12 months.